THE EVOLUTION OF SOCKET BAYONET MANUFACTURE

THE EVOLUTION OF SOCKET BAYONET MANUFACTURE

From Hand-Craft to Mechanisation 1770–1860

PETER G. SMITHURST

Pen & Sword
MILITARY
AN IMPRINT OF PEN & SWORD BOOKS LTD.
YORKSHIRE – PHILADELPHIA

First published in Great Britain in 2025 by
PEN AND SWORD MILITARY
An imprint of
Pen & Sword Books Limited
Yorkshire – Philadelphia

ISBN 978 1 03613 719 9

A CIP catalogue record for this book is available from the British Library.

Typeset in Times New Roman 10/12 by
SJmagic DESIGN SERVICES, India.
Printed and bound in the UK by CPI Group (UK) Ltd.

The Publisher's authorised representative in the EU for product safety is Authorised Rep Compliance Ltd., Ground Floor, 71 Lower Baggot Street, Dublin D02 P593, Ireland.
www.arccompliance.com

For a complete list of Pen & Sword titles please contact
PEN & SWORD BOOKS LIMITED
George House, Units 12 & 13, Beevor Street, Off Pontefract Road,
Barnsley, South Yorkshire, S71 1HN, England
E-mail: enquiries@pen-and-sword.co.uk
Website: www.pen-and-sword.co.uk

or

PEN AND SWORD BOOKS
1950 Lawrence Rd, Havertown, PA 19083, USA
E-mail: uspen-and-sword@casematepublishers.com
Website: www.penandswordbooks.com

MIX
Paper | Supporting responsible forestry
FSC® C013604

Contents

Preface viii

Acknowledgements x

Chapter 1 Manufacture of the French M.1777 bayonet at Klingenthal 1

1.1 Introduction 1

1.2 Forging the Socket (douille) 1

1.3 Reaming the socket 8

1.4 Attaching and forging the blade 8

1.5 Grinding, Polishing and Burnishing 14

1.6 Grinding 15

1.7 Polishing 16

1.8 Burnishing 17

1.9 Inspecting and testing the blade 18

1.10 Cutting the mortice slot 20

1.11 Filing the socket body and bead 21

1.12 Making the locking ring (virole) 22

Chapter 2 Manufacture of the Russian Model 1808 bayonet at Tula 27

2.1 Introduction 27

2.2 Forging the socket 28

2.3 Rough-boring the socket 29

2.4 Facing the ends of the socket 31

2.5 Turning the outside of the socket 32

2.6 Filing the machined surface of the socket 35

2.7 Filing the socket behind the neck 36

2.8 Cutting the mortice slots in the socket 38

2.9 Cutting the mortice in the bridge 41

2.10 Turning the bridge ... 44
2.11 Creating the hole for the stop pin. ... 46
2.12 Making the locking ring ... 48
2.13 Making the locking ring screw ... 48
2.14 Grinding and Polishing the blade ... 54
2.15 Finishing the socket ... 56

Chapter 3 Manufacture of the Enfield Pattern 1853 socket bayonet ... 57
3.1 Introduction ... 57
3.2 Specifications for Manufacture ... 59
3.3 Welding the socket and blade ... 62
3.4 Socket bridge roughly shaped by hand forging ... 65
3.5 'Drawing-out' the blade ... 66
3.6 Forming the hollows in the blade ... 67
3.7 Stamping the socket ... 72
3.8 Machining the socket to length ... 74
3.9 Socket drilling ... 75
3.10 Socket reamed ... 78
3.11 Socket turned from neck to ring bead ... 80
3.12 Centre-hole drilled in squared tip of trimmed blade ... 80
3.13 Neck turned in a copying lathe ... 81
3.14 Socket behind neck machined ... 81
3.15 Machining the blade ... 87
3.16 Edges (corners) of blade milled ... 87
3.17 Top face next to elbow planed and shoulders formed on other two faces ... 89
3.18 Planing the faces of the blades ... 90
3.19 Blade hollows and curved tip milled ... 92
3.20 Front of socket turned ... 93
3.21 Bending the blade at the neck into its final position ... 94
3.22 Socket turned from locking ring bead to bridge ... 95
3.23 Bridge turned in a copying lathe ... 95
3.24 Hole drilled for locking ring stop pin ... 97
3.25 Locking ring stop pin fitted and squared ... 98
3.26 Mortice slots cut ... 98
3.27 Hardening, tempering, grinding and polishing ... 99

CONTENTS

3.28 The locking ring 100
3.29 Inspection and proof 101

Conclusions 104

Appendix 1 Weights and Measures 105
Appendix 2 Procédés de la fabrication des armes blanches, publié par l'ordre du Comité de salut public (édition de 1793) with translation 107
Appendix 3 *The Guardian*, 1855, 10th Jan, p.6 187
Appendix 4 Bayonet steel supplied by Thomas Firth and Sons, Sheffield 190
Appendix 5 Pattern 1853 rifle muzzle diameters 196
Appendix 6 Three patents relating to manufacture of a socket bayonet in one piece 197
Endnotes 204
References 207

Preface

In the case of military muskets and rifles the bayonet was, and still is, an integral part of the 'weapon system'. There have always been collectors of bayonets, and their interests are catered for by many excellent books covering the history of the bayonet in its myriad varieties adopted and used by the armed forces of the world. These books provide a wealth of detail on national variations and often include many rare, and in some instances, bizarre bayonets. They focus on the end of the bayonet's story and do not cover its beginning – the conversion of more or less amorphous pieces of iron and steel into finished products. That is the focus of this publication.

It might be asked why, out of all the bayonets of the world, these three have been selected since at first sight they appear very ordinary and mundane when compared with some of their more 'exotic' brethren. There are various reasons. As with the arms they were fitted to, they are the only bayonets whose manufacture is described in varying degrees of detail in contemporary publications. They also share a kinship. As in the case of the weapons they fitted, the Russian M.1808 is a direct copy, and the Enfield Pattern 1853 bayonet a descendant of, the French M.1777 which was a major landmark in socket bayonet design with its medial locking ring, becoming the prototype for many, if not all, socket bayonets which followed.

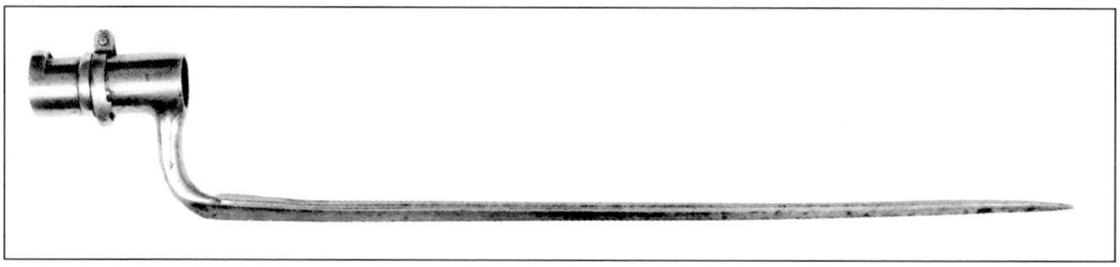

Fig. 1. The French Model 1777 bayonet. (Author's collection)

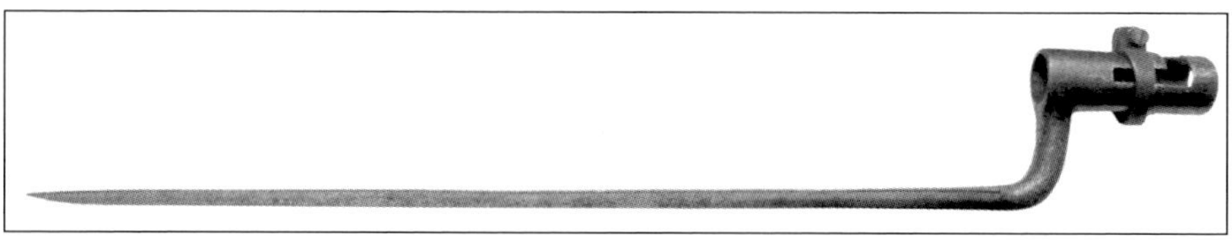

Fig. 2. The Russian Model 1808 bayonet. (Courtesy Graham Priest)

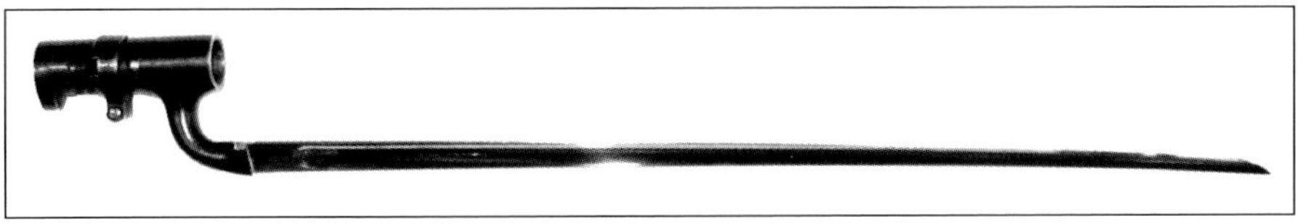

Fig. 3. The Enfield Pattern 1853 bayonet. (Author's collection)

That kinship also provides a basis for comparison of the technologies employed in their manufacture. While accounts of the manufacture of the French M.1777 and Russian M.1808 bayonets provide greater detail, the shorter accounts of the manufacture of the Enfield Pattern 1853 bayonet lack certain details or present a confusing narrative; in such cases these gaps have been filled and confusions re-interpreted by the provision of newly created sketches. However, they are also supplemented by an extensive and unique collection of specimens representing almost every stage in its manufacture held by Birmingham City Museum. Although these represent processes and practices in the 'private trade' fulfilling government contracts, they nevertheless provide valuable insights of procedures omitted from the accounts describing the processes at Enfield. These specimens have been studied and will be published here for the first time. It should be noted that these specimens retain the black bitumen-like preservative possibly applied at the time of transfer to the museum in the later 19th century, which obscures some details. Socket bayonets have obvious differences from 'sword' and 'knife' bayonets, but their manufacture still has many points in common and is, to some degree, 'transferrable technology'.

Before embarking upon details of their manufacture, for those who may not be familiar with bayonets, the terminology used in Britain in describing the features of the socket bayonet is shown in Fig. 4. National variations in the terminology will be highlighted as they are encountered.

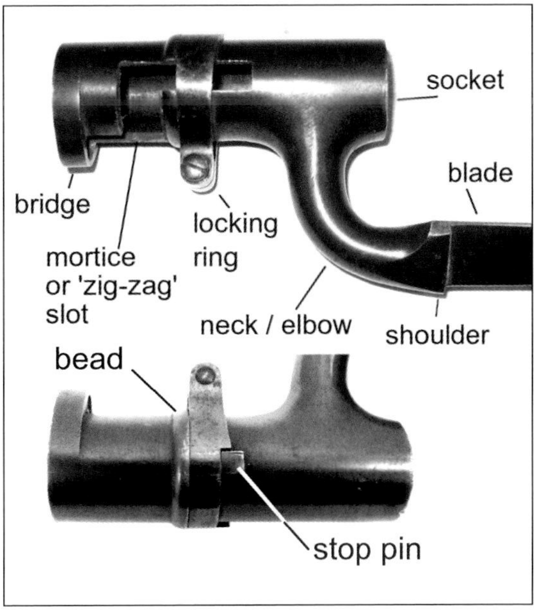

Fig. 4. The terminology of the Enfield socket bayonet. (© P. Smithurst 2025)

Acknowledgements

First to the staff of Birmingham City Museum for providing access to the bayonet specimens collection, allowing me to photograph them, and to Nadine Lees, Digital Media and Rights Officer, for granting permission for use of photographs.

To Graham Priest for provision of images of the markings on very rare American-made and other 'foreign' contractors' Pattern 1853 bayonets.

And, as always, to Royal Armouries for my continued role as Curator Emeritus and to colleagues who provide assistance in many ways.

Finally, I accept responsibility for any errors in the translation of the document in Appendix 2.

Chapter 1

Manufacture of the French M.1777 bayonet at Klingenthal

1.1 Introduction

This bayonet was designed by Honoré Blanc for his Model 1777 musket and was the first to employ a locking ring set mid-way along the socket. It was more effective than other methods used on sockets and was widely copied in many countries. Fortunately, the earliest comprehensive source of published information is a French text, Rauch's *Procédés de la fabrication des armes blanches, publié par l'ordre du Comité de salut public,* [Processes of the manufacture of bladed weapons, published by the order of the Committee of Public Safety] published in Paris in 1793, which contains extensive detail on the processes and tools used in its manufacture. A transcript and translation of the relevant text, which does not seem to have appeared in print, is included as Appendix 2.

The apparent lack of much in the way of mechanisation suggests the methods may have varied little, if at all, from 1777. As noted by Rauch, *There are three parts to consider; the socket and the ring which are iron, and the blade which is steel. Also, they must be considered in two states; 'black', that is to say, as they come out of the hands of the forger, and 'white', as they come out, as to the socket and the ring, from the hands of the filer, and as for the blade, the hands of the grinder, after having passed through those of the hardener.*

1.2 Forging the Socket (douille)

The socket forger's anvil, accompanied by a vice capable of holding very hot metal, is shown in Fig. 1.1.

Work commenced with the making of the elbow or neck which connected the socket to the blade. The starting material was a bar of iron approximately 18 lines (40mm) wide and around 7-8 lines (16–18mm) thick. In the first heating to white heat, approximately 25mm of the end was reduced in width and lengthened to form a square section around 50mm long. A portion of this square 'shank' was then rounded by the use of dies, one of which was set in a dovetail slot in the anvil face. The other, held in position by the master forger by its handle, was struck by the

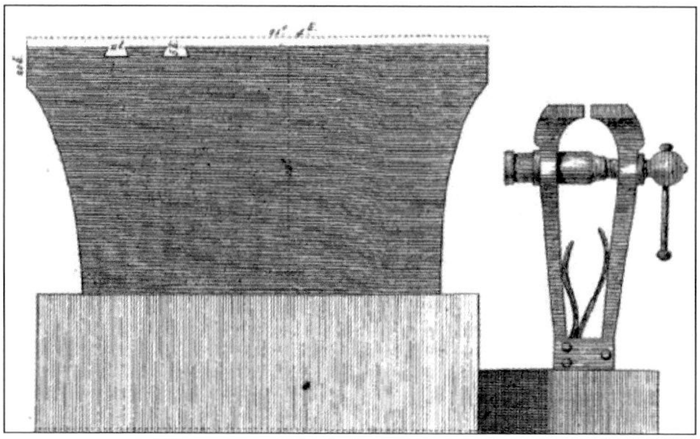

Left: Fig. 1.1. The socket forger's anvil. (Rauch, 1793, Pl. I, Fig. 5)

Below: Fig. 1.2. *Left*. The swage set in the anvil. (Rauch, 1793, Pl. I, Fig. 5); *Right*. Sketch showing it in use with the upper swage. (© P. Smithurst)

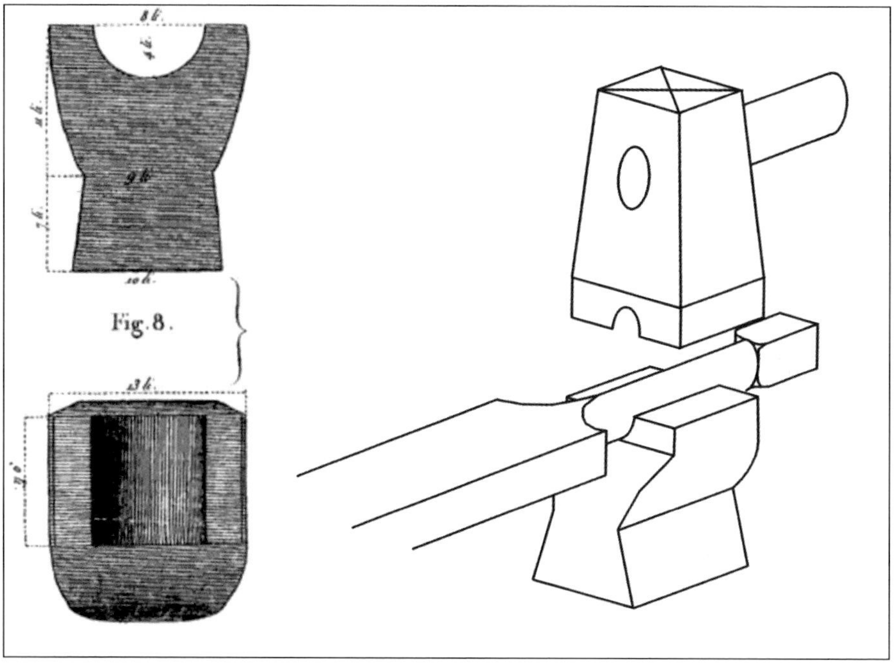

assistant, leaving around 8 lines (10mm) of the original squared section untouched, Fig. 1.2.

While still hot, it was cut almost through with a chisel, leaving a length of 25mm of the original 40mm wide bar. The forger bent it to ninety degrees where it had been cut, and the rounded portion of the shank was immediately grasped in the circular cut-out in the vice jaws, Fig. 1.3.

The long bar was moved up and down to detach it followed, if necessary, by striking the wide stub-end with a large hammer from above to 'square' the shoulders against the flat top face of the vice jaws, Fig. 1.3. The sequence is shown diagrammatically in Fig. 1.4 and the finished forging is shown in Fig. 1.5.

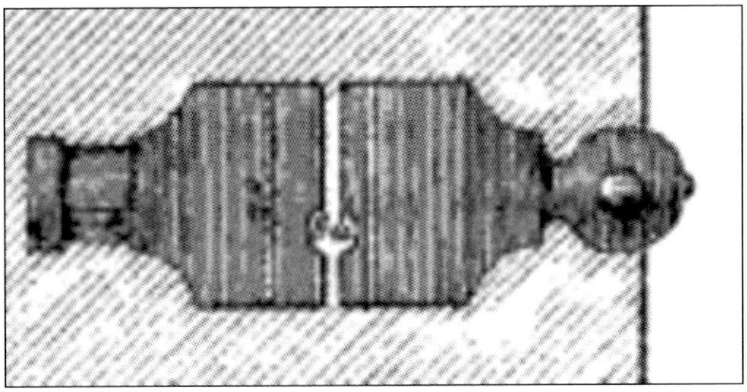

Fig. 1.3. The socket forger's vice in plan view showing the cut-out into which the shank of the elbow was fitted. (Rauch, 1793, Pl. I, Fig. 5)

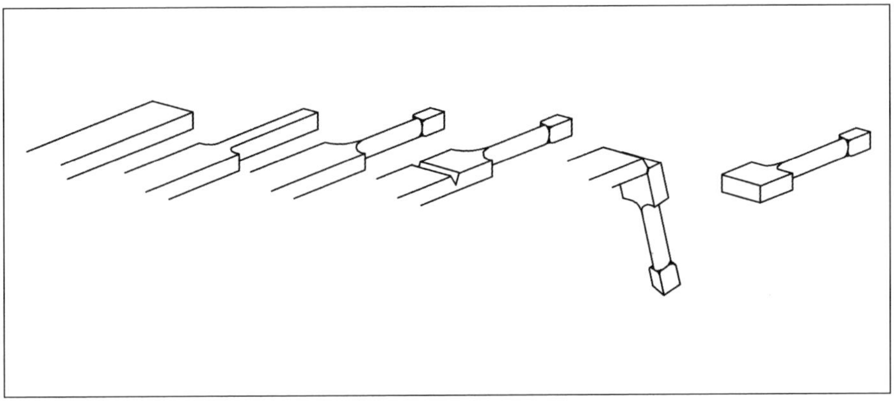

Above: Fig. 1.4. Sketch showing the sequence of operations. (© P. Smithurst)

Right: Fig. 1.5. The neck, or elbow, forging. (Rauch, 1793, Pl. III, Fig. 15)

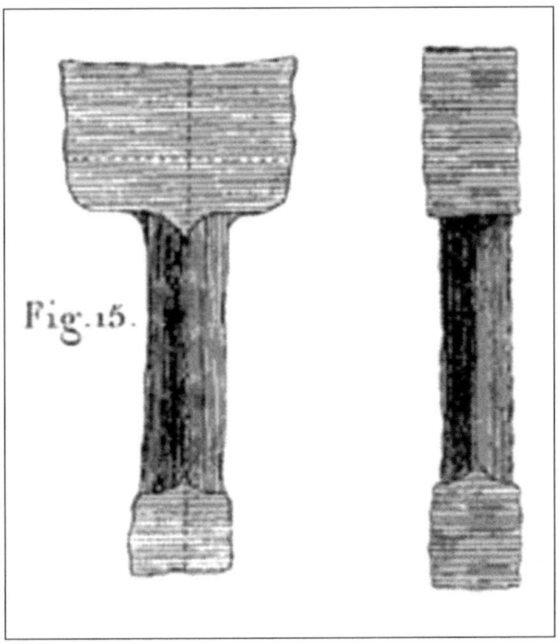

The large portion in Fig. 1.5 was then ready to be transformed into the socket. The roughly forged elbow was placed in the hearth and the portion which would form the socket brought up to temperature. It was then placed on the anvil and the master forger began to flatten it. It was then bent over at right angles to the elbow shank and again clamped in the circular cut-out in the vice jaws. There the partly flattened portion was given a glancing blow to take the metal slightly over the junction with the elbow shank and then the remainder flattened and spread to the required degree. Rauch provides no illustrations of these stages so a sketch representing them is shown in Fig. 1.6.

In the next stage the forging was returned to the hearth, re-heated, and the forging of the plate continued in such a way as to 'reserve' a thickness of metal in the centre and at the corners.[1] These were to form the central bead against which the locking ring rested and the *bridge* which reinforced the opening in the socket. Again, these stages are not illustrated so the sketch (Fig. 1.7), has been prepared to illustrate what it is thought Rauch was describing.

Whilst forging this side of the plate would have been more difficult, it would result in these 'reserved' portions being on the outside as required when the plate was folded

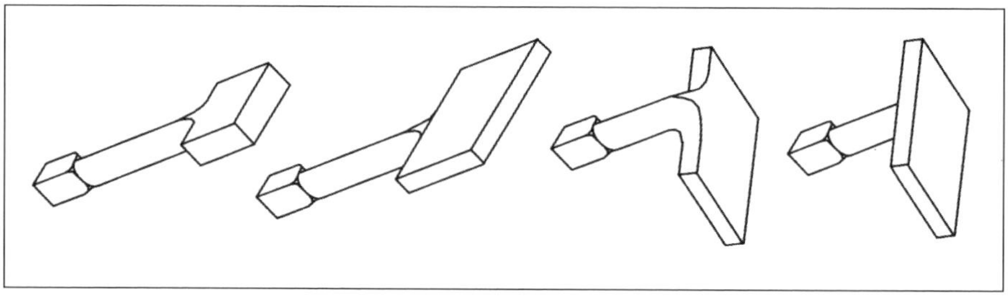

Fig. 1.6. Representation of the presumed steps in the second stage in the forging of the socket. (© P. Smithurst)

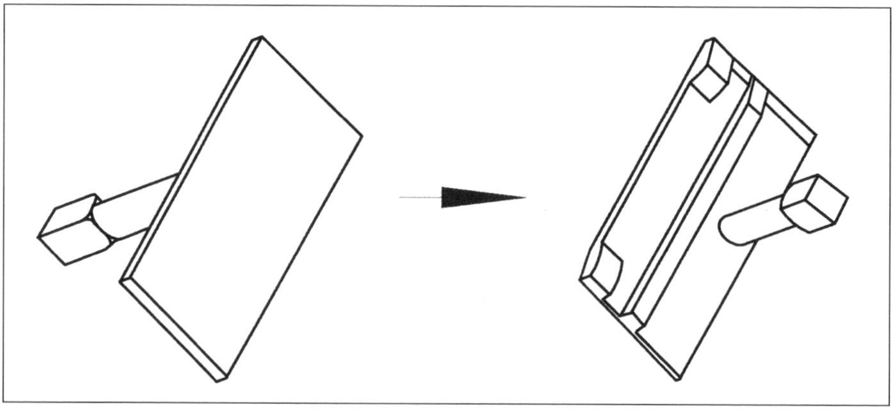

Fig. 1.7. The finished plate ready for 'wrapping' into a tube, showing the 'reserved' portions. (© P. Smithurst)

to form the socket. The 'plate' was heated to 'cherry-red' and the lateral extremities chamfered on the special die block, Fig. 1.8, set into the top face of the anvil.

After heating to 'cherry red' again, the round shank was clamped in the vice and the forger began to fold or 'wrap' the 'plate' with a hammer. He then placed it on the anvil and continued folding or wrapping into a tube with the chamfered edges overlapping. After inserting his thinnest mandrel, the forming of the tube continued, resulting with around 8 lines (20mm) of overlap. Finally, still on its mandrel, the forming of the tube was finished using the special die, Fig. 1.9, set in the top face of the anvil.

This created a tube which was ready for welding as shown in Fig. 1.10, although the 'reserved portions' are not in evidence.

The welding of the tube constituted the third stage in the manufacturing process and

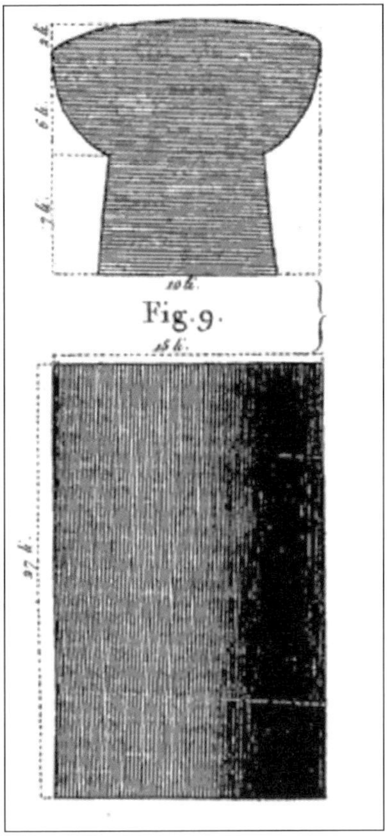

Right: Fig. 1.8. Elevation and plan of die block used for chamfering. (Rauch, 1793, Pl. II, Fig. 9)

Below left: Fig. 1.9. The die /swage used in the last stage of 'wrapping' the tube. (Rauch, 1793, Pl. II, Fig. 10)

Below right: Fig. 1.10. The roughly prepared tube ready for welding. (Rauch, 1793, Pl. III, Fig. 16)

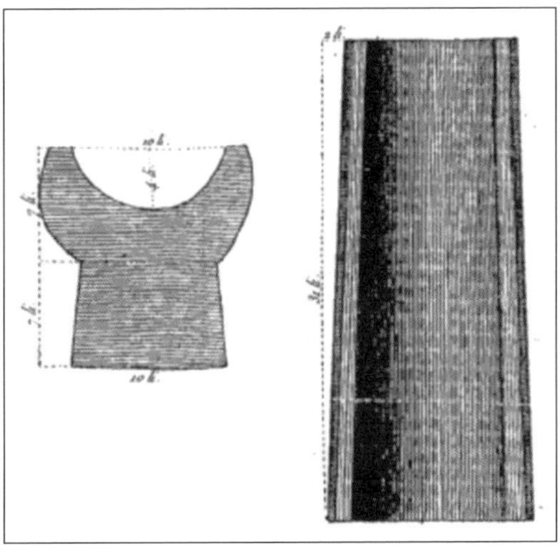

required three heats; two to weld the upper and lower extremities and one to weld the middle portion. When finished, the welded socket had the appearance as in Fig. 1. 11.

While still hot, the welded socket on its mandrel was placed in the die, Fig. 1. 12, which was secured in a channel in the top of the anvil, and was lengthened while at the same time, by the use of a matching top die, forming the 'bead' against which the locking ring would be seated.

The die was short enough not to interfere with the junction of the socket with the elbow, so this portion was finished with the pein of the hammer, as was the opposite end where the 'bridge' was formed. The finished socket forging is shown in Fig. 1.13.

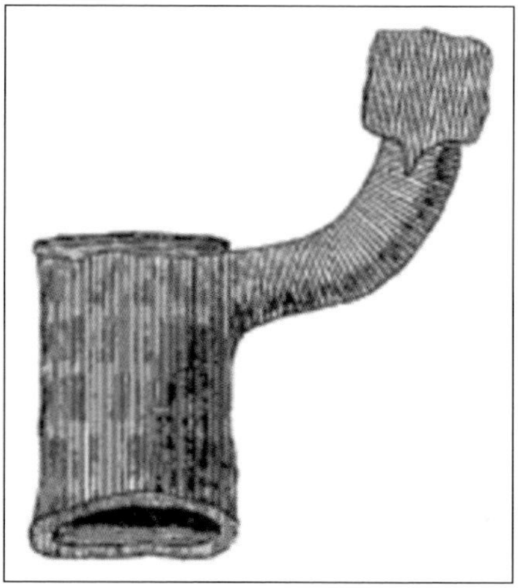

Fig. 1.11. The welded socket. (Rauch, 1793, Pl. III, Fig. 17)

After annealing, the assistant filed the top and bottom edges of the socket to make them square with its axis and it was then sent for inspection at the 'black-weapons',

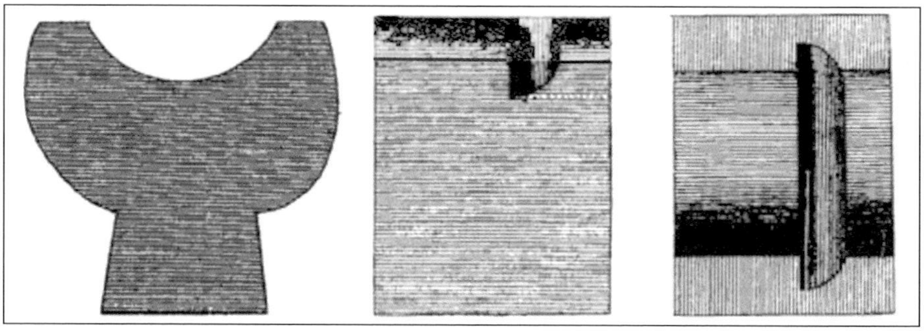

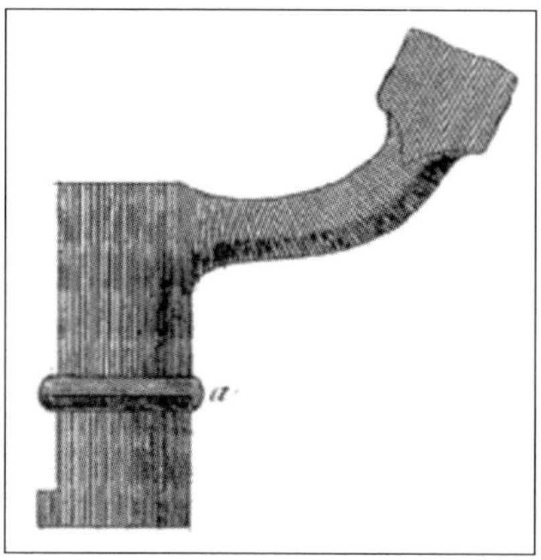

Above: Fig. 1.12. The bottom die used to form the 'bead'. (Rauch, 1793, Pl. III, Fig. 13)

Left: Fig. 1.13. The finished socket forging. (Rauch, 1793, Pl. III, Fig. 18)

i.e. forgings, store. The inspector examined the bore to make sure there were no defects that would not be removed by machining. He visually checked it for size and if he was uncertain, he would use the gauge, Fig. 1.14. As can be seen, this can check a variety of features.

The original illustration is annotated with the various features to be measured but unfortunately not all are legible. With regard to the socket forging, it will be seen that portions are marked *Douille de la Bayonette noire* – socket of the bayonet 'in the black', – which is taken to mean they are applicable to the forging, Fig. 1.15.

The large opening was for measuring the outside diameter of the socket, while the small one was for checking the diameter of the elbow. Another was used to gauge the geometry of the socket in relation to the bridge and the rib for the locking ring, Fig, 1.16.

If satisfactory, the socket would be stamped with the mark of the inspector on the portion of the 'elbow' to which the blade was to be welded.

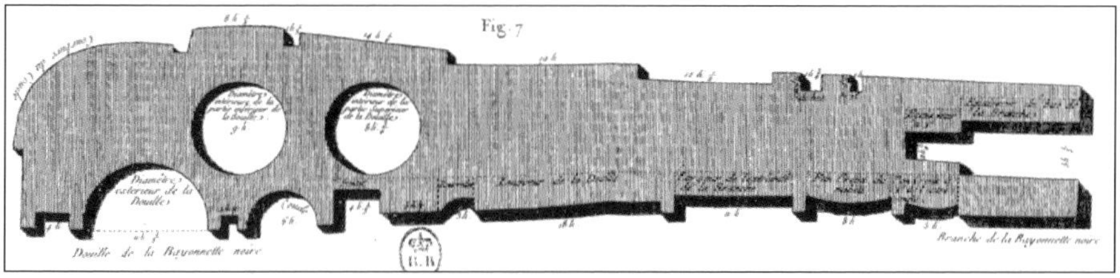

Fig. 1.14. The bayonet gauge. (Rauch, 1793, Pl. II, Fig. 7)

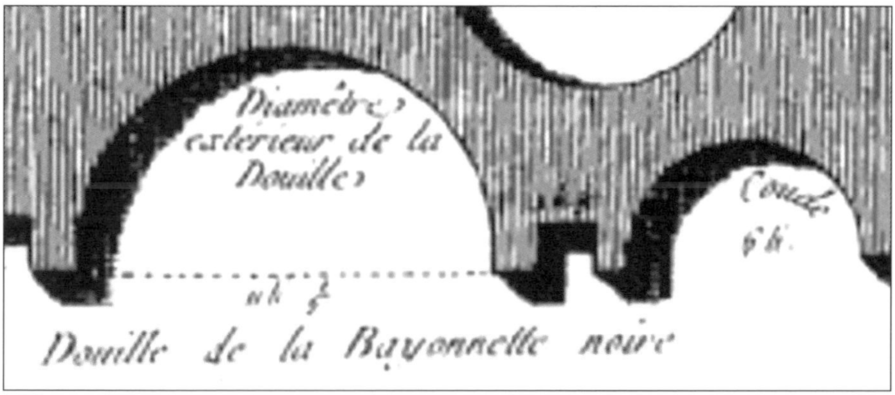

Above: Fig. 1.15. Detail of part of the gauge in Fig. 1.14.

Right: Fig. 1.16. The gauge for socket geometry with an actual socket alongside to illustrate its use.

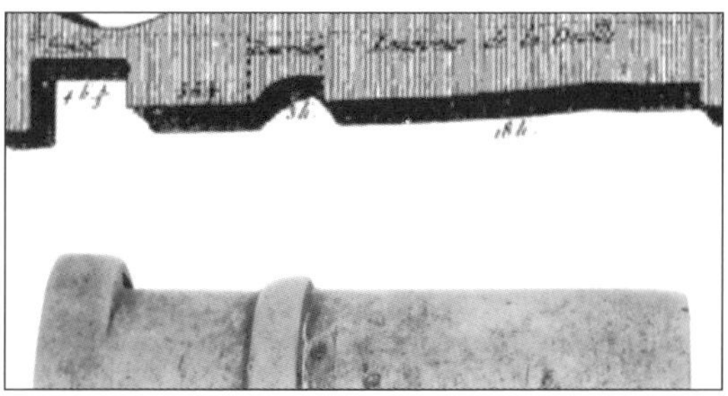

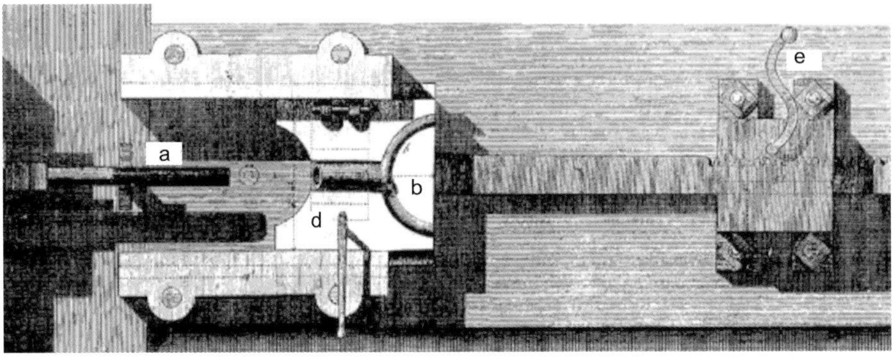

Fig. 1.17. Plan view of socket reaming machine: a: reamer; b: sliding carriage; d: clamping device; e: operating handle for the rack feed. (Rauch, 1793, Pl. IV, Fig. 20)

1.3 Reaming the socket

The next stage, reaming the socket, was carried out using a water-powered machine, Fig. 1.17.

According to Rauch,[2] this operation was carried out by children aged ten to twelve years. The process began by securing the socket in the clamping device, d, on the carriage, b. Using the rack and pinion arrangement, the socket was then fed onto the reamer, revolving at approximately 110–140rpm, until the largest diameter portion of the reamer passed through, indicated by the resistance ceasing. The account[3] is a little confusing at this point. On the one hand it implies that six different sized reamers were used; on the other hand, it implies a tapered reamer, whose largest size was that of the finished diameter, was employed. While the reaming was taking place, the second child was lubricating the reamer with a feather dipped in oil, and the outside of the socket was cooled by a stream of water. It was acknowledged that operating the rack feed on the machine was arduous work for a child and so the children took it in turns. Two hundred sockets were reamed daily. They were inspected once more and those accepted were stamped with the mark of the 'contrôleur d'armes noires' on the elbow.

1.4 Attaching and forging the blade

The making of the blade, like the socket, was a straightforward and simple process to those engaged in it. Describing those processes, even though there are the descriptions provided,[4] is far from simple, partly because some terminology is obscure.

As can be seen from Figs. 1.18 and 1.19, the blade had a medial rib running the full length at the rear, creating a 'T'-section. This allowed a reduction in weight over conventional triangular-section blades prevalent at the time the Model 1777 was created, but without any loss in strength, in the same manner as a 'T'-section steel beam.

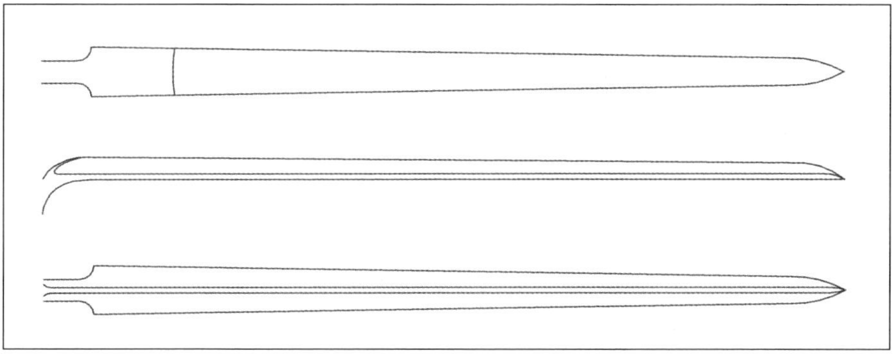

Above: Fig. 1.18. Drawings of the blade showing top, side and underside views. (© P. Smithurst)

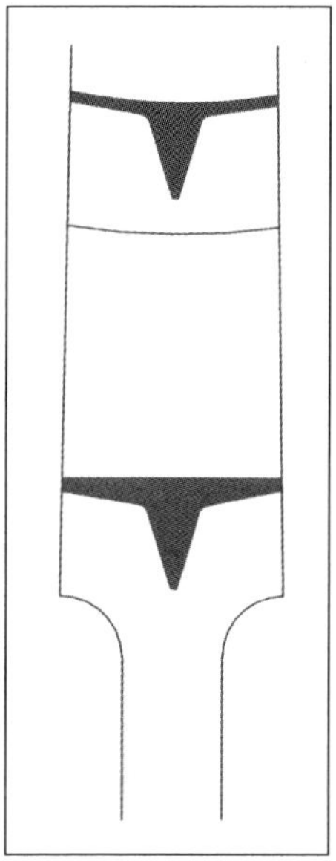

Right: Fig. 1.19. Sections of the blade; at the *root* of the blade, it has a flat top surface, the remainder being slightly concave. (© P. Smithurst)

The blade began as a steel bar eight lines (18mm) wide, six lines (13.5mm) thick and approximately seven inches long, requiring six and a half ounces (203 grams).[5] The end of the bar was forged to a taper to give an approximate shape to the 'mood' or 'mould' from which the blade proper would be formed. This seven-inch length was then cut off and the wide end bevelled in readiness to be welded to the bevelled end of the elbow. This sequence is interpreted in Fig. 1.20.

Prior to attaching the blade, the assistant had sorted all the prepared sockets into groups of 'correct weight', 'slightly over-weight' and 'slightly under-weight', and matched those with steel bars so that their combined weights were correct. Any bars that were too heavy or light were discarded. The first step in creating the blade was to weld one of the steel bars to the elbow of the socket. This commenced by taking a socket, heating the end of the elbow to a 'cherry red' and chamfering the end of the elbow, turning the bias [slope] towards the socket.[6] At the same time, the assistant was bevelling the end of the steel bar. They were returned to the hearth and the bevelled parts heated to a sparkling white heat, removed, the bevelled ends overlapped and

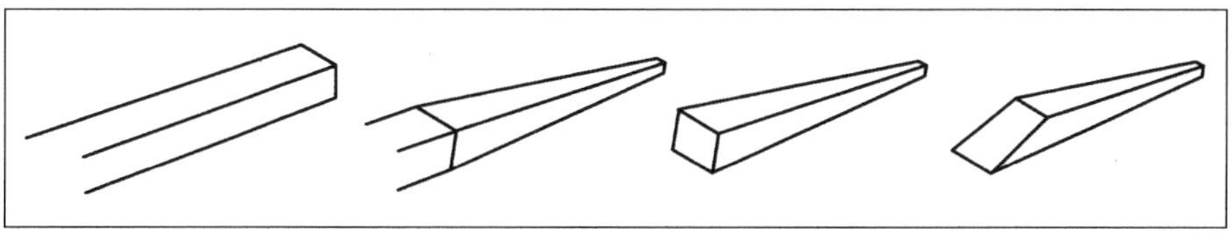

Fig. 1.20. Creating the *mood* from which the blade is formed. (© P. Smithurst)

welded by a series of fast, light hammer blows. This weld can be seen on the example shown in Fig. 1.21 where the iron of the elbow has become etched over the years while the steel blade portion remains relatively smooth.

The same phenomenon can be found on table knife blades, prior to the advent of stainless steel, where the steel for the blade was welded to an iron tang and was known in the Sheffield cutlery trade as the 'thumb-mark', Fig. 1.22.

When the master deemed the weld complete, and while the metal was sufficiently hot, with his assistant he began to forge the first third of the blade.[7]

> *He then places the elbow and the socket in the fixed dresser, and with the hand-dresser applied close he twists the model* [blade mood] *at its root, so as to place one of the edges to the right of the socket. This one will be flattened in the continuation of the work; but the opposite square will form the stop of the back of the blade.*[8]

The 'dresser' is the 'fork' set in the block on which the anvil stands, Fig. 1.23, but elsewhere in the text[9] is incorrectly referred to as a *tranchoir,* which is actually a chisel-like cutter.

No illustration of this stage is provided, but it is imagined to be of the form shown in the sketch in Fig. 1.24, in which the blade 'mood' has been twisted in relation to the socket.

Above: Fig. 1.21. An example showing the weld junction between the iron elbow and steel blade, delineated by the 'rough' and 'smooth' areas. (© P. Smithurst)

Left: Fig. 1.22. The 'thumb-mark' on a steel table knife blade welded to an iron tang. (© P. Smithurst)

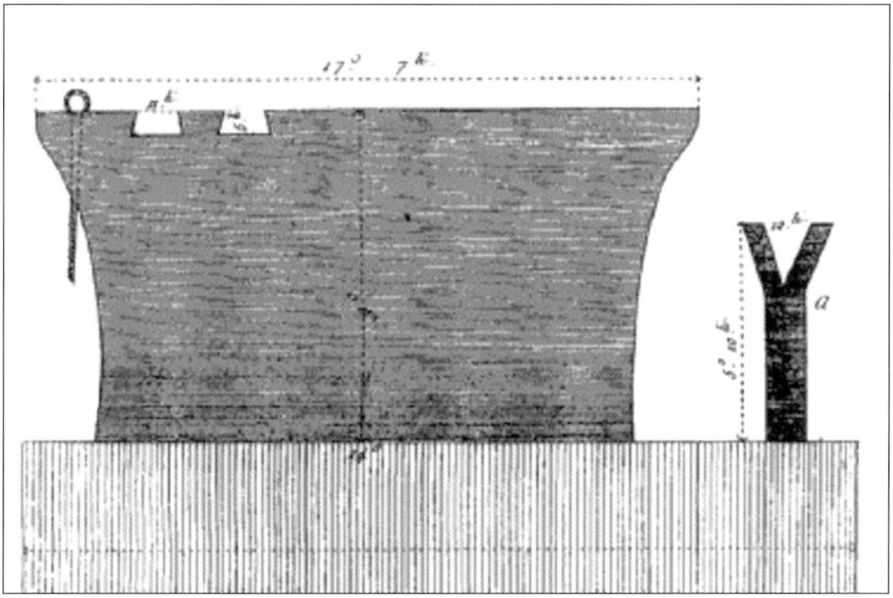

Fig. 1.23. The blade forger's anvil. (Rauch, 1793, fig. 21, pl. V)

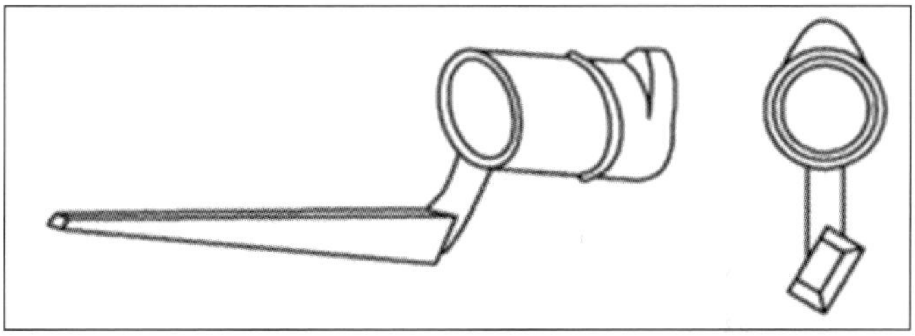

Fig. 1.24. Sketch showing the blade twisted in relation to the socket in preparation for forging. (© P. Smithurst)

The reason for this becomes apparent in a subsequent stage. First, the shoulder of the blade where it joins the elbow is formed using a die, or swage, Fig. 1.25, striking obliquely on the two upper faces of the blade, driving the metal towards the swage.

It would be expected that this would create a 'square' shoulder, whereas those shown in the illustrations have a definite curved form, and may therefore be a later modification.

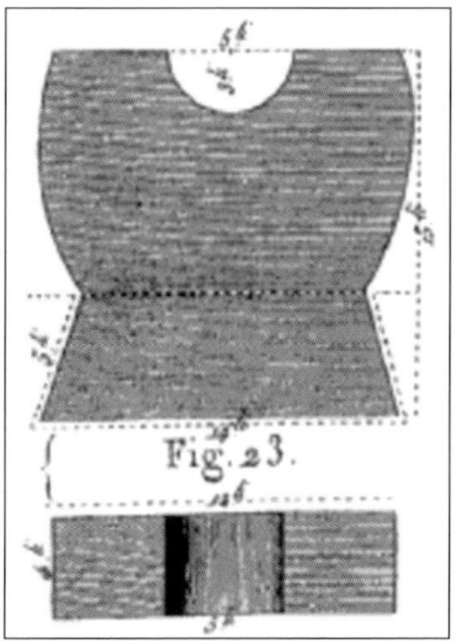

Fig. 1.25. The die, or swage, used to form the shoulder of the blade. (Rauch, 1793, fig. 23, pl. V)

At this point, the forger began to form the flat and the back of the blade which would ultimately be the 'T'-section already referred to. This he did using the pein of his hammer and working on both of the two exposed faces; the phrase quoted earlier can be recalled – *so as to place one of the edges to the right of the socket. This one will be flattened in the continuation of the work; but the opposite square will form the rib of the back of the blade.*[10] Whilst the description is vague, this process is presumed to be that shown in Fig. 1.26 since it is difficult to conceive of how otherwise a rectangular section might be transformed into the required triangular section by a simple forging operation.

It will be noticed that for this to be accomplished, the socket had to lie below the anvil face. Forging continued, drawing the blade to its full length of eleven inches (see Appendix 1 for comparison of the Paris inch with the Imperial inch). Work on creating the back of the blade then commenced, using the die shown in Fig. 1.27 which was fixed to the top of the anvil.

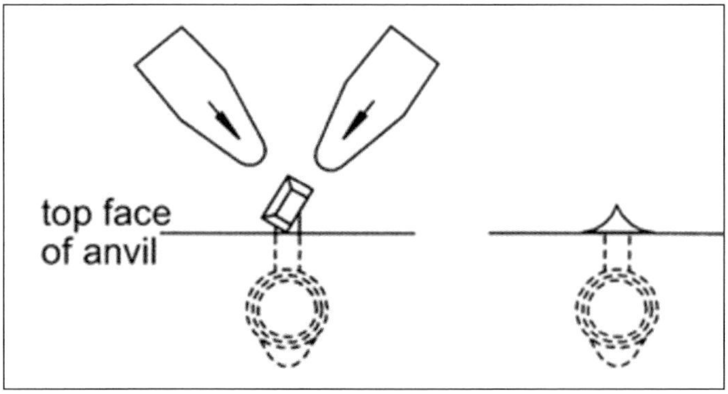

Fig. 1.26. The flat 'inner' face of the blade being formed and preparation of the 'back edge'. (© P. Smithurst)

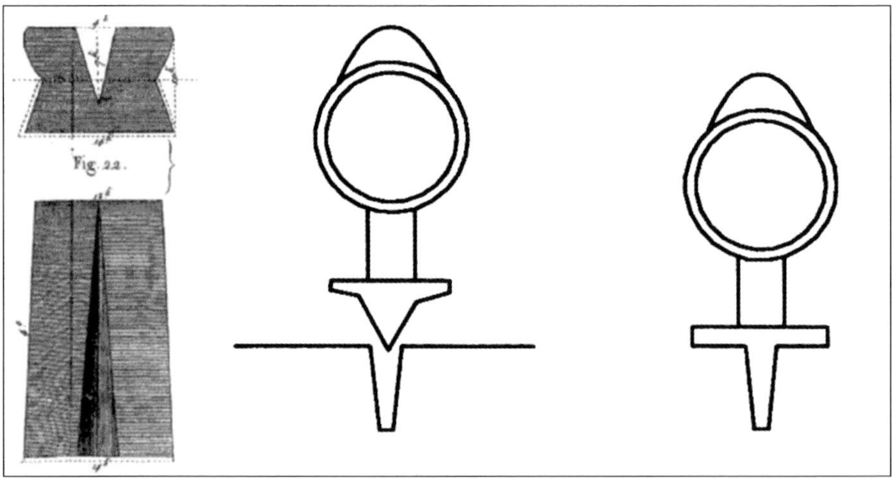

Fig. 1.27. *Left*; the die used. (Rauch, 1793, fig. 22, pl. V) *Right*; the transformation of the triangular section to a 'T' – section. (© P. Smithurst)

The heated blade was hammered on the die to form the roughly 'T'– section, moving it longitudinally in the process. Using a die graduated in depth and shorter than the blade would have required considerable skill to create a blade whose features tapered uniformly along its length. The die was *greased with shuttle oil or lard at the outset, and whenever it is deemed necessary. It is necessary to clean the bottom of the die every time, and it is best to grease it also each time.*[11]

Cleaning the bottom of the die, where flakes of iron scale accumulated and were compacted, was achieved using a steel spike kept close to hand. This forming of the back of the blade was usually carried out in two stages and when completed any imperfections were corrected by the forger using either hammer or dresser or both. The next operation was to create the 'hollow' on the inner, flat, face of the blade and was carried out using a series of graduated fullering tools, Fig. 1.28.

The blade was heated to 'cherry-red' and the back of the blade placed in the die used to create it, which acted as a support, and the forger – *placed on the opposite side the stamp used from above, fig. 24, whose flat shape, or at least very little curvature, is moulded on this face at the root of the blade,*

This almost flat face extended for about one inch.

Having performed that operation -

> *Here one operates on about two thirds of the blade, from the flattened face which was formed in the previous heating. The master uses the two top stamps, fig. 26 and 27. It starts at the narrowest point, which the master extends better, and makes it better penetrate into*

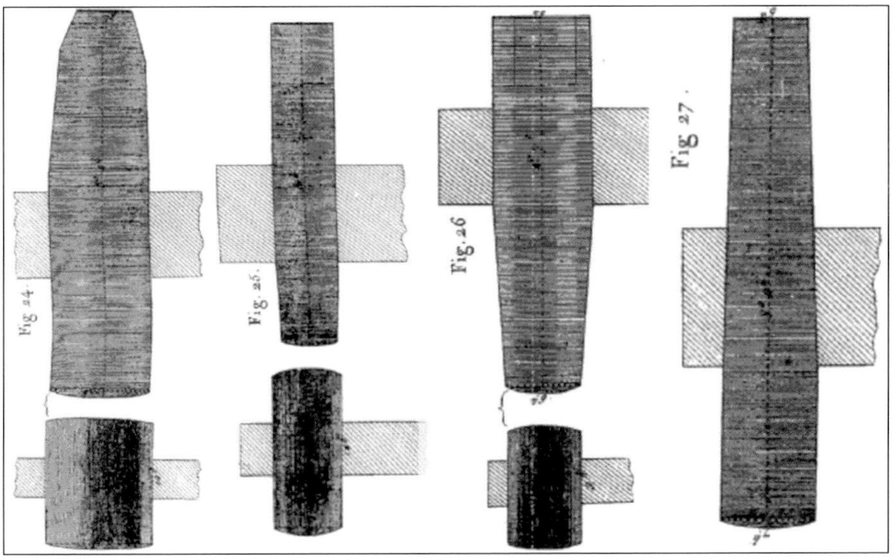

Fig. 1.28. The set of fullering tools, reorientated to show them in their functional position. The three on the left are also shown at bottom in plan view. (Rauch, 1793, pl. V, composite)

> *the angle of the stamp below, and then employs the widest, the form of which is better adapted to the concavity that the inner side of the blade must have, especially towards the base.*
>
> *It only remains to complete the preceding operation up to the point, with the same two rounded stamps, and to bring the blade to the prescribed length. – He works on the last third of the blade, and his object is to perfect the whole form. The stamp is used, fig. 25, which is the narrowest of the four.*[12]

Two marks were struck on the flat face of the blade, one of the blade forger and the other of the steel supplier. It once again went for inspection by the *contrôleur d'armes noires* who checked the dimensions of the different parts of the blade and for any defects which could not be removed during grinding, and, if satisfactory, received his mark on the elbow.

The blade was then hardened by heating to a 'cherry-red', withdrawing from the hearth and

> *passed twice through moistened iron scales which are heaped up on a small board placed on the edge of the trough, and he plunges it into the water in this same position, that is to say, starting with the point and keeping it inclined while it is submerged.*[13]

Following hardening, it was tempered by being held close above the hot charcoal and heated to what was considered the correct temperature. This was judged by its colour, depending on the nature of the steel used, and to confirm his judgement, on removing it from the hearth the craftsman would rub it with a rag to remove any scale so he could better examine it in the daylight. Then, whilst still hot, the blade was straightened if necessary, followed by quenching in water.[14]

1.5 Grinding, Polishing and Burnishing

The blade was now ready for its finishing treatments of which there were three:

> *that of grinding itself, that of polishing with emery and that of burnishing with charcoal. but it is necessary to distinguish also the work to be done on the back of the blade from that on its inside face.*[15]

There was however no straightforward progression, each process, except burnishing, being interspersed.

There are some questions arising around the interpretation of various terms used in the original document. For instance, *aiguisage* is often translated as 'sharpening' but in this context more logically means 'grinding to shape/size'. Others are *brunissage* and *brunit,* both of which can be translated as *burnishing* or *browning.* Both are applicable to arms, but 'browning' is out of place in grinding and polishing operations and therefore these two terms assuredly refer to 'burnishing'. Finally, *canelure* can be taken to be a 'rib' or a 'groove' and used in the context of grinding wheels, either might be applicable. However, in comparison with grinding wheels used in some of the Sheffield trades, such as the grinding of round and triangular files, 'groove' would seem to be the most appropriate meaning.

1.6 Grinding

A variety of grinding wheels were used – a large sandstone wheel about seven feet diameter and 7 to 8 inches wide turning at around 160–200rpm and two more sandstone wheels of 6 and 3 inches diameter.[16] At this point contradictions begin to be encountered. According to this same statement there is a *millstone of soft granite with grooves of about twenty-four to thirty inches in diameter for the edges of the blade*, whilst elsewhere four 'medium' wheels of soft red granite ranging from 15 inches to 30 inches diameter and grooved on their peripheries, operating at 400–500rpm, are referred to.[17] The confusion does not end there. There is a choice between four polishing wheels or three polishing wheels, one of twenty-four inches in diameter; another six inches, and the last of those three inches.[18] Despite this confusion over the number of 'wheels' used the more important aspect is *how* they were used.

The first step was to make the blade the correct length and this was done by holding the tip against the flat side of one of the 'grooved' grinding wheels, using a wrought iron 'scabbard' mounted on a piece of wood to check the length.[19] This seems a very unlikely material for a bayonet scabbard at this time and was probably one specially made to act as a gauge for use by grinders.

The grinder then transferred to the large grinding wheel and sitting in front of the edge rotating towards him, ground square, i.e. at 90° to the longitudinal axis, across the face and two edges of the blade, and also the edge of the rib at the back of the blade. He also formed the point using the edge and two side faces of the grindstone. Again, a 'scabbard' was used to check the maximum widths. This was the only work carried out on the large grindstone.

He then returned to the grooved grinding wheels. These, it will be recalled, were made from soft red granite and the various grooves formed on their periphery matched different features of the blade. He began by grinding the two faces adjacent to the rib along the back of the blade, grinding one side then the other for the lower two-thirds of the blade. This was done in two stages because of the heat generated and the need to quench the blade to prevent the temper being destroyed. This alone suggests the grinding was carried out 'dry' (see appendix 4), as opposed to using a stone fed with a stream of water. Then the final third towards the tip was ground in a narrower groove. These features were checked against a gauge as and when necessary, but the gauge is not illustrated.

It was then that the inner face of the blade received attention. The concavity consisted of three parts; at the base of the blade, adjacent to the elbow, it was virtually flat for about one inch; from there to the centre of the blade it had a slightly more pronounced hollow, and from the centre to the point the hollow was even more pronounced. For the first inch of the blade, he therefore used a small grindstone of sandstone or soft granite about six inches diameter. We are told that *these grinding wheels are liable to vary greatly in their quality: the one that bites the best is the best for this operation.*[20] This same wheel was used to 'whiten' the blade all over, i.e., remove the oxidised 'black' surface to reveal the bare metal. It is perhaps easy to understand from this comment why edged weapons are referred to as 'armes blanche', although French gun barrels were also finished 'white'.

For the portion from the 'flat' base to the centre, a wheel of three inches diameter was employed. Finally, the portion up to the point was ground longitudinally on one of the grinding wheels with a raised curved rib. At each stage the curvature could be checked against a gauge and after grinding, the blade was checked against a scabbard which it had to just enter.[21] The edge of the blade was rounded by grinding lengthwise in a groove and finally the grinder struck his mark on the 'flat' portion.

1.7 Polishing

The blade was now ready for polishing, and it has been noted that the polishing wheels were made of oak. Indeed, very specific guidelines are given for the type of oak to be used:

> *We should choose old oak with a fine grain, and preferably one which grows towards the top of the mountains on the southern side and had its trunk exposed to the rays of the sun: we advise to leave it a year or eighteen months in water before using it, so that it does not warp, but often one does not have this foresight. There must be no knots in the polishing wheels.*[22]

The wheels were composite, constructed of segments so that the grain of the wood ran along the periphery. Often the edges of the wheels would need cleaning of embedded emery, especially in moving from polishing to burnishing, and this was done by applying a chisel to the rotating wheel, as in turning.[23] This is very similar to practices in the Sheffield cutlery trades where such wheels were used in a process referred to as 'glazing' – the replacement of the coarser grinding marks by finer ones as a prelude to polishing fine blades.

First to be polished was the back of the blade and this was performed using the large wheel of 24 to 30 inches diameter and up to two inches wide rotating at up to 1,000rpm. A paste of emery and oil was applied to the 'hollow' sections on the back, and they were polished lengthwise. They were done in stages because the heat generated made it impossible for the grinder to apply hand pressure on the middle of the blade after polishing to continue polishing up to the point. The blade was then sprinkled with 'fine sand or powdered ash', wiped over with a rag to remove the oil and then polished again all along the back. That process was repeated, after which the face of the blade was polished.

For this the large polishing wheel needed a more rounded edge than for the previous process and the grinder shaped it by turning it with a joiner's chisel, or a piece of sabre blade. A paste of emery and oil was applied from the mid-point of the blade to the tip and it was polished lengthwise, angling it slightly so the socket did not come into contact with the wheel.[24] This was a consequence of geometry as shown in Fig. 1.29, the socket making it impossible to polish more than half of the blade lengthwise on the large polishing wheel.

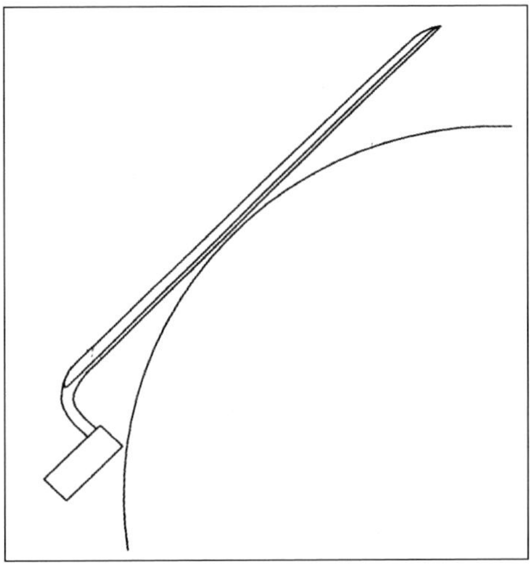

Fig. 1.29. Diagram to show the limitations of grinding the inner face of the blade on a large diameter wheel. (© P. Smithurst)

As will be seen, smaller polishing wheels were available and could have been used to polish lengthwise so why they were not used for that purpose remains unknown. At the conclusion of this process, the blade was sprinkled with sand or ashes, wiped, and polished again, this process being repeated one more time.

1.8 Burnishing

The blade was then ready for burnishing. The large polishing wheel was again 'turned' with a chisel to prepare it for burnishing the back of the blade. The rim of the rotating wheel was rubbed with alder or beech charcoal and then the rim polished with a piece of agate or hard red haematite. The 'hollows' in the back of the blade were burnished, re-charging the wheel with charcoal and polishing with agate if necessary. The polishing wheel was then turned with the chisel to suit the upper half of the blade, and this was burnished in the same way.

The final operation was to polish the lower half of the blade, but unlike the upper half, this was polished crosswise. This operation was postponed until this time so that the burnished upper half of this face is clearly separate from the simply polished lower half. The first one-inch 'flat' portion was smeared with emery and oil and polished with a six-inch wheel. The three-inch wheel was then used in the same manner to polish up to the half-way point, leaving a line of demarcation between the burnished and polished regions. The blade was again sprinkled with sand or ashes and wiped over. This demarcation in the surface finishes between two sections of blade was not uncommon. The Sheffield cutlers I knew referred to it as 'crossing' and it was to be found on many blades including that of the Enfield

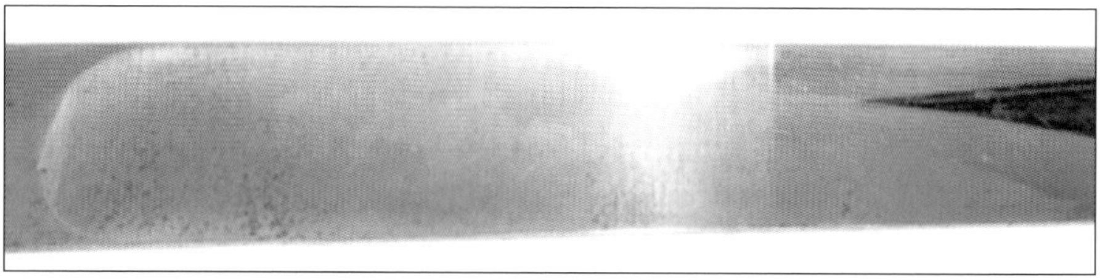

Fig. 1.30. Portion of an Enfield 1853 bayonet showing the demarcation between surface finishes. (© P. Smithurst)

Pattern 1853 bayonet, Fig. 1.30, although it was a visible feature soon lost in the bayonet's service life.

Explaining these processes makes them appear long and drawn out and in reality it was quite a slow process. Each stage was carried out on a batch of bayonets:

> *The grinder usually operates on fifty or sixty bayonets, which is two days' work for him and his assistant. Each operation is done on all successively.*[25]

1.9 Inspecting and testing the blade

The bayonet was subjected to another inspection with a particular focus on the blade, the length, widths and inclination being checked using the scabbard mentioned previously, and if there were any doubts about the shape of the other parts, the gauge could be used. The relevant part of the gauge shown in Fig. 1.31 with the metric equivalents, measured using an actual example, from left to right, the widths of the blade at the base, one-third of the length and at the tip before it curves to a point.

The quality of the polishing and burnishing were also inspected, and the blade was subjected to a bending test using a special jig although the description, in translation, lacks some clarity.[26] However, the description and the nature of the test has led to only one conclusion of how the device functioned. The point of the

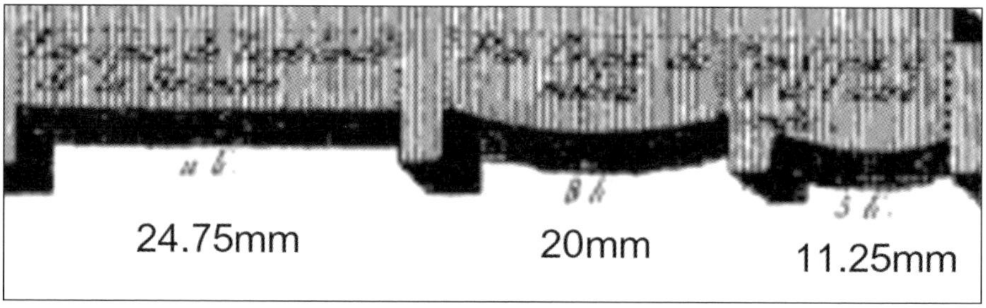

Fig. 1.31. Part of the bayonet gauge shown in Fig. 1.14 used for checking blade widths with modern metric equivalents from an actual specimen added.

blade was placed in the opening in the block A, and the middle of the blade rested on block B, shown in Figs. 1.32 and 1.33.

The dimension shown on the drawing for the height of the top face of B, although not fully distinct, would appear to be 17 lignes – 38.25mm. Interestingly, this results in the same degree of bending applied to the Enfield pattern 1853 bayonet and which will be discussed later. The sketch below shows how it is envisaged to have functioned.

If all was acceptable, the inspector stamped his mark at the base of the flat portion of the blade, supporting it in the appropriate groove in a brass 'cushion', Fig. 1.34.

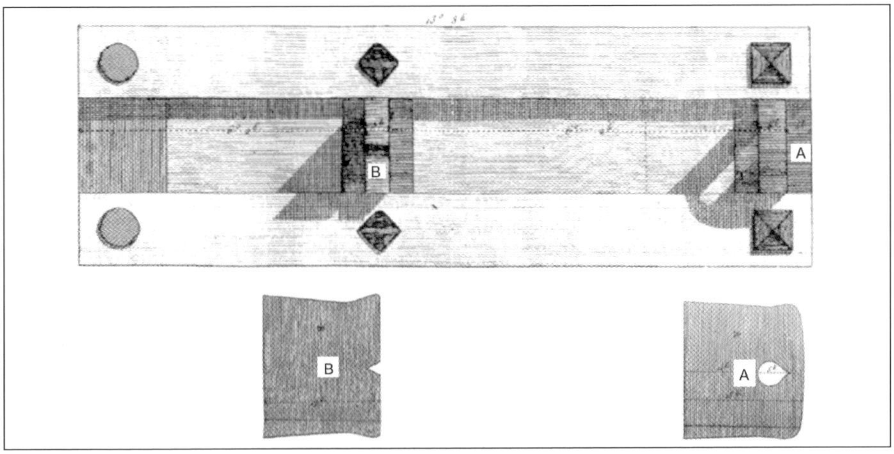

Fig. 1.32. The 'bending test' appliance. (Adapted from Rauch, 1793, fig. 29, pl. 6)

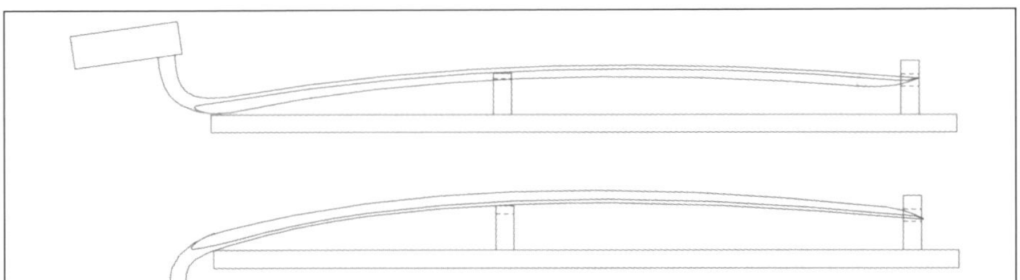

Fig. 1.33. Sketch of the bend-testing fixture in use. (© P. Smithurst)

Fig. 1.34. A portion of the brass 'cushion' on which the bayonet blade and elbow were supported for stamping. (Rauch, 1793 Fig. 19, pl. 3)

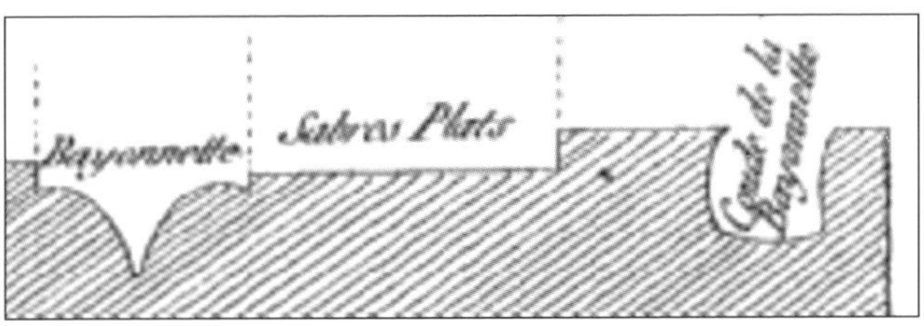

1.10 Cutting the mortice slot

A number of operations still remained to be carried out, including the cutting of the 'zig-zag' mortice slot in the socket to receive the tenon on the barrel and by which, in conjunction with the locking ring, the bayonet was held in place, and the manufacture of the locking ring and its screw and the fitting to the socket of the 'stop-pin' to prevent over-rotation of the ring.

First, the socket was filed to the correct length, using the gauge to ensure correct placement of the orifices relative to the bead. The slot was then cut. Its nature is shown in Fig. 1.35; it creates an opening in the 'bridge' of the socket and then extends with a 'dog-leg' into the socket walls, cutting through the bead against which the locking ring is seated. The opening through the bridge is described as being first cut with a chisel.[27] A mandrel carrying a hardened steel cutter two and a half lines (5.6mm) wide, Fig. 1.36, was then inserted into the socket, the cutting edge aligned with the opening in the bridge, then driven by hammer blows to cut the first leg of the slot.

The cross slot forming the first part of the 'dog-leg' was then made using the edge of a coarse file followed by finishing with another coarse file two and a half lines thick. It will be realised that filing the walls of a tube across its axis would

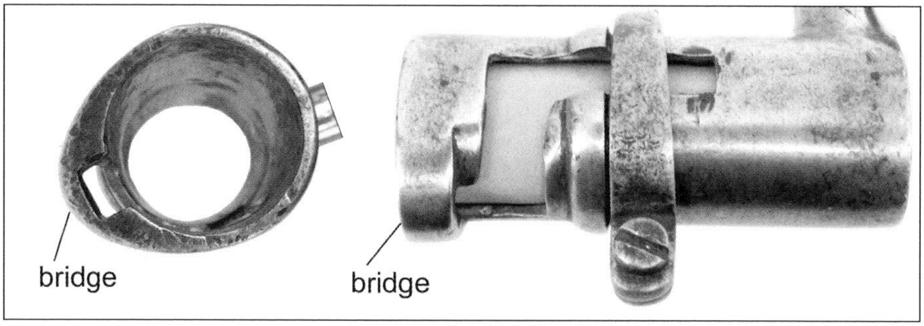

Fig. 1.35. Showing the nature and position of the slot into which the tenon on the barrel passes. Since the tenon is beneath the barrel, the bayonet when fitted has its blade to the right when the musket is held in the firing position. (© P. Smithurst)

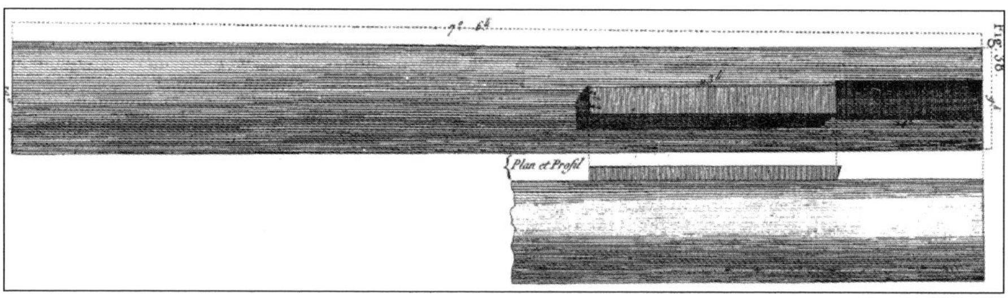

Fig. 1.36. The mandrel, more in the nature of a 'drift' or 'broach', with its inserted cutter (Rauch, 1793, fig. 38, plate 7).

create a rectangular opening without the need for additional tooling. Finally, the third leg of the slot was commenced by filing the appropriate portion of the bead flush with the walls of the socket and then delineating the slot with a chisel, followed by the use of another mandrel with a short inserted hardened steel cutter, fitting into the socket with the cutter passing through the slots already created. The socket was then placed so that its upper edge rested on the jaws of the vice and the mandrel struck with a hammer to remove the metal to form the third leg of the slot. Any burrs left from these operations were removed with files.

1.11 Filing the socket body and bead

It then remained to clean the body of the socket and the bead using coarse files, the operation being attended with frequent use of the gauge to ensure correct dimensions.[28] The shape of the body and bead were then perfected using a special hinged tool, Fig. 1.37, fitted with two hardened steel inserts whose inner semi-circular faces match the required profile of socket and bead and are cut with teeth resembling that of a fine burr or rasp rather than file teeth.

Making this would have required a high degree of skill to maintain the correct sizes of the socket body. The tool was used by first fixing a mandrel, to which the bayonet socket was fitted, in the vice with the blade pointing downwards. The tool was then clamped around the socket and turned vigorously with both hands.[29] Although not stated, it is presumed that when the jaws were fully closed,

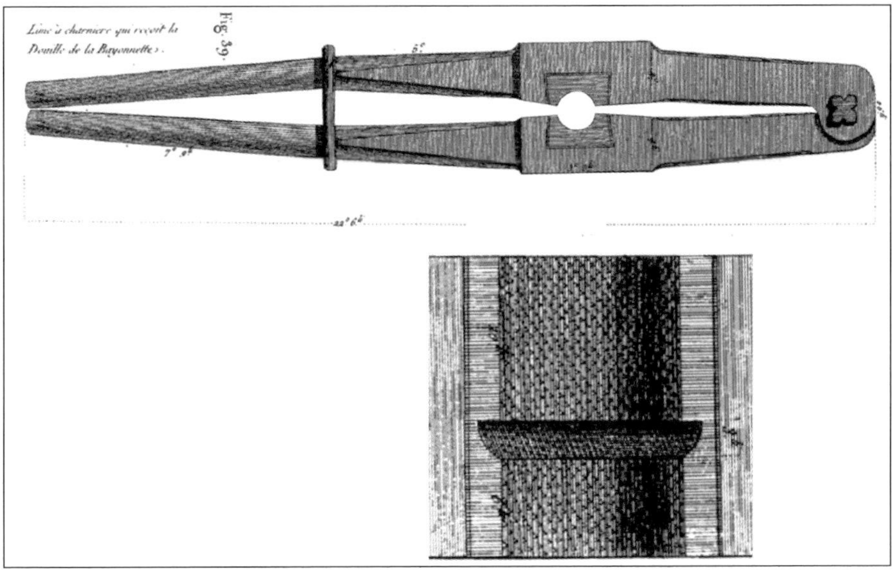

Fig. 1.37 *Top:* Special 'clamp' filing tool for the socket; *Bottom:* detail showing the profiled inner face of an insert cut with file teeth. (Adapted from Rauch, 1793, Fig. 39, plate 7 with shadows removed for clarity)

the correct dimensions had been reached. This process is the forerunner of 'clamp milling' in which relatively simple profiles of circular cross-section were formed to pre-determined sizes using hollow milling cutters in a lathe or milling machine.

1.12 Making the locking ring (virole)

The locking ring, whilst seemingly a simple device, required a high degree of accuracy in its geometry and, therefore, in its forging and finishing.

When finished, the 'ears', which were brought together to form the 'head' when the ring was bent to shape, had to meet without a gap and when clamped with the screw, the ring had to rotate freely, but not be loose, on the socket. The 'stop', which engaged with the 'stop-pin' and limited rotation of the ring, had to be in the correct position. The notch in the 'bridge', which allowed passage of the barrel tenon, had to be of correct size and correctly aligned with the bridge on the socket.

The ring commenced as a small bar of iron three and a half (Paris) inches (94.8mm) long, four lines (9mm) wide and two lines (4.5mm) thick.[30] Then, by use of a simple former, Fig. 1.39, it was forged to correspond with the forging shown in Fig. 1.40.

The simple shape and size alongside the need for accurate geometry of the ring forging would have made it an ideal candidate for die-forging, both as a means of speeding the process and ensuring repetitive accuracy. After re-heating to red heat, a hole at least one and a half lines in diameter (3.375mm), for the shank of the screw, was then punched in one 'ear' and in the other ear a hole, one line in diameter (2.25mm) was punched and which was subsequently tapped.[31] After heating again, the forging was placed with the central boss in the channel usually reserved for fitting

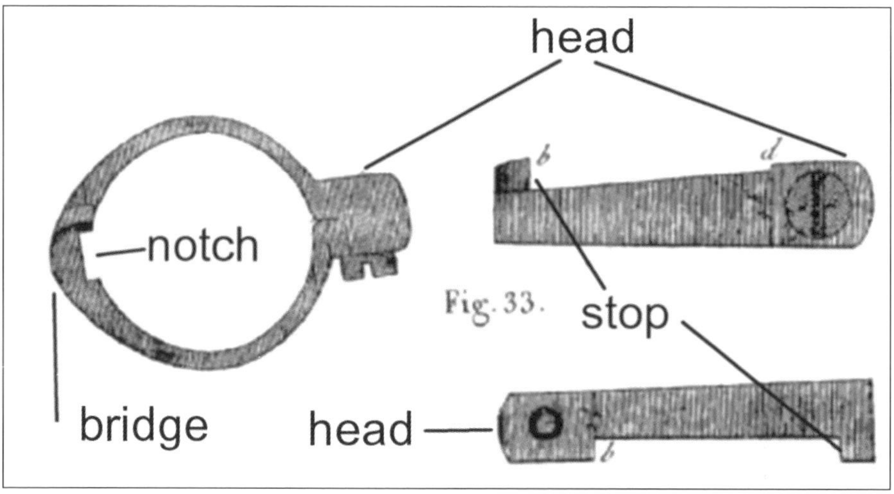

Fig. 1.38. The features of the ring. (From Rauch, 1793, Fig. 33, plate 6)

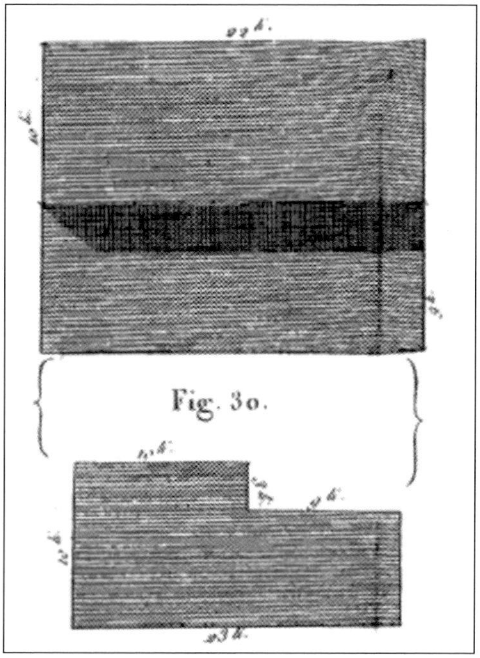

Right: Fig. 1.39. The former used in forging the ring. (Rauch, 1793, Fig. 30, plate 6)

Below: Fig. 1.40. The ring in its forged state. (From Rauch, 1793, Figs. 31 & 32, plate 6)

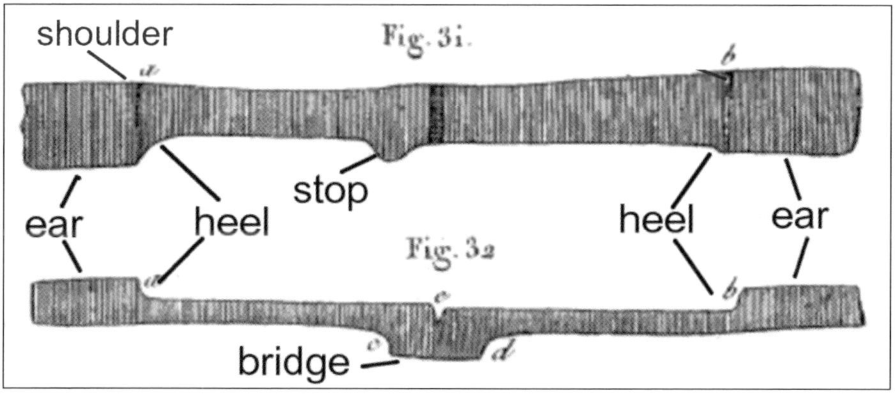

tooling on the anvil face and was struck with the pein of a hammer. This roughly formed the rectangular notch in what would become the bridge and at the same time commenced folding the forging into a ring. A further heating allowed the forging to be placed on a mandrel whose diameter was the same as the outside diameter of the socket and after shaping it as much as possible by hand, the forger:

> *then put it on the die,* [Fig. 1.41 on next page], *to complete rounding and to form the two folds that are necessary to put the heels at the ends in contact, as they must be, to accommodate the screw that must pass through them.*[32]

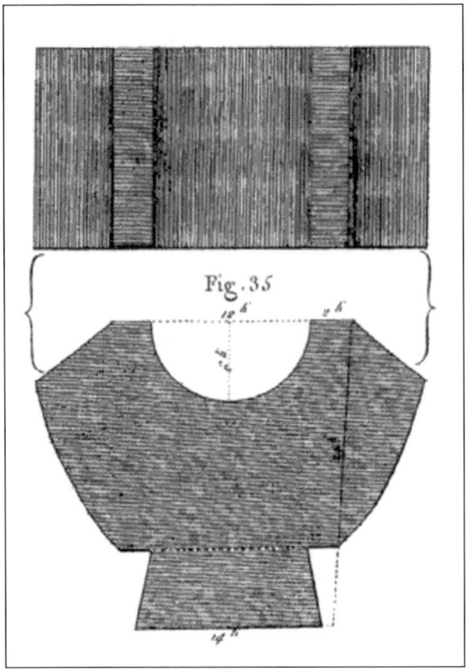

The finished form of the ring after this stage is shown in Fig. 1.42.

Considering the form of the ring, it is difficult to conceive from Rauch's description how the required result could be achieved, although something may have been lost in translation. The geometry of the die does not match that of the ring. Whilst the diameter of 12 lines (27mm) corresponds to the outer diameter of the circular portion of the ring, the periphery of the ring is not wholly circular with the lobe which will form the bridge, Fig. 1.43. Nor would it allow the forming of the two 'ears' which, when brought together, form the head of the ring.

The only way envisaged that the die could work would be by opening the ring along its axis into a short helix. This would allow the 'lobe' to clear the die and the 'ears' to be bent preparatory to forming the 'head', Fig. 1.44.

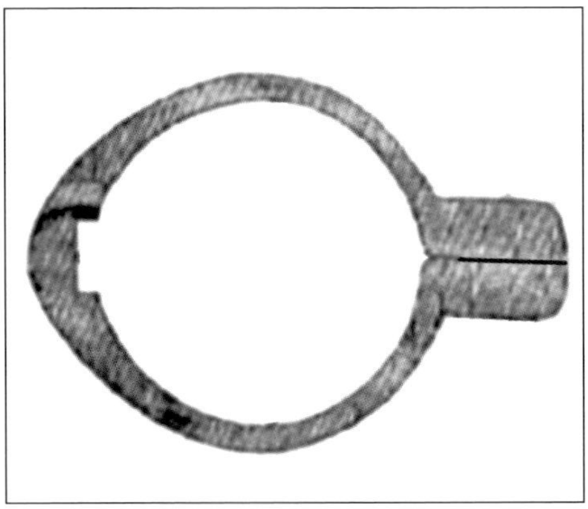

Above: Fig. 1.41. The die used to form the ring. (Rauch, 1793, Fig. 35, Pl. 6)

Left: Fig. 1.42. The finished ring forging. (Rauch, 1793, Fig. 33, Pl. 6)

Below: Fig. 1.43. The die and ring superimposed do not fit. (© P. Smithurst)

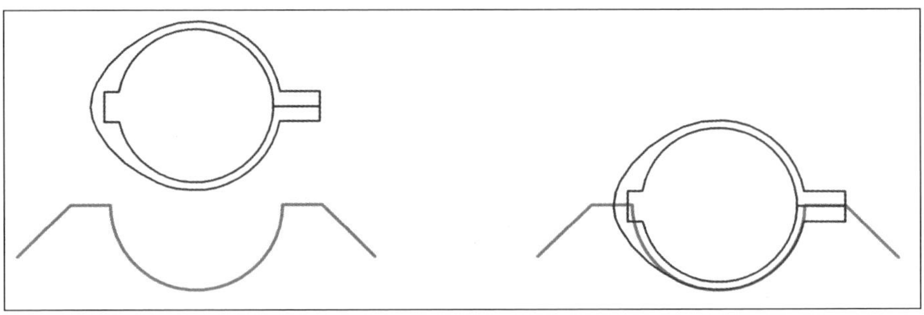

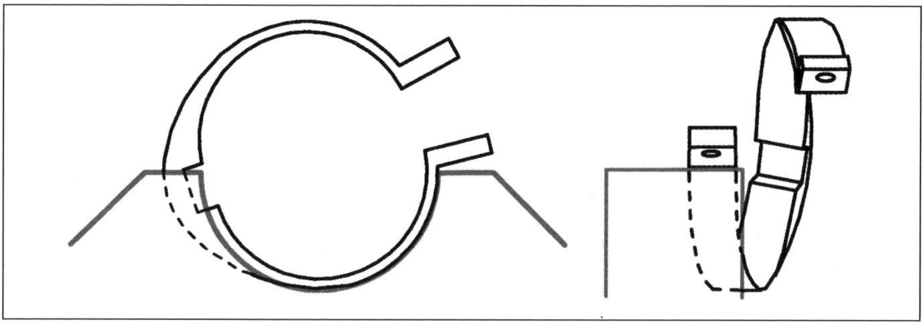

Fig. 1.44. Opening the ring to form a short helix would allow the die to fulfil at least part of its function. (© P. Smithurst)

The description continues:

> *To achieve this last object* [forming the 'head'], *the forger places alternately several times, the outer face of each of these folds on the two flattened flanges of the stamp, and strikes first with the pein of the hammer, and then of the head, on the opposite side of the other fold. He takes care in joining the two folds, which will be called ears thereafter, to align the two holes.*[33]

Again, using the die shown, it would seem difficult since the ears could not be bent to lie on the top flat face of the die as this would give the wrong angle for their subsequent mating together. The only way that can be envisaged would be to have one of the flat faces flanking the die cavity lowered by the thickness of the 'ears'.

However, Rauch makes no mention of such procedures being followed so we are left to wonder exactly how this stage of the manufacture was performed. From his previous statement, the forger:

> *takes care in joining the two folds, which will be called ears thereafter, to align the two holes*

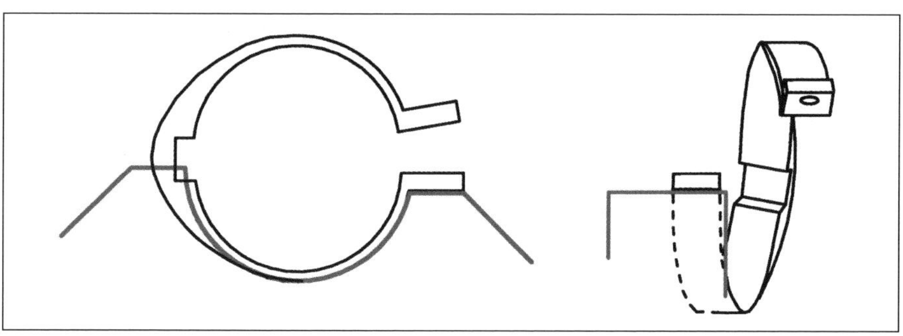

Fig. 1.45. Lowering one flat face flanking the die would allow the 'ears' to be set at the correct angle. (© P. Smithurst)

and that in itself would have been a difficult undertaking whatever procedure was used, requiring the holes to have been perfectly positioned in the first place, before any bending took place.

After annealing:

> *The filer takes the ring as it leaves the forge; he clasps it in the vice by the edges of the one of the two 'ears' which must be tapped; and to be free to do it, he turns away the other; he perfects the hole of the first with a hand-held square broach, which has a handle like a gimlet, and then he taps this hole. He withdraws this ear from the vice, and puts the other in it, to pass the same broach, which being conical, can also perfect the hole, though of a half-line greater.*[34]

The words *he turns away the other* is taken to mean that the ring was opened up into the shallow helix as suggested. The flat mating faces of the 'ears' were then filed, and great care was needed to ensure that when closed together again, the holes for the screw were properly aligned, tested by fitting the screw, and that when screwed together, the ring was able to rotate on the socket without being too loose or exhibiting any binding. The ring was then fixed in the vice by the ears so that the face which mated with the bead on the socket was horizontal and the forger carefully filed that face and the corresponding edges of the ears. Then the inside edge of the ring was slightly chamfered so that the ring would fit snugly against the bead. The ring was reversed in the vice and its upper profile filed. The edge-views of the ring shown in Fig. 1.38 do not quite concur with reality since studying an actual ring, Fig. 1.46, shows that one upper edge slopes from the 'head' to the bridge whilst the other edge, which engages with the stop-pin on the socket, steps down at the head and runs parallel until it reaches the projecting 'stop'.

To file those edges accurately and without damaging the one opposite would have required great care. The filed edges were then treated with a fine file followed by burnishing with a hardened steel burnisher having a single handle.[35]

These were important elements and to avoid extensive repetition suffice it to say that, in the case of the ring and the screw, they were first forged using simple dies, followed by filing to create correct contours and dimensions and finally they were polished and burnished. The 'stop-pin' was simply cut from a piece of suitable iron wire, threaded for an appropriate distance, a hole in its correct position in the socket having already been prepared to receive it. All of that required careful forging and the judicious use of the file.

Fig. 1.46. The 1777 bayonet locking ring. (Author's collection)

Chapter 2

Manufacture of the Russian Model 1808 bayonet at Tula

2.1 Introduction

In his own words Gamel notes that the musket is the Model approved by His Majesty the Emperor in 1808,[1] and hence the bayonet is given the same designation. Gamel also notes that the military hierarchy were aware of Cotty's publication of 1806[2] and, given the many close similarities, there can be little doubt that the French M.1777 was the inspiration for the Russian M.1808. Unfortunately, the Russian M.1808 bayonet has proved to be a particularly rare item in Britain, despite the fact that 487 flintlock muskets were captured in the Crimean War,[3] but whether with their bayonets is not stated. The only example it is possible to illustrate is that in Fig. 2.1.

It will be seen to have lost its bridge over the entrance to the mortice slot at some point but its kinship with the French M.1777 is clear.

It would appear that prior to 1818/19 operations at Tula were similar to those at Klingenthal but at that time bayonet making at Tula was extensively mechanised with machines introduced by Pavel Dmitrievich Zahava (1779-1839), a mechanic at the Tula factory.[4, 5] The procedures at Tula therefore provide interesting comparisons in view of the Russian bayonet being basically a copy of the French Model 1777 bayonet. Manufacture at Tula commenced with two pounds of wrought iron and one pound of steel (approximately 0.9 pounds avoirdupois, 409 grams).

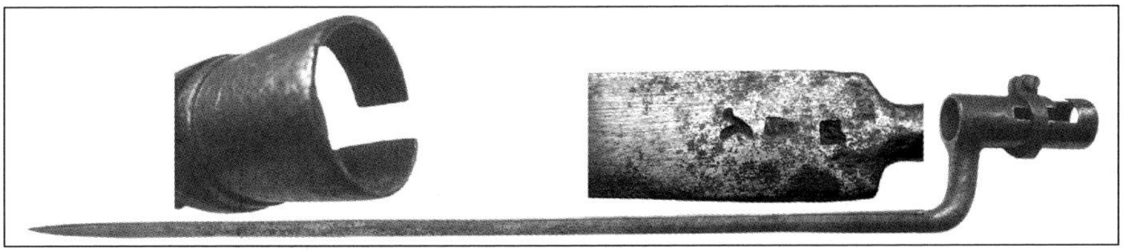

Fig. 2.1. The Russian M.1808 bayonet. (Courtesy of Graham Priest)

2.2 Forging the socket

A portion of the iron bar was cut off, hot-forged and wrapped to form a tube, then welded along the seam in the same way as in barrel making. The remaining piece of iron was further divided and a *neck with a tongue* and a *lump* were prepared. These were then welded to the tube, diametrically opposed, to create the bayonet socket, Fig. 2.2.

The steel bar was then welded to the neck, presumably by a 'scarfed' joint in the traditional way, and forged to form the blade.

After this stage, the bayonet was adjusted to a gauge, the nature of which was not specified but considering the rudimentary state of the bayonet at this point gauging would have been very simple, checking such things as the offset of the elbow and that there was sufficient metal in the socket and blade for them to be finished to correct size. All this work was carried out in the private forges at the homes of the craftsmen, who, with the help of the assistant, forged around 6 bayonets per day.

Curiously, the blade was hardened at this stage by heating to red heat and then dropping it into a trough of cold water.[6] The blade was then tempered by

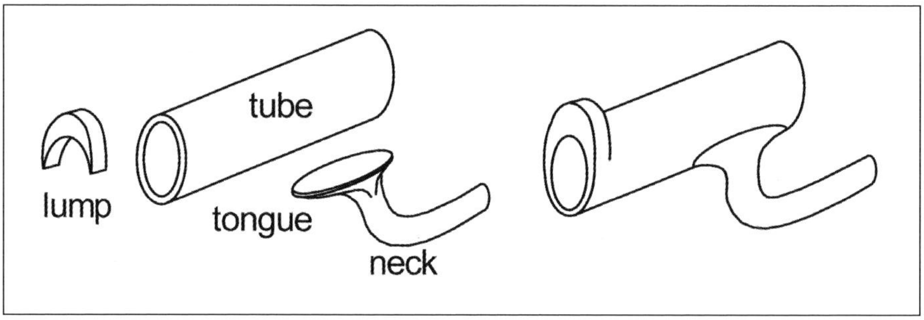

Fig. 2.2. Interpretation of Gamel's description. (© P. Smithurst)

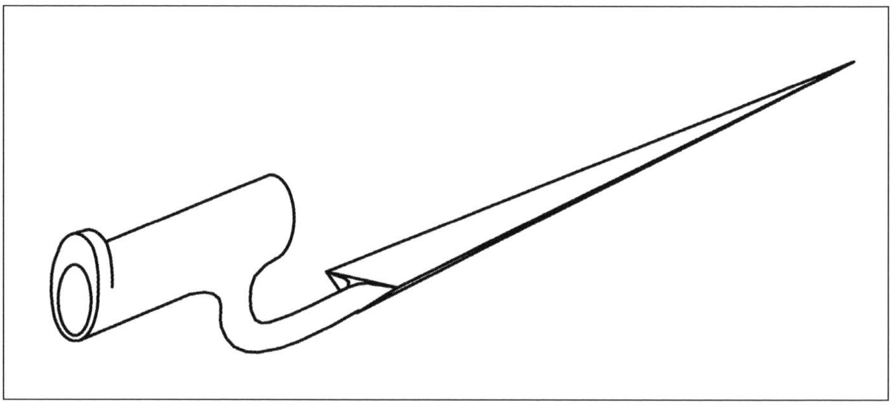

Fig. 2.3. The blade attached and shaped. (© P. Smithurst)

heating to a pre-determined lower temperature and the blade straightened if necessary. It is not stated that the blade is quenched after tempering but one would imagine that if it were not, and allowed to cool naturally, the blade would become too soft.

2.3 Rough-boring the socket

After this hardening and tempering, the socket underwent its first, or *rough* drilling operation. This was carried out in the barrel drilling workshop using the same tools and methods. Since the socket tube internal diameter had to be ultimately equal to the outer diameter of the muzzle, larger drills were required and up to twenty could be used in this first drilling operation, a gauge being used to determine the correct size.

The second, or *finish* drilling operation was carried out on one of the recently introduced machines, Fig. 2.4.

The machine consists of basically, two parallel beds on which two bayonets were mounted by fixing their sockets in the clamps on each of the sliding carriages. The bayonet shown in position on the rear bed may not be readily visible so an

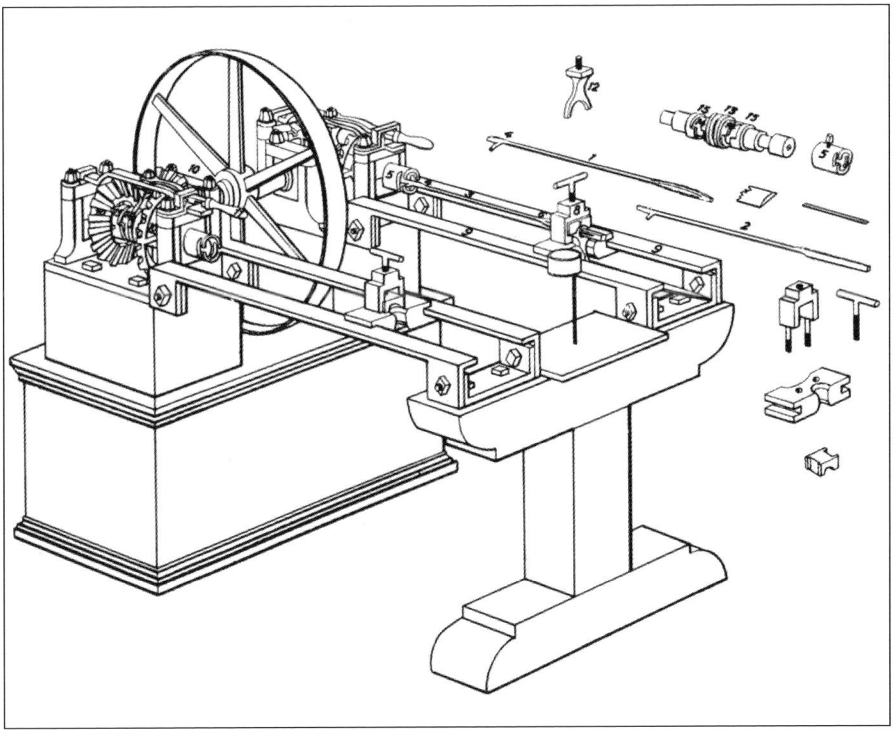

Fig. 2.4. The machine used at Tula for finish drilling the bayonet sockets. (Gamel, 1826, Fig. XV)

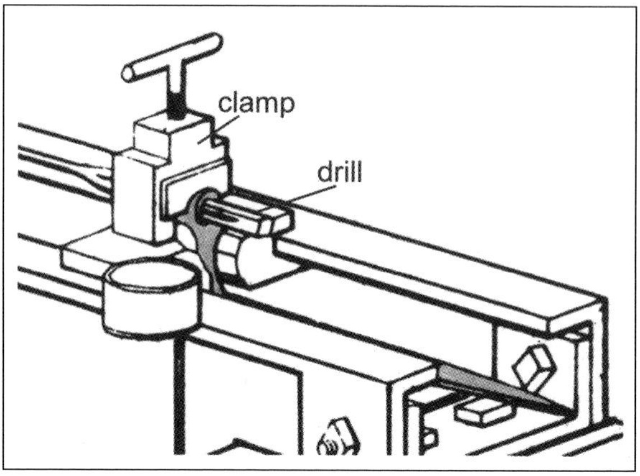

Left: Fig. 2.5. Detail of the drilling machine shown in Fig. 2.4 with the bayonet (grey) in the process of being drilled. (Gamel, 1826, Fig. XV)

Below: Fig. 2.6. The 'self-closing' drill used at Tula. (Gamel, 1826, Fig. XV – part)

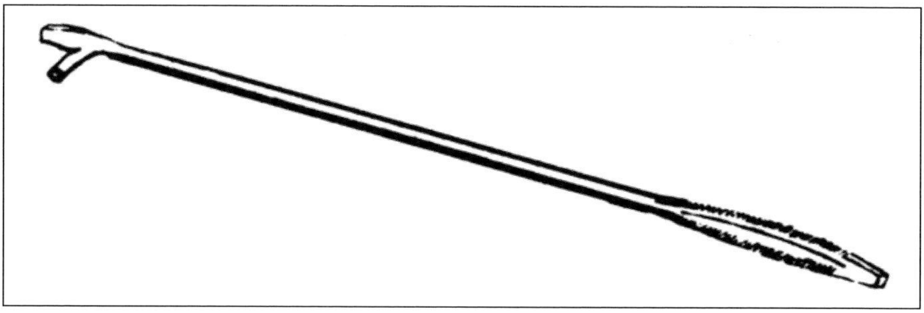

annotated detail of this portion of the machine, with the bayonet highlighted in grey, is shown in Fig. 2.5.

The first drill to be used is referred to in the Tula Report as a 'self-closing' drill and is shown in Fig. 2.6.

The drill had a plain round shank with a peg projecting radially at one end, which fitted into the socket on the spindle nose, the drive being transmitted by means of this peg. At the cutting end the drill was split and opened outwards for a short length, similar to the eye of a needle. It is presumed that this cutting portion is of steel and that being split in this way allowed it to be compressed when entering the socket and the 'spring' allowed it to be used several times in the socket, gradually enlarging the hole to the required size each time it passed through.

The second drill, or more correctly the second and third drills, were square section and, in the same manner as some of the barrel drills, had teeth along their edges arranged in a helical pattern like a screw thread. The third drill had finer teeth. They were sharper than the self-closing drill and, as in barrel drilling, were used in conjunction with a convex slip of wood shown enlarged in Fig. 2.7. If extra pressure was needed, a strip of paper was added.

As in barrel drilling, the drills pulled the socket tube onto them during drilling and the machines were also reversible. Again, it raises the question that if the drills acted as a threading tap how could they create a bore without threads? The finished

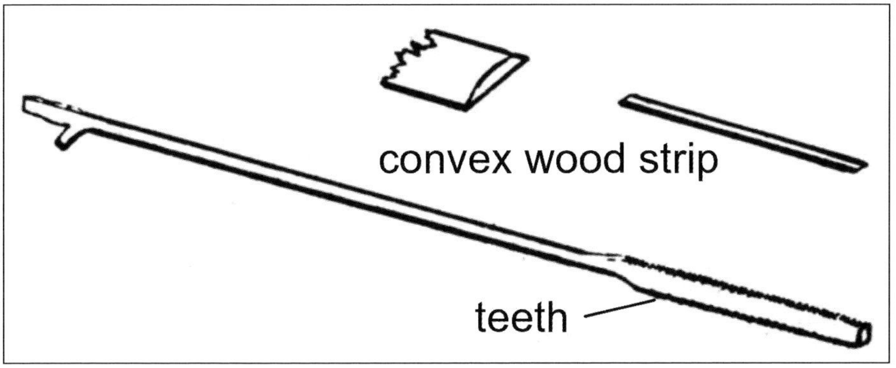

Fig. 2.7. The square drill used for finishing the bayonet socket, shown with the slip of wood and strip of paper used to push the cutting edge into contact with the bore of the socket. (Gamel, 1826, Fig. XV)

bore size was checked against a cylindrical gauge equal in size to the muzzle diameter and Gamel's Report tells us four of these machines operated by four men drilled two hundred and seventy-five bayonet sockets per day.[7]

2.4 Facing the ends of the socket

The ends of the socket tube were then faced to correct length in the machine in Fig. 2.8.

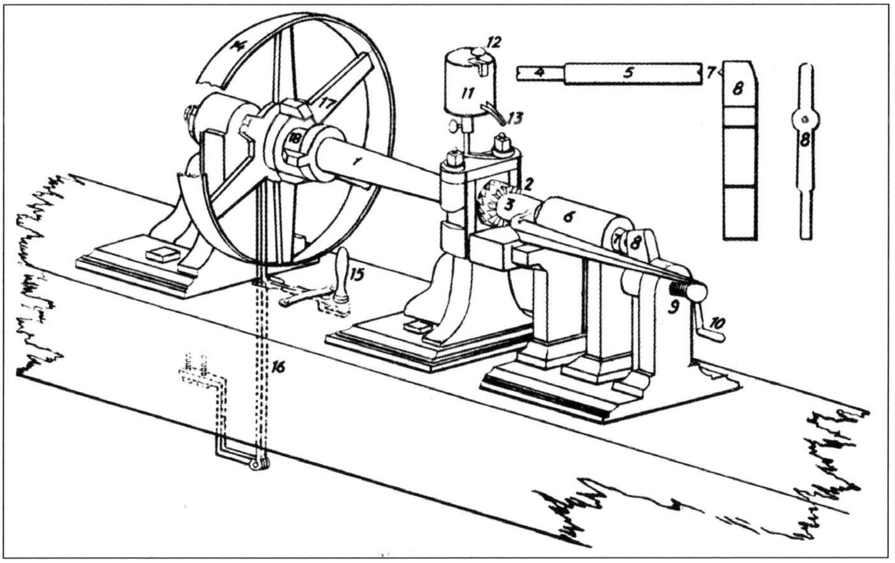

Fig. 2.8. The machine used at Tula for facing the ends of bayonet socket tubes. (Gamel, 1826, Fig. XVI, top)

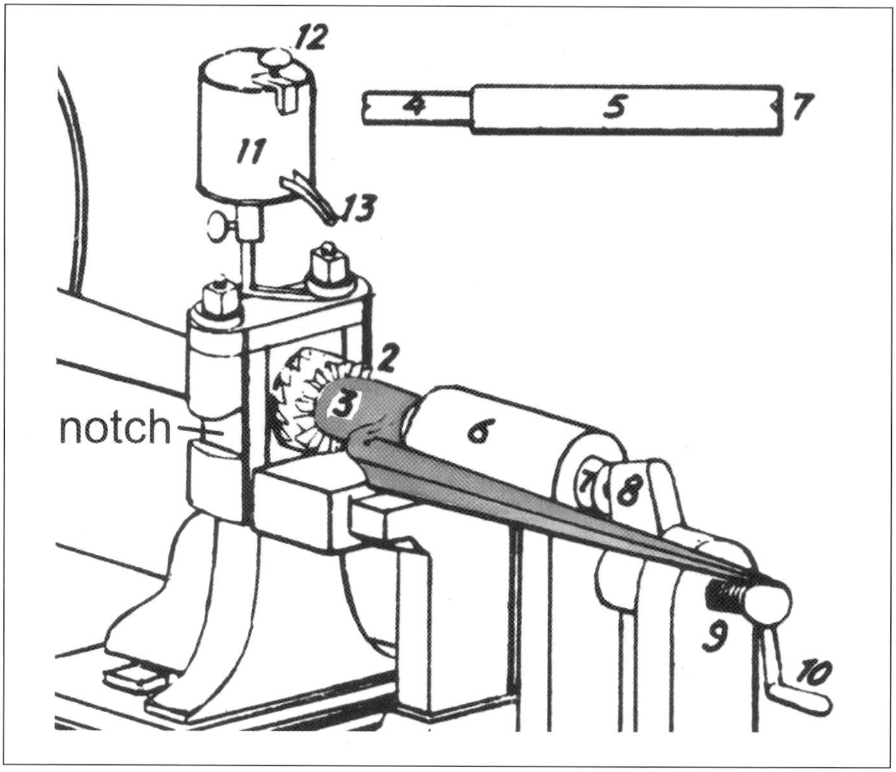

Fig. 2.9. Detail showing the fixing of the bayonet in the machine.

The bayonet socket was mounted on the narrow end, 4, of an arbour, 5, so that its end bore against a shoulder, Fig. 2.9.

This arbour was carried in a 'tailstock', 6, with a forward projecting ledge upon which the blade rested to prevent rotation. By operating the screw, 9, the arbour was pushed forward by the action of the lever, 8, so that the end of the socket tube was brought to bear against the rotating cutter, 2. This cutter had teeth cut on its face as with a face mill, similar to that used for facing the breech-end of the barrel and rotated at high speed, being fed with cooling water from the canister mounted above it. The bayonet was then reversed on the mandrel, the blade fitting into the notch to prevent rotation, and the front end of the socket faced in the same manner.

2.5 Turning the outside of the socket

A similar machine was then used to turn the accessible part of the socket between the elbow and the lower rim, Fig. 2.10.

The bayonet socket was fitted onto the reduced diameter portion, 19, of the mandrel, 20.

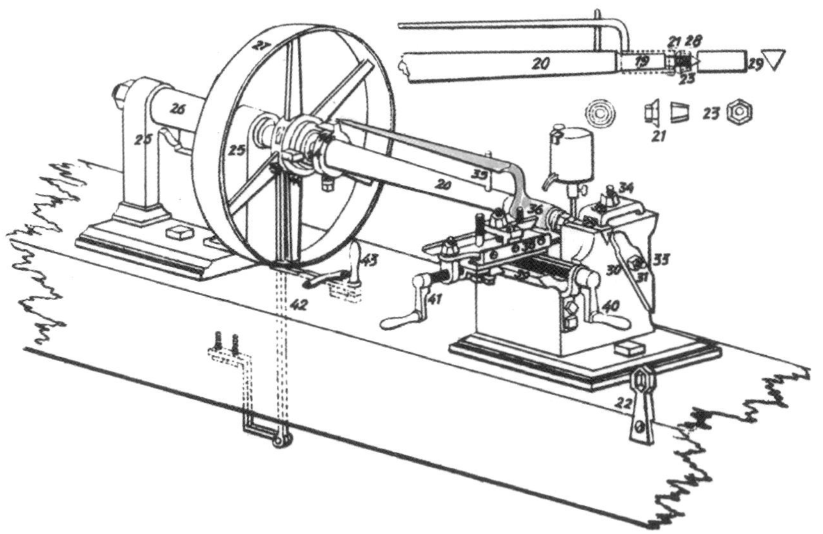

Fig. 2.10. Machine at Tula for turning the outside of the bayonet socket. (Gamel, 1826, Fig. XVI, bottom)

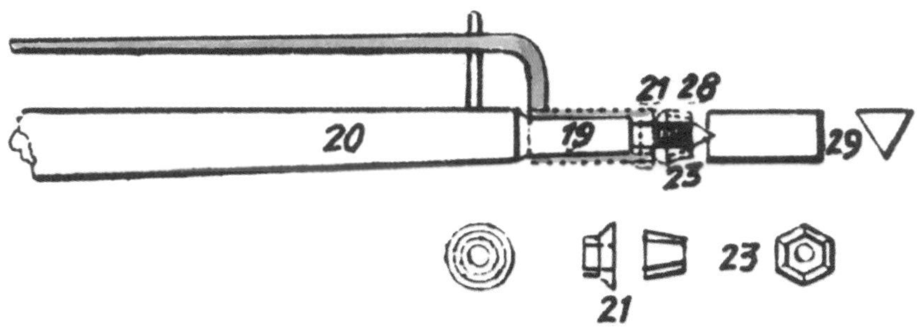

Fig. 2.11. The mandrel and components for securing the bayonet. (Gamel, 1826, Fig. XVI)

The shoulder between these larger and smaller diameters was conical. The diameter of the mandrel was then further reduced and threaded and terminated in a point. A conical sleeve, 21, was then fitted, followed by a securing nut and by this means the bayonet socket was 'self-centering' and securely fixed. The mandrel, 20, with the bayonet mounted and a 'drive-dog', 46, Fig. 2.12, attached to the headstock end, was then fitted to the machine by means of the two centre points at each extremity of the mandrel entering into conical holes in the the headstock shaft and tailstock.

The headstock, Fig. 2.12, comprised a shaft, 26, fixed in the supports, 25, and on which was fitted a rotating drive pulley, 27. By means of the lever, 43, the pulley could be slid forwards so that the 'drive-dog', 24, on the pulley engaged with the 'drive-dog', 46, on the mandrel, thus causing the mandrel-bayonet assembly to rotate.

The 'tailstock', Fig. 2.13, exhibited some very unusual features but ones totally in keeping with the purpose of the machine.

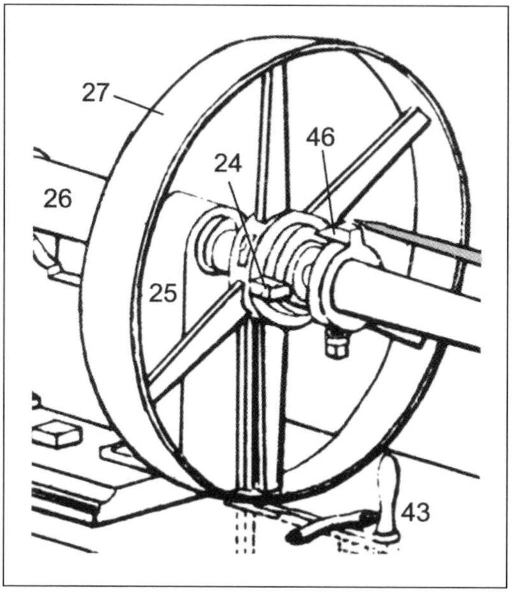

Left: Fig. 2.12. The 'headstock' of the turning machine. (New annotations for clarity) (Gamel, 1826, Fig. XVI)

Below: Fig. 2.13. The 'tailstock' of the socket turning machine. (socket highlighted in grey and new annotations for clarity) (Gamel, 1826, Fig. XVI)

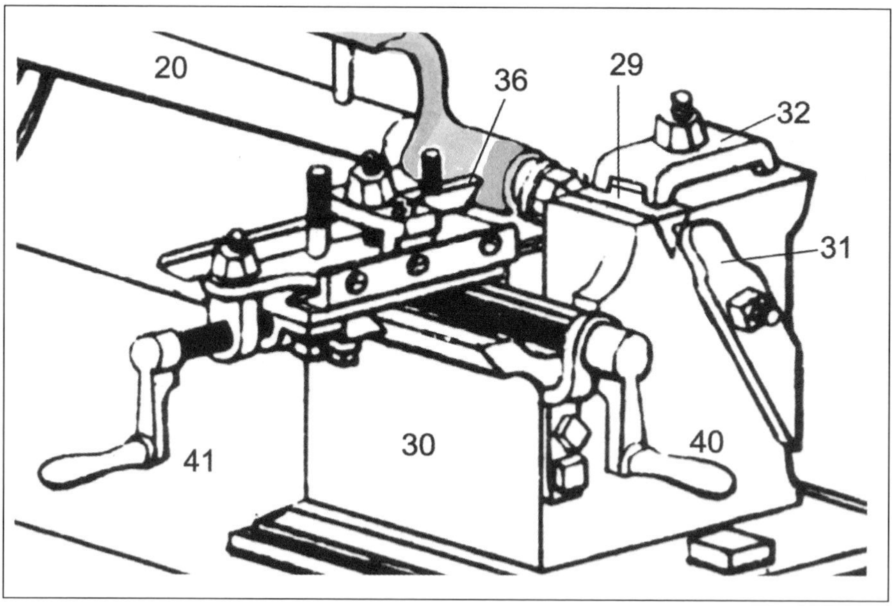

What would be termed the 'barrel' in a conventional tailstock was in the form of a triangular steel bar, 29, its left-hand end having a centre-hole into which the pointed end of the mandrel fitted. It was pressed forward by the lever, 31, operated on by a nut carried on a threaded stud in the tailstock body, so that the centre points at each end of the mandrel were secured in their respective centre-holes. This triangular bar was then secured in its housing in the tailstock body by the clamp, 32. A forward projection of the tailstock body was formed to carry a compound slide which, in a conventional lathe, would be mounted on the saddle. A transverse screw-feed, operated by the handle, 41, allowed the turning tool, 36, to be brought into contact with the socket of the bayonet. It may have been noticed that the bayonet in the illustrations to this point fails to show the 'bead' against which the locking ring abuts. Then the tool could be fed along the socket body, taking into account the 'bead', by the screw feed operated by the handle, 40. Two turning tools were used; one a wide pointed tool with a radiused cutting edge and another with a similar but smaller radius, which gave the socket a slightly 'ribbed' surface. Sizes were checked by a gauge. The final surface finish was corrected in the next operation. Six of these machines turned 275 sockets per day.[8]

2.6 Filing the machined surface of the socket

A machine similar to the socket turning lathe, Fig. 2.14, was used to remove the marks left by the turning process by the use of files.

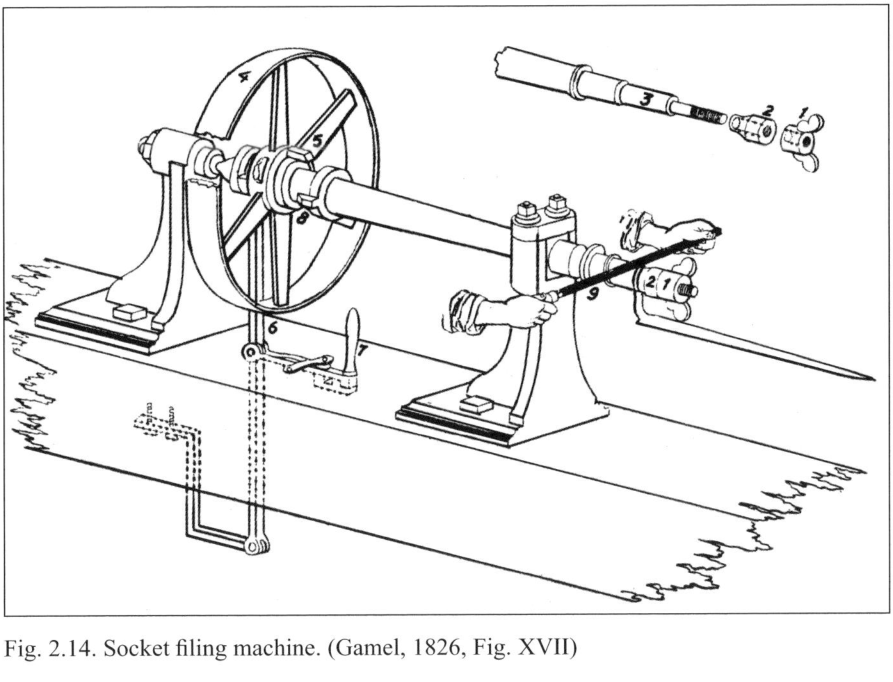

Fig. 2.14. Socket filing machine. (Gamel, 1826, Fig. XVII)

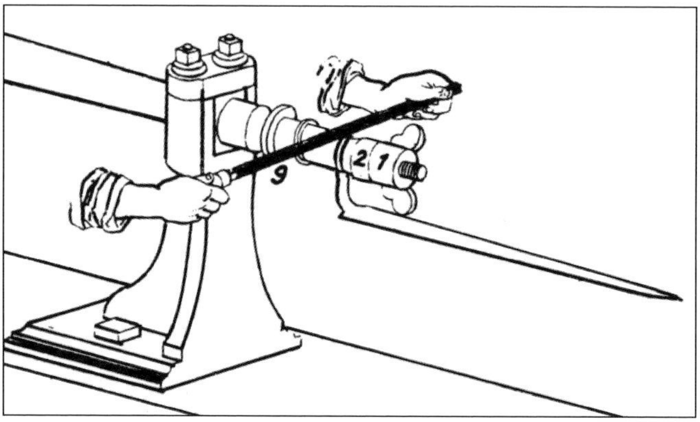

Fig. 2.15. Socket filing machine – detail. (Gamel, 1826, Fig. XVII)

As with the turning machine, the bayonet was fitted to a shaft by means of a conical sleeve, 2, and a nut, 1, and rotated by means of a flat-belt pulley wheel fitted with a 'stop-start' arrangement identical to the machine in Fig. 2.11.

A 'coarse', followed by a 'medium', and finally a 'smooth' file were used to finish the socket outer surface and the bead.

2.7 Filing the socket behind the neck

Gamel refers to a 'boss' on the socket[9] but which is actually the part prohibited from ordinary turning by being opposite the neck, and filing was carried out on the machine in Fig. 2.16.

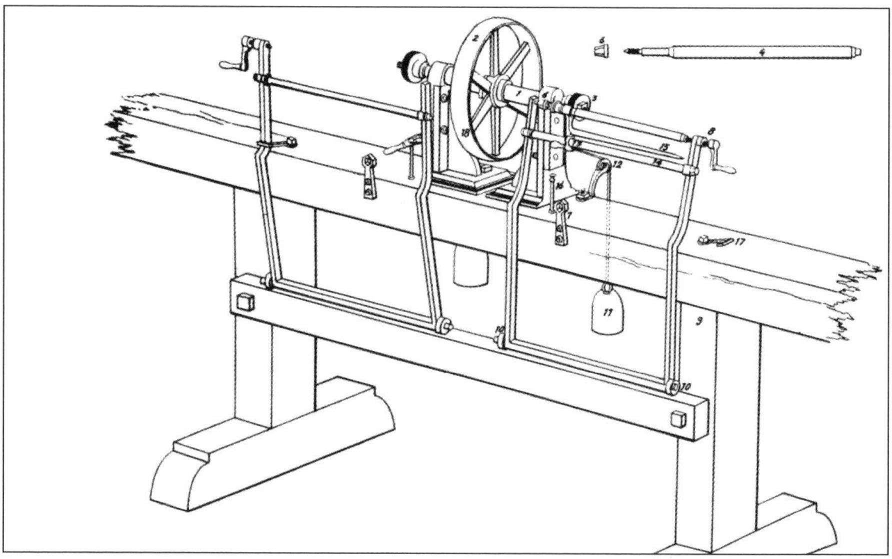

Fig. 2.16. The machine for filing the socket behind 'the neck'. (Gamel, 1826, Fig. XVII, part)

It was a double ended machine allowing 2 sockets to be worked upon and, as with the preceding machines, the bayonets were fixed on a mandrel in the same way. In this case, the bayonets did not revolve but the shaft, 1, Fig. 2.17, carrying the drive pulley, 2, was fitted at each end with two rotary files, 3. The bayonet on its mandrel is fixed between 2 points in a 'rocking' iron frame by the screw, 8.

This iron frame is acted upon by a weight which pulls the frame and the bayonet towards the rotating file.

The frame was manually controlled by the workman who grasped the blade and rotated the socket against the rotary file, taking care that it did not make contact with the elbow. When finished, the frame was drawn away from the file and secured by a hook to prevent it from falling away, and the bayonet removed and replaced by another for filing.

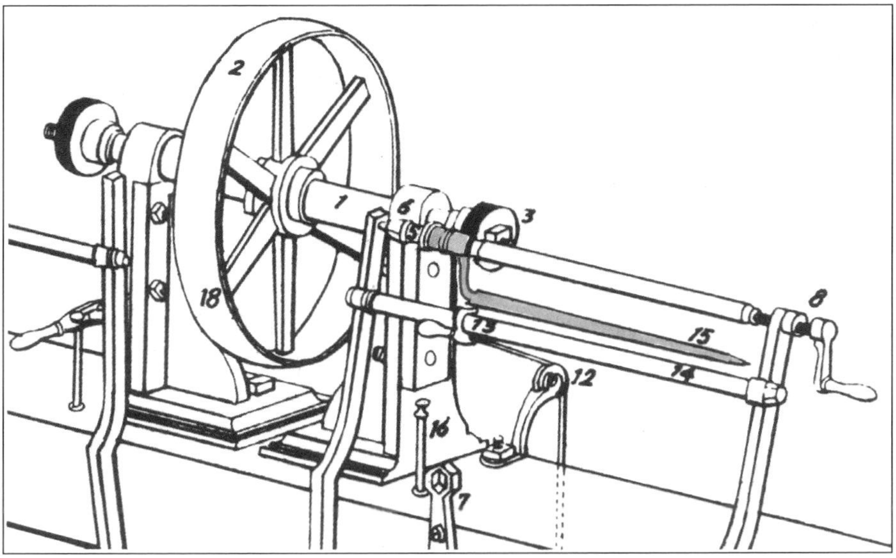

Above: Fig. 2.17. Detail of the machine for filing the socket behind 'the neck'- highlighted in grey.

Right: Fig. 2.18. Close-up of the machine for filing the socket behind 'the neck'.

2.8 Cutting the mortice slots in the socket

This was carried out in four separate operations, three of which were to cut the slots in the wall of the socket and the fourth to extend the first leg of the slot through the bridge, which Gamel refers to as the 'lump'. For cutting the slots in the wall, three screw presses, as shown in Fig. 2.19, were used. These 'fly presses' were constructed in the traditional manner in having a screw carried in a strong cast iron body. The lower end of the screw could be fitted with the appropriate punch and its upper end was fitted with a large diameter 'flywheel' and handle. The thread was a 2-start thread which meant, all else being equal, it travelled twice as fast as a conventional screw thread of the same size and this, combined with the momentum imparted by the flywheel, enabled it to punch through the cold wrought iron.

The first step was to punch the upper leg of the mortice which cut through the bead against which the locking ring seated. This was the longest of the mortice slots and this fact, combined with the need to cut through the bead as well, incurred extra force and a special fixture was used to support the socket.

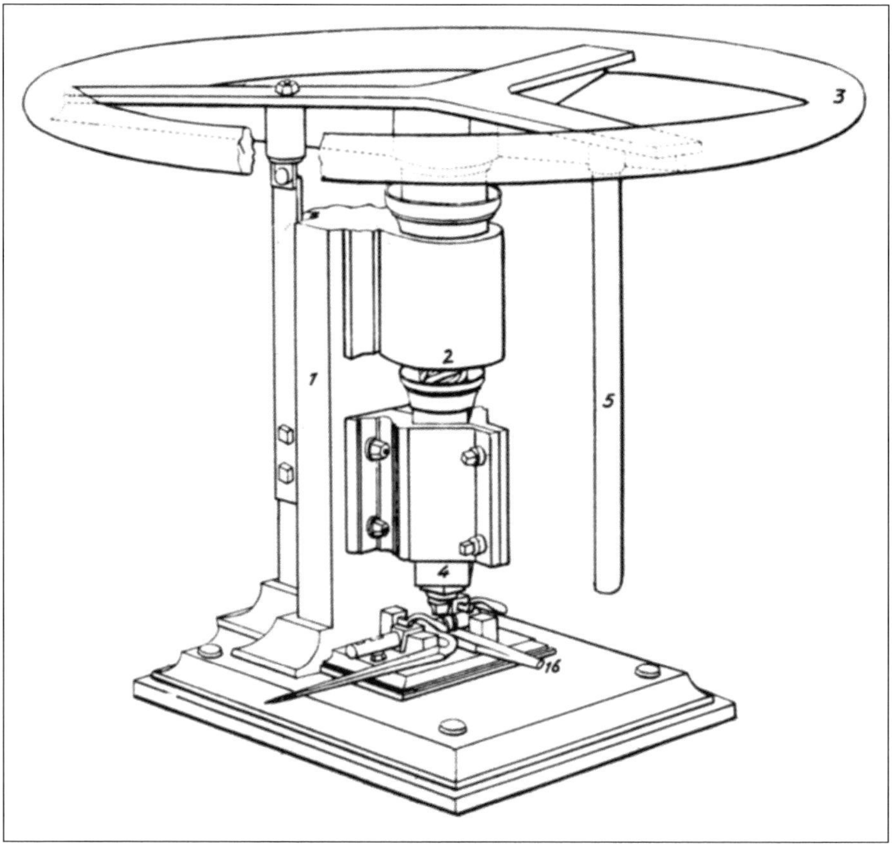

Fig. 2.19. Fly press used for punching out the mortice slots. (Gamel, 1826, Fig. XIX, part)

The components of the fixture and assembly are shown in Fig. 2.20.

Item 9 is the punch to form the long slot, 6, in the socket. The socket was fitted to a mandrel, 12, which was reversible and had a matching slot, 13, at each end. When fitted to the mandrel this sub-assembly was fitted to a fixture which Gamel refers to as a 'nest',[10] item 14, where it was clamped in position by two wedge-like keys, 15 and supported by a wedge, 16, shown in Fig. 2.18. This only becomes fully clear when Fig. 2.18 is examined in greater detail, as shown in Fig. 2.21.

It can be seen that the block at the centre of the mandrel straddles one of the fixture supports and the wedge, 16, is placed under the socket to provide support during punching.

The second slot, parallel to the first and close to the bridge was produced next using the items shown in Fig. 2.22.

Again, the socket was mounted on a cylindrical mandrel, 17, having appropriate slots at either end and which was fixed in the supporting block, 19, and secured by a screw, 18. For this operation the elbow and blade clearly had to be vertically below the punch so the mounting block had to be sufficiently high to allow for this. However, since the applied force was much less than that needed to cut the first slot, there was no requirement for additional support of the socket.

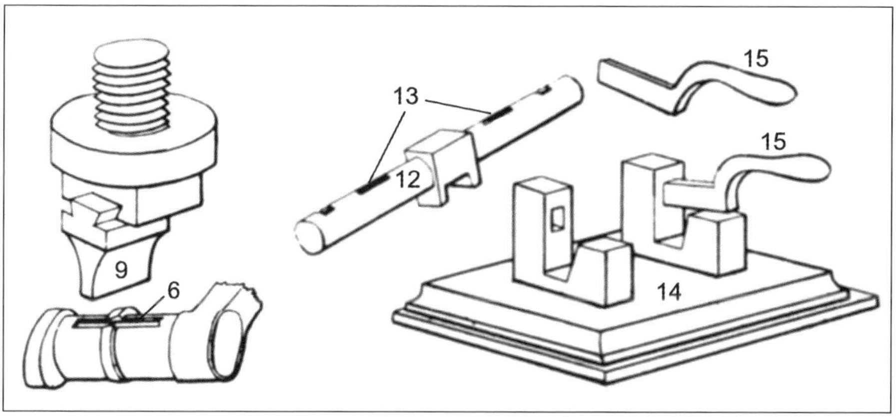

Fig. 2.20. The components of the fixture. (Composite image and new annotations from Gamel, 1826, Fig. XIX)

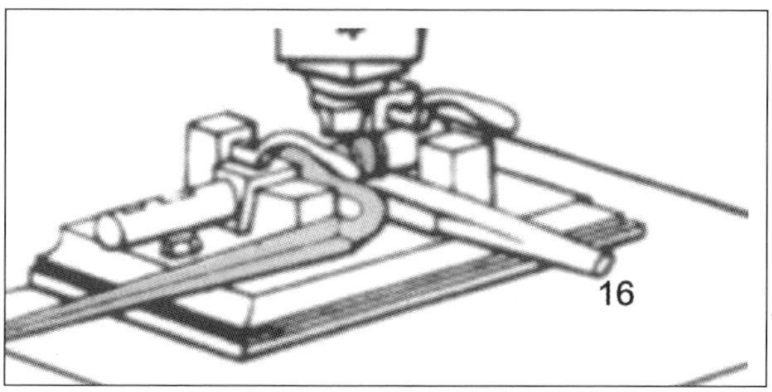

Fig. 2.21. Detail of the assembly for punching the long leg of the slot, with the bayonet highlighted in grey. (Gamel, 1826, Fig. XIX, detail)

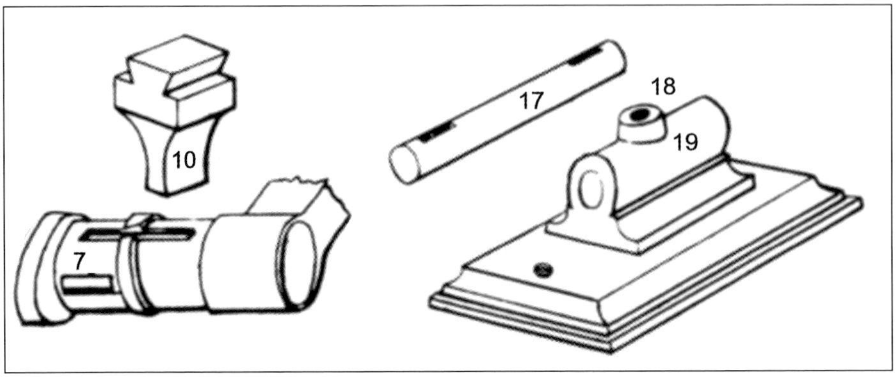

Fig. 2.22. Equipment used in punching the second slot. (Composite image and new annotations – from Gamel, 1826, Fig. XIX)

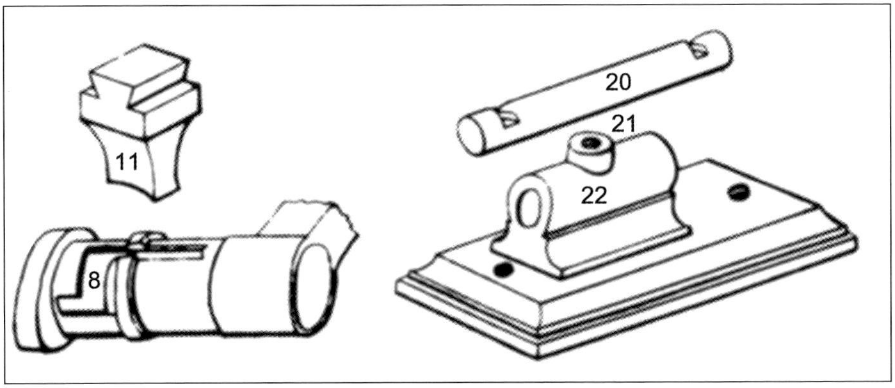

Fig. 2.23. Fixtures used in cutting the third slot. (Composite image and new annotations from Gamel, 1826, Fig. XIX)

The third and last slot was transverse and connected the two slots already cut and for this a similar set-up was used, Fig. 2.23.

Gamel notes that these presses are set up close to the bayonet socket turning (and presumably the filing machines) and "the masters can punch very easily the triple slot for the bayonet tenon in any number of sockets finished up to that stage of manufacture."[11]

2.9 Cutting the mortice in the bridge

This operation also was carried out using a special machine, Fig. 2.24, capable of handling 4 bayonets. This is a more complex machine than those just examined and even at a large scale, the functional elements and the annotations are difficult to decipher. So, some enlargements of important details have been prepared and in some cases combined, along with an additional sketch to provide greater understanding.

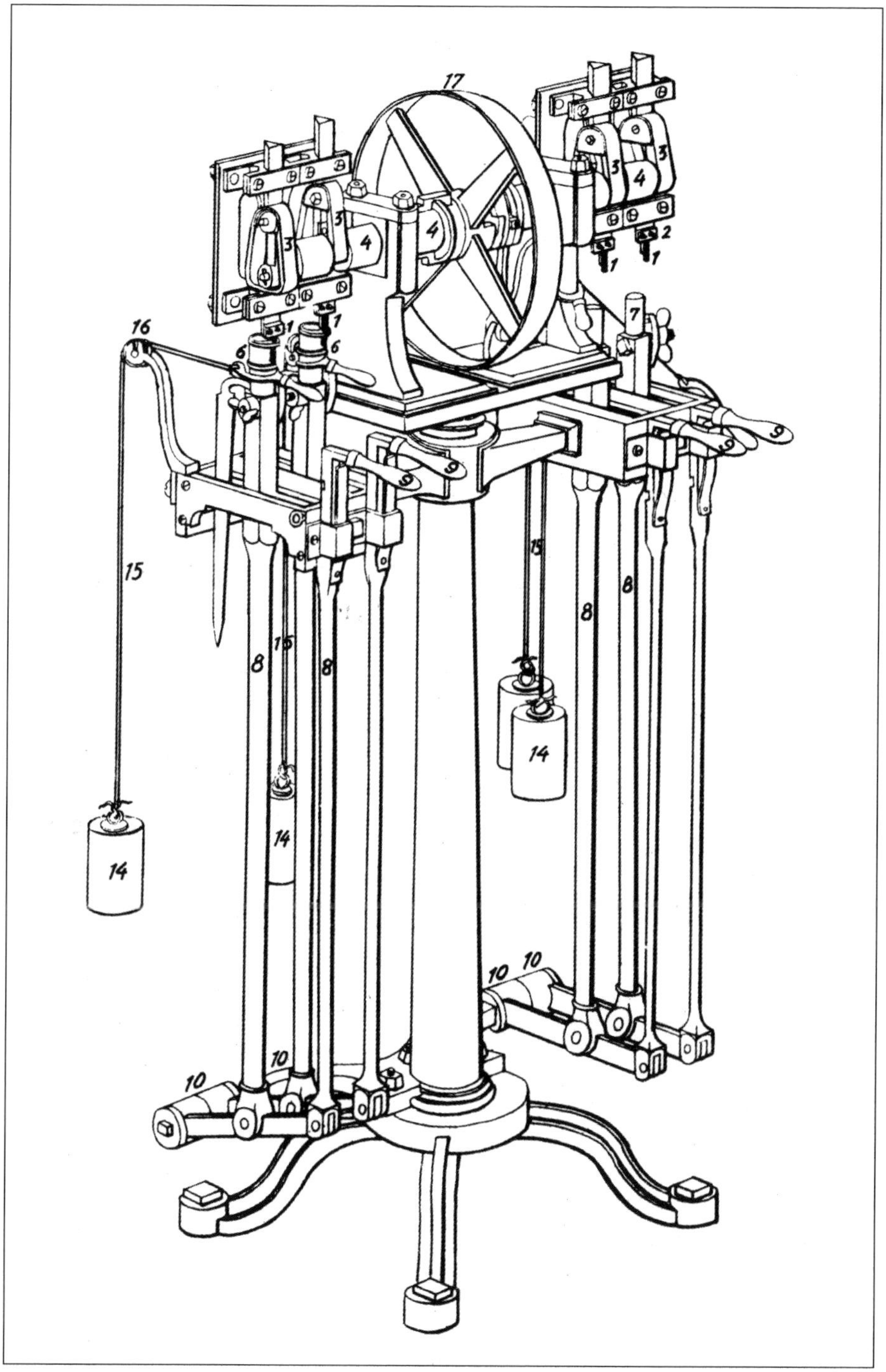

Fig. 2.24. The bridge notch filing machine. (Gamel, 1826, Fig. XX)

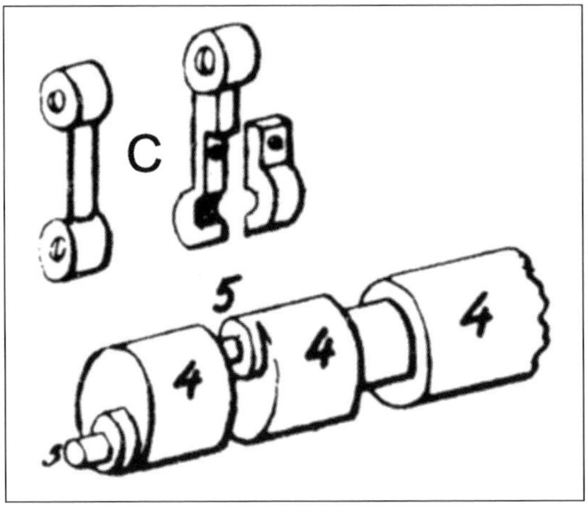

Fig. 2.25. Crankshaft and connecting rods. (Gamel, 1826, Fig. XX, detail)

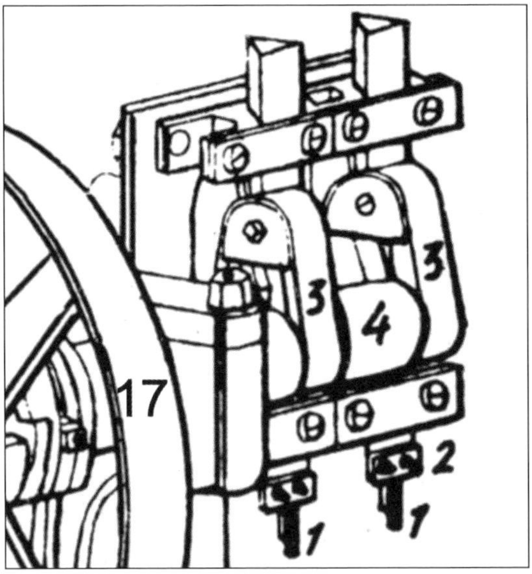

Fig. 2.26. One end of the crankshaft with its fittings. (Gamel, 1826, Fig. XX, detail)

The principal element of the machine is the crankshaft, 4, driven a pulley. The nature of this crankshaft is shown in Fig. 2.25.

The crankshaft, 4, by its very nature, has off-set crank-pins, 5, to which are attached the lower ends of the connecting rods not referred to by Gamel and newly annotated as C. A further detail Fig. 2.26, shows the drive pulley and one end of the crankshaft along with its fittings.

Gamel's description of its functions lacks certain details. For example, he states files, 1, are fixed to the 'loops', 3, by means of screws, 2, and that the 'loops' are mounted on an eccentrically turned shaft, 4, having a crank, 5, moving the files up and down. That is fine as far as it goes, but he omits to mention that within the 'loops' there is a connecting rod having its upper end fitted to a guide bar and its lower end fitted to the crankpin, Fig. 2.25. Also, that the upper end of the 'loops', 3, is fixed to the upper end of the connecting rod, C, and the lower ends are attached to the reciprocating files which also acts as a guide bar so that it has a vertical motion, Fig. 2.27.

As shown in Fig. 2.28, the bayonet was mounted on the cylindrical end of a rod, 8, which could be lifted by the handle, 9, so that the file, 1, was brought to bear on the bridge of the socket, 6, when the machine was in operation. Contact between the file and the socket was maintained by a weight attached by the rope, 15, to a hook, H, placed on the socket.

Some means of controlling the depth of the notch filed in the bridge would have been needed, such as a simple 'stop' to prevent further movement of the rod, 8, but is not mentioned.

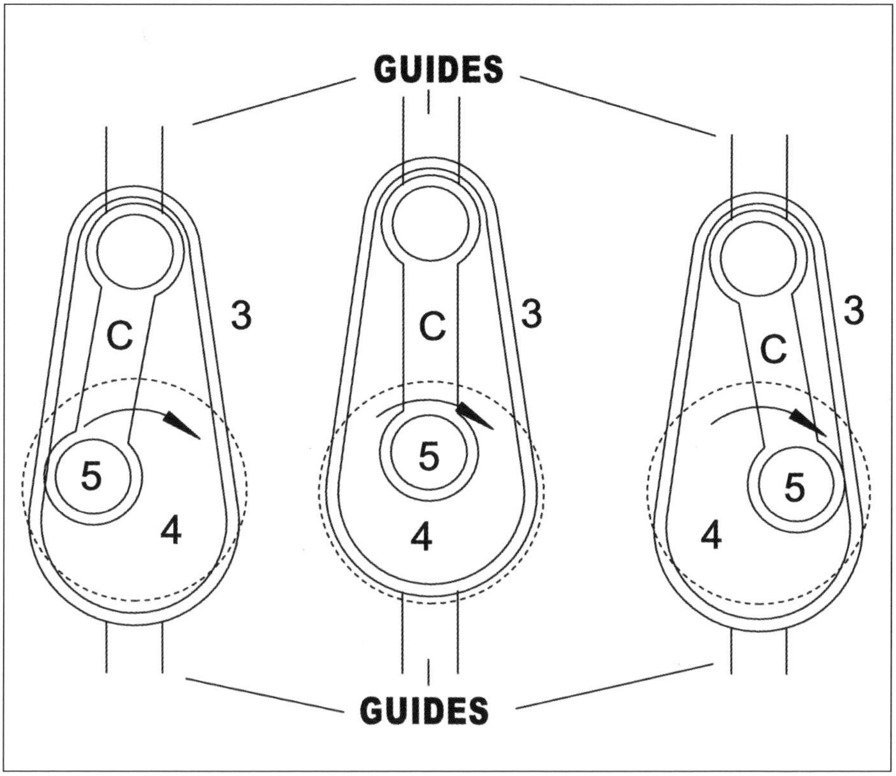

Above: Fig. 2.27. Showing the need for anchoring the upper and lower ends of the loops, 3, to a guide bar to allow them to move vertically. (© P. Smithurst)

Right: Fig. 2.28. Detail showing the machine set up for operation. (Gamel, 1826, Fig. XX, detail)

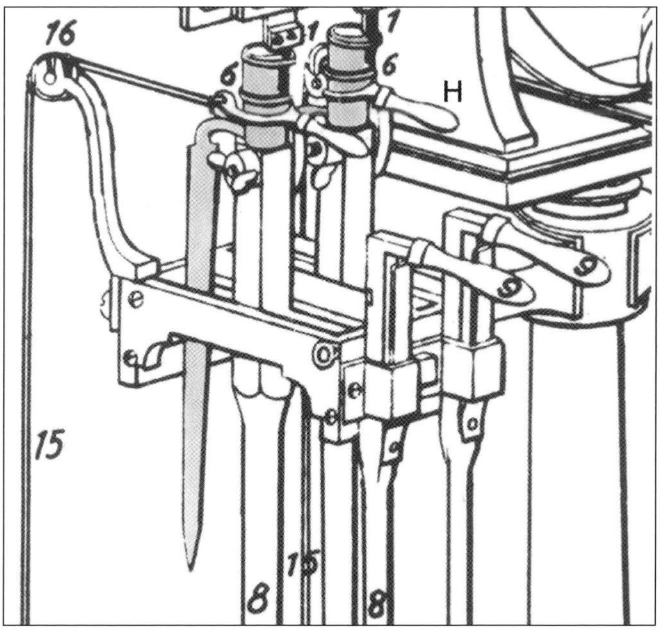

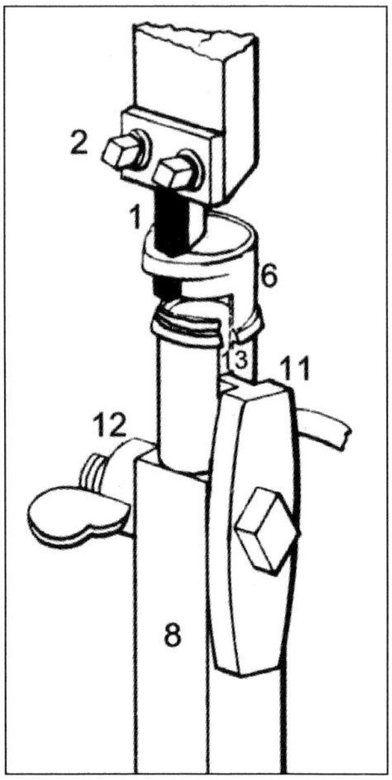

Fig. 2.29. Detail showing the method of mounting the bayonet on the machine. (Gamel, 1826, Fig. XX, detail)

Further details of the mounting of the bayonet are shown in Fig. 2.29. It was of course crucial that the bridge and the slot leading to it were in correct orientation to the file. This was accomplished by the socket, 6, being mounted on the cylindrical extension of the rod, 8, by a clamp, 11, having a projection which fitted into the slot, 13, in the socket and which was secured by the nut and bolt, 12. If all of the preceding operations had been carried out correctly, this would have placed the bridge and the slot leading to it in correct juxtaposition to the file, 1.

Such a system in which each operation depends upon the accuracy of the one preceding it is a core requirement of interchangeability and would require a system of gauging to verify each stage. While Gamel mentions the use of gauges in the early stages of bayonet manufacture he does not do so in describing these operations, but it is difficult to imagine how this could have been achieved without them. With this machine it was possible to file the bridge notches of two hundred and seventy five bayonets per day[12] – a strange number considering they were done in batches of 4!

2.10 Turning the bridge

Having created the mortice, the bridge was then turned, which, having a non-circular profile required a very specialised machine, Fig. 2.30. Gamel's description of the details of this machine are somewhat loose and are not made clearer by the illustrations which obscure some of these features. Basically, this is a copying lathe. The shaft upon which the socket is mounted is very similar to those in the previous machines just described with two exceptions. One is that a 'small rise is made'[13] which fits into the notch of the bridge, and the other is that on the 'outside [of] the tube [socket] an oval part is made on the cylinder having the same configuration that should be acquired by the lump [bridge]'.

These are not readily visible in Fig. 2.30 so a sketch, Fig. 2.31, has been prepared to show them. Gamel's 'small rise' is taken to be a key to fit the notch in the bridge and his 'oval part' is taken to be a cam matching the desired profile of the bridge and correctly juxtaposed when the socket is mounted on the shaft. It is conceived that a shoulder, the same diameter as the socket body, would also be needed to avoid the socket being directly up against the cam with the risk of consequent damage to either by giving clearance to the cutting tool.

To function as a copying lathe, this cam needed a follower attached to the toolpost and a means of advancing the tool as turning progressed. This was

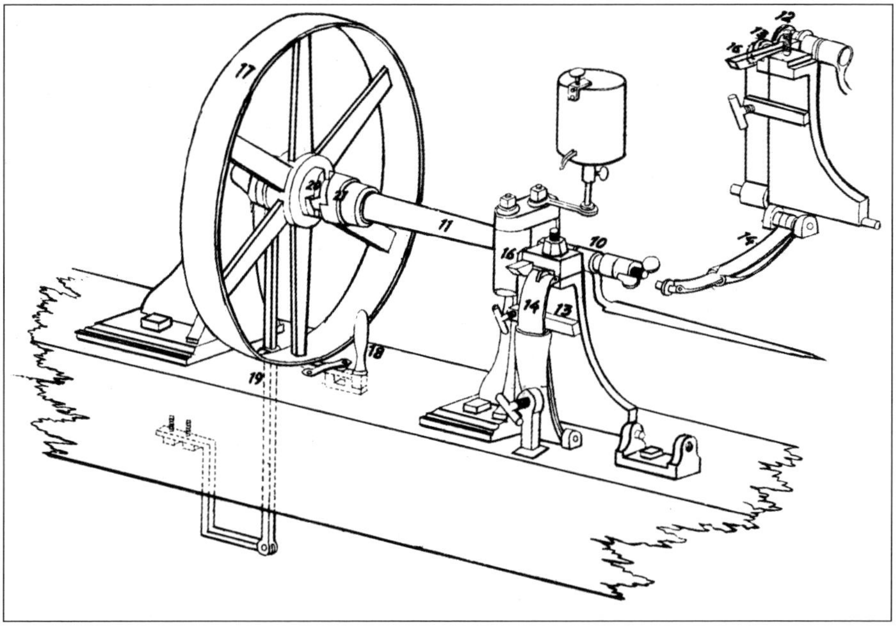

Above: Fig. 2.30. The machine for turning the bridge. (Gamel, 1826, Fig. XVIII)

Right: Fig. 2.31. Suggested form of the shaft end for mounting the socket. (© P. Smithurst)

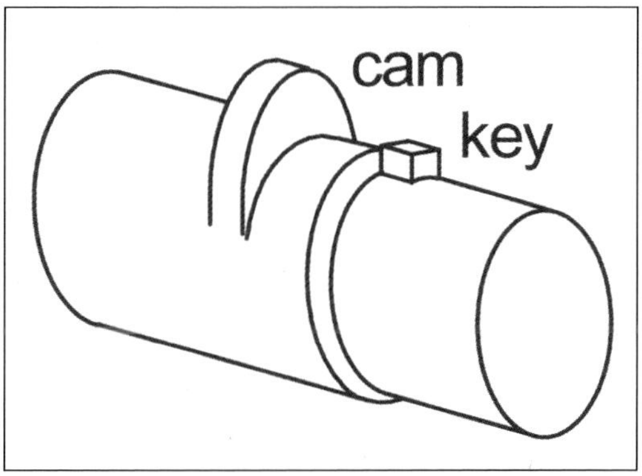

accomplished by the ingenious device in Fig. 2.32 (on next page). Unfortunately, in Gamel's Fig. XVIII (Fig. 2.30), the same key number, 13, has been assigned to two different features so, in re-annotating, this has been corrected to what is believed to be Gamel's original intention.

In Fig. 2.32, 12 is the 'oval' [cam] formed on the shaft upon which the bayonet is mounted. Item 13 is the cam follower. Gamel notes that: *On rotation of the cylinder* [shaft] *the oval part* [cam] *comes into contact with the rib of a small block, 13, fitted to the upper part of the spring, 14, of the supporting block, 15, with a tool, 16.* Study of the detail of the illustration, Fig. 2.33 (on next page) shows this is clearly an error but might be attributable to the translation.

The spring, 14, certainly has what appears to be a roller at its upper end but when assembled correctly on the machine, Fig. 2.33, it is nowhere near the 'cam'.

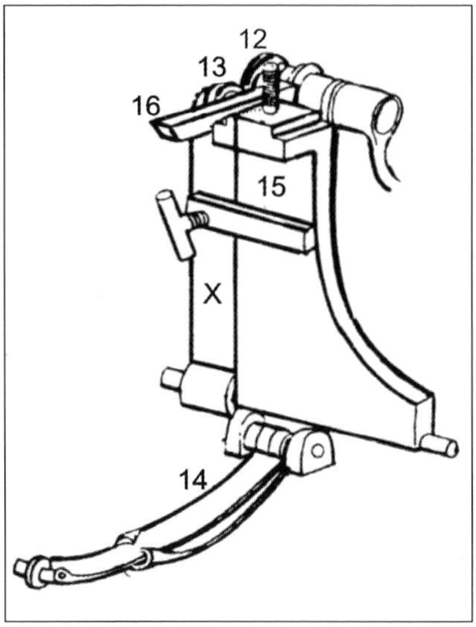

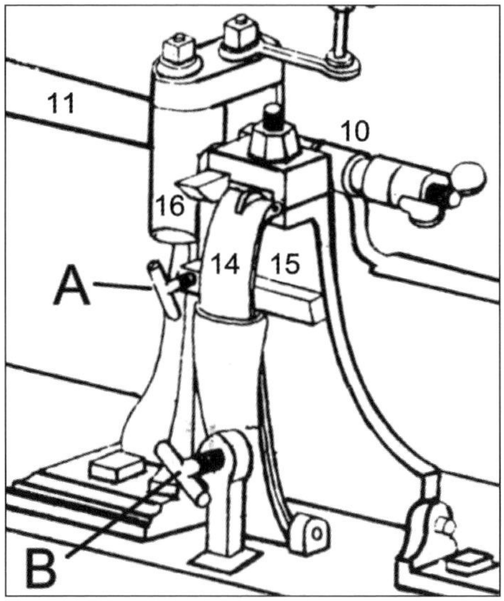

Above left: Fig. 2.32. The device acting as toolholder and support for the cam follower. (Reannotated – from Gamel, 1826, Fig. XVIII)

Above right: Fig. 2.33. The device acting as toolholder and support for the cam follower in position on the machine. (From Gamel, 1826, Fig. XVIII)

On the other hand, the item noted as 'X', Fig. 2.32, pivoted on the same axis as the 'supporting block' [tool holder] 15, has a similar device at its upper end, 13, which is in line with the 'cam'. The item X, and the tool support, 15, can move independently so that in operation, the upper end of X is in contact with the cam and, because it is born upon by an arm attached to item 15 and fitted with a screw, causes this to follow accordingly. Pressure on the spring, 14, bearing upon the tool block, 15, and via this on the cam follower on X, is adjusted by the thumbscrew B to maintain positive contact. When starting, once the bayonet socket, 10, had been secured in place the screw, A, would be unscrewed to 'back-off' the turning tool, 16, and the screw B operated to bring the cam follower, 13, on X, into positive contact with the cam. When the machine was set in motion, the screw, A, would be turned to bring the cutting tool into contact with the bridge on the socket, and advancing the tool continued until the correct dimension had been reached. Two hundred and seventy-five bridges were turned on one machine each day.

2.11 Creating the hole for the stop pin

As a reminder, the stop pin on the socket is to both limit the rotation of the locking ring and to keep it against the 'bead'. In the absence of an example of the Russian M.1808 bayonet, a French M.1777, albeit very worn, will serve, Fig. 2.34.

As noted when dealing with the M.1777 bayonet, the exact positioning of the stop pin was important insofar as at one extreme position of the locking ring, the notch in its bridge had to coincide with the long mortice in the socket to allow passage of the tenon on the musket barrel; at its other extreme the locking ring had to 'wedge' up against the tenon to secure the bayonet.

Fig. 2.34. The socket with its stop pin, (© P. Smithurst)

The hole was punched using the same press used for creating the mortice slots and had a special fixture allowing the socket to be correctly aligned, Fig. 2.35.

Gamel's description of this tooling is scant. He simply notes: *The socket is mounted on the cylinder, 24, which is fixed in the supporting block, 25, by a screw, 26. The spring, 27, has a recess on its inner surface in which the crown* [bead] *of the socket fits so that the hole is punched always at a convenient* [fixed?] *distance from it.*[14] This is bordering on meaningless. Examination of the 'cylinder, 24' shows a projection in addition to the hole at the nearer end. It would make more sense if this were a block, replicating the tenon on the musket barrel, allowing the bayonet to be fitted to this 'cylinder' in the same fashion. The tenon fully entered into the mortice slot would then provide a suitable datum for the positioning of the punch and the hole in the cylinder into which it would pass, Fig. 2.36.

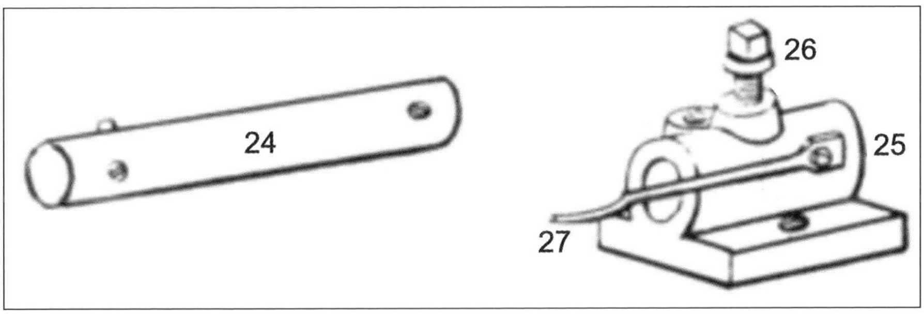

Fig. 2.35. The fixture for punching the stop pin hole. (From Gamel, 1826, Fig. XIX)

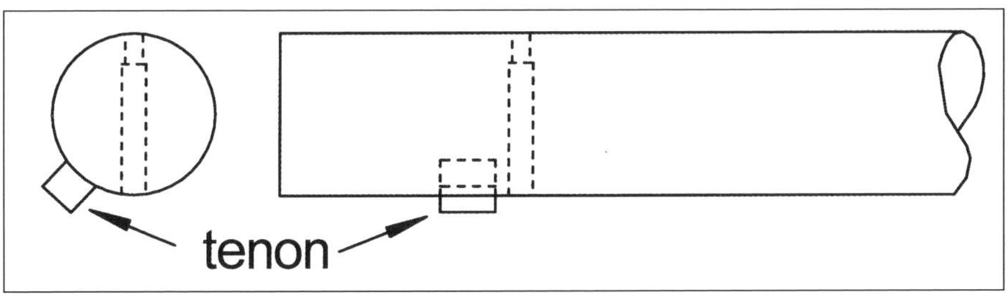

Fig. 2.36. Suggested nature of the fixture for mounting the socket for punching the stop pin hole. (© P. Smithurst)

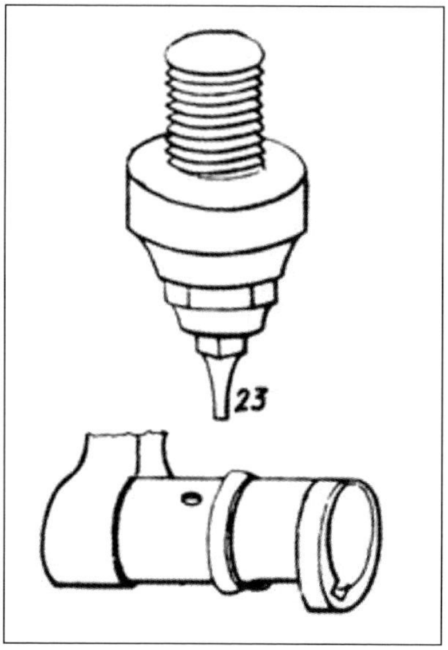

Fig. 2.37. The punch tool for the stop pin hole. (Gamel, 1826, Fig. XIX)

By using such a device there would be no need for the spring since the bayonet could be manually pressed against the tenon, which would also prevent the risk of misalignment and guarantee the required outcome.

It is also suggested that with such a small hole, the hole in the fixture would need to be initially only slightly larger than that of the punch nose to allow free passage, but would then need to become wider to avoid becoming blocked with the punched-out pieces.

This hole was then threaded. The stop-pin, referred to in the translated version of Gamel's book as the 'nipple',[15] was made from wire clamped in a hand-vice, threaded with a screw-stock and screwed tightly into the hole. It was then cut off and the external portion filed to its correct size and any inner projection of the stop pin filed flush with the socket using a fine file.

2.12 Making the locking ring

Prior to 1826 the locking ring had been hand-forged, but die-forging had been introduced around this date. Gamel states that the 'tongues of the sleeve' – by which is taken to mean the 'ears' of the ring in the French terminology – were forged in this die and were dressed with first a medium, and then a smooth file. The holes were either punched or drilled, followed by the appropriate one being tapped, and the 'groove' [recess] in which the stop-pin operated, finished with a file. The 'inclined' step on the opposite edge, which bore against the tenon on the barrel, was filed. In the translated version this tenon is erroneously referred to as the 'backsight'![16]

2.13 Making the locking ring screw

This entailed the use of a special lathe, Fig. 2.38, which has many features resembling later 'screw machines'.

The main elements of this machine are shown in Fig. 2.39.

The making of a screw like the one in question is fairly basic but unfortunately, Gamel's description of the machine and its operation is lacking in some details. The screw was made from an iron bar, 1, which was passed through a hole running the full length of the lathe spindle, 2, projecting at the end and was clamped by the screws, 3, and was the same diameter as the screw head, Fig. 2.39. The machine

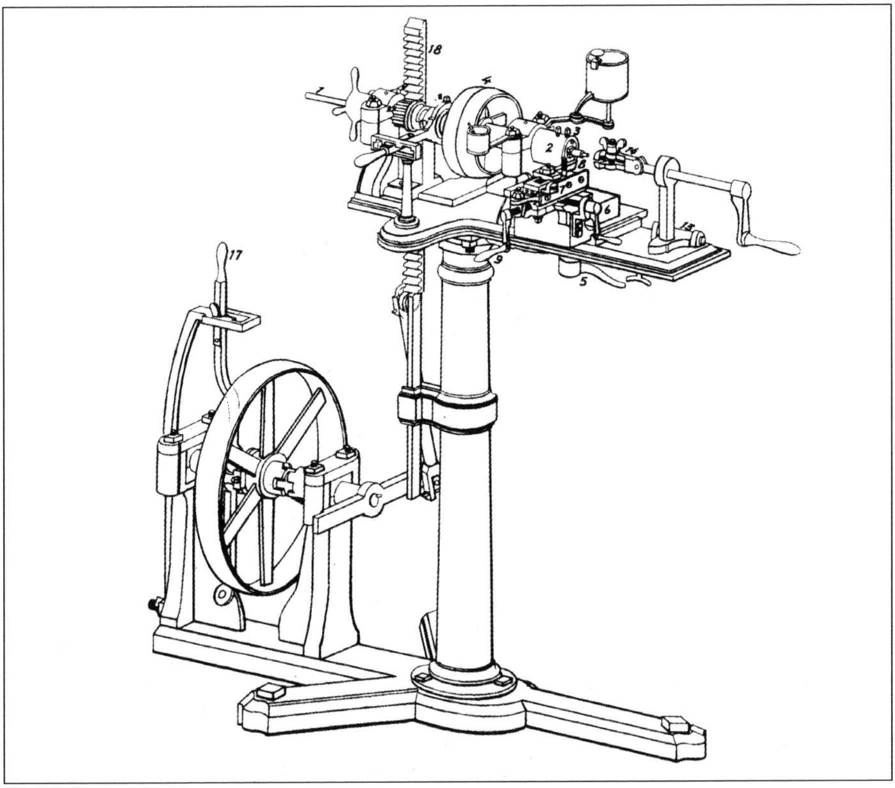

Fig. 2.38. Machine for making locking ring screws. (Gamel, 1826, Fig. XXI)

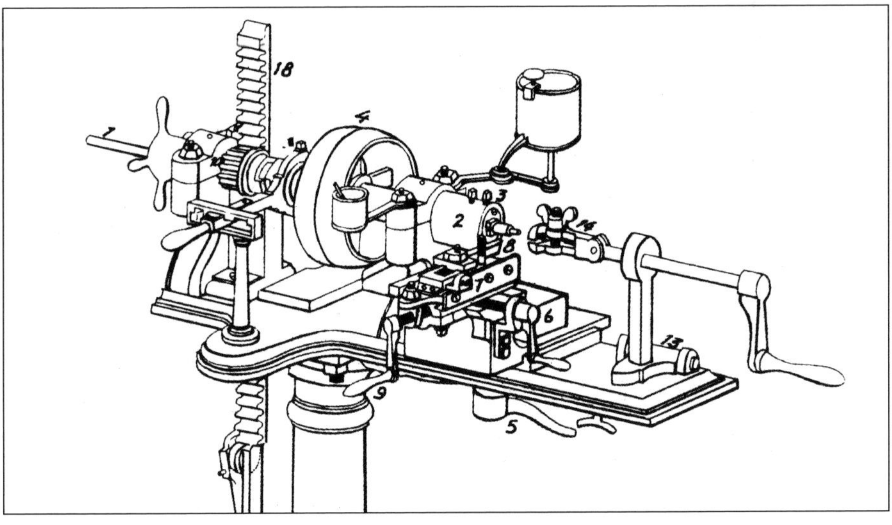

Fig. 2.39. The machine in detail. (Gamel, 1826, Fig. XXI)

was fitted with a typical compound slide on which was mounted the cutting tool and which, by use of the handles, 6 and 9, could be moved parallel or at right angles to the spindle axis. Gamel also refers to a template, Fig. 2.40, designed to limit the travel of the cutting tool in turning the screw shank and head:

> *with a recess corresponding to the depth of the head of the cut screw, is fixed to the moveable carriage* [compound slide] *and its motion is hindered by the upright piece. When the template strikes against the upright piece in the supporting block* [top slide] *at its widest part, 11, the cross travel of the tool is stopped and the head of the screw is cut. When the upright piece is in contact with the narrower part, 12, of the template, the cutting tool moves further and cuts the stem of the screw.*

This seems unfathomable and is not aided by the illustrations in which the template is barely visible. In making a screw, the stem is first turned, followed by the head – not as in the procedure described by Gamel.

To illustrate the principle of what is a simple copying lathe using a template for making a screw, four explanatory drawings have been prepared. In the first, Fig. 2.41, the compound slides are shown. The lower one, here referred to as the traversing slide, is operated by a screw using the handle, 6, and moves parallel to the lathe axis. The upper one, mounted on the traversing slide and referred to here as the cross slide and to which is fitted the cutting tool, is operated by a screw using the handle, 9, and moves at right angles to the lathe axis. These two motions, in conjunction with a template, allow the stem and head of the screw to be cut to correct lengths and diameters.

Now to describe the machining operations to form the screw. The first stage is the machining of the screw stem and for simplicity, the guide pin and cutting tool have been made the same width.

In Fig. 2.42 the guide pin is moved to bear against the appropriate portion of the template. In this position the cutting tool, fixed to the cross slide, is then adjusted so that the correct diameter and length of the stem will be turned, possibly using a 'dummy screw' as a setting gauge, and the cutting tool locked in place. The guide pin/cutting tool will remain in this correct juxtaposition throughout the process.

With the machine set in motion the traversing slide carrying the top slide with the tool/guide pin assembly is then moved parallel to the axis so that the stem is turned to the correct diameter and length determined by the guide pin coming into contact with the step in the template.

In stage 2, Fig. 2.43, the cross slide has been withdrawn to a 'stop' on the slide so that the left hand edge of the guide pin just clears the top of the step on the template.

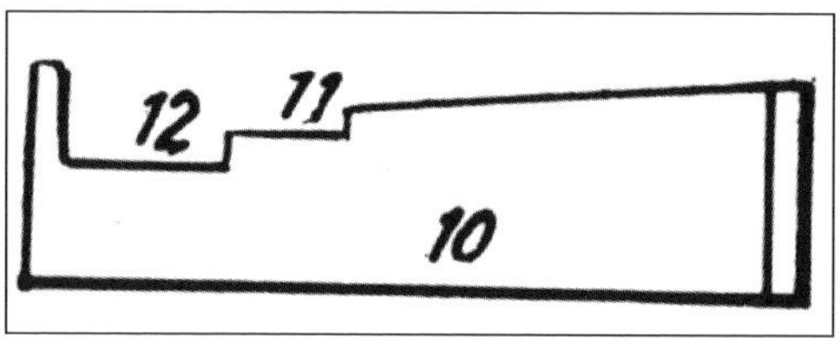

Fig. 2.40. The template. (From Gamel, 1826, Fig. XXI)

Right: Fig. 2.41. Diagrammatic representation of the two slides. (© P. Smithurst)

Below: Fig. 2.42. Diagrammatic repetitive turning of a screw stem using a template. (© P. Smithurst)

Bottom: Fig. 2.43. The cross slide withdrawn so that the guide pin is in contact with the top of the step and the head of the screw machined. (© P. Smithurst)

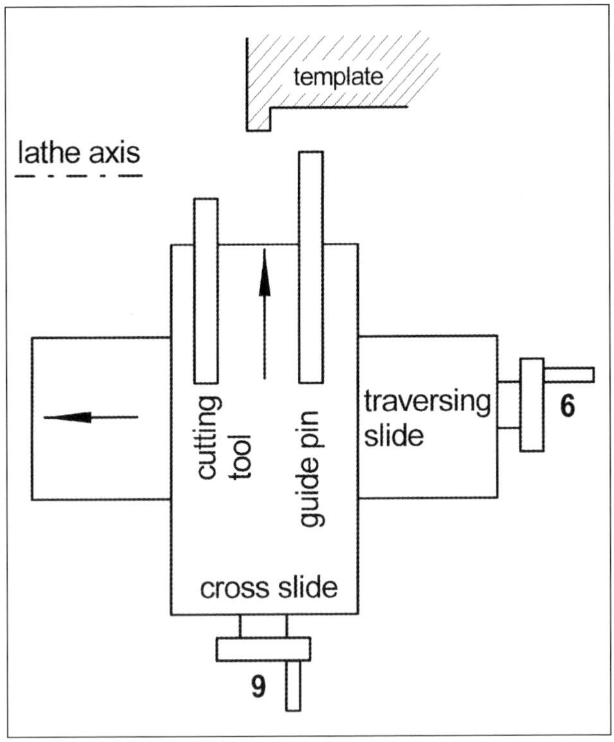

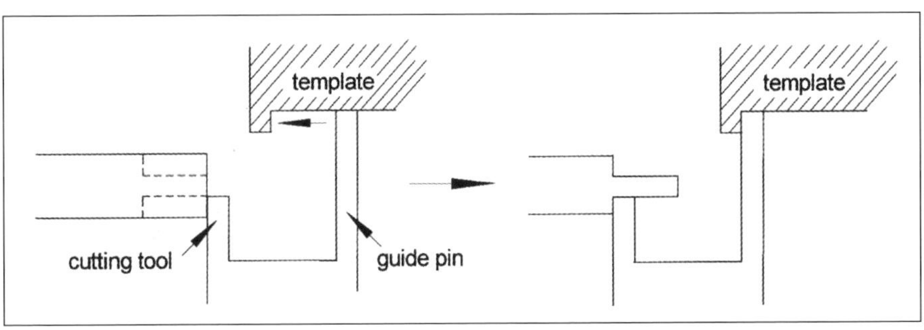

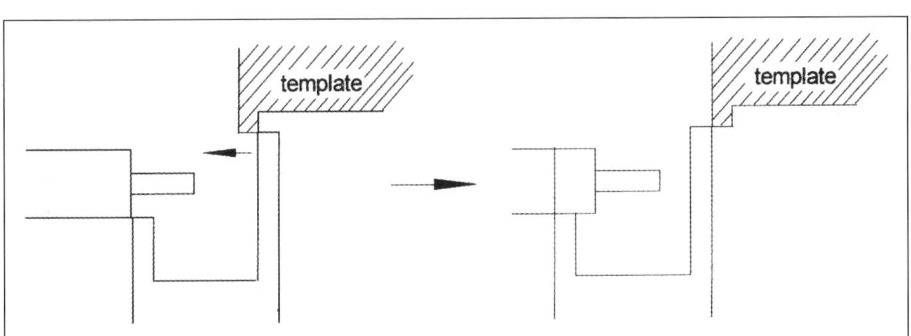

By operating the bottom traversing slide once again, the head of the screw is turned, and its movement is continued until it comes into contact with a 'stop' on the machine such that the right hand edge of the guide pin has just cleared the step on the template.

Before the screw could be separated from the round bar, the stem had to be threaded. A detail of the screw machine, Fig. 2.44, shows a rudimentary 'tailstock' hinged at the rear, 13, and carrying a shaft fitted with a handle and a 'pin vice', 14, which has threading dies, 16, inserted in the jaws. While machining the screw, the 'tailstock' was hinged backwards and when ready for threading, the cross slide carrying the cutting tool was withdrawn and the 'tailstock' was hinged forwards to bring the dies into line with the stem of the screw.

Being fitted with a handle suggests the threading operation was done by hand – but not according to Gamel, and his description needs to be considered alongside some details of the machine, Fig. 2.45.

Gamel states that once the stem of the screw was 'clamped in the jaws of the vice', threading was undertaken by putting the rack, 18, into motion by moving the lever, 17, so that the pulley wheel, W, engaged with the crank and connecting rod arrangement. This raises a number of questions which are not addressed. Clearly, the wheel, W, had to be driven by a different belt from that used to operate the lathe. Also, why such a complicated arrangement was used when threading could have been easily accomplished by hand is not stated. Also, why was a backward and forward rotary motion needed for threading – admittedly it is usual for threading to be carried out with an occasional partial reversal of the dies to clear any swarf, but not a full reversal. Also, were the dies of such a size that when the vice jaws were closed it corresponded to the correct thread diameter? No answer to these questions is supplied by Gamel.

The last stage was cutting off the screw from the bar, Fig. 2.46.

This last stage is also illustrated by Gamel, Fig. 2.47.

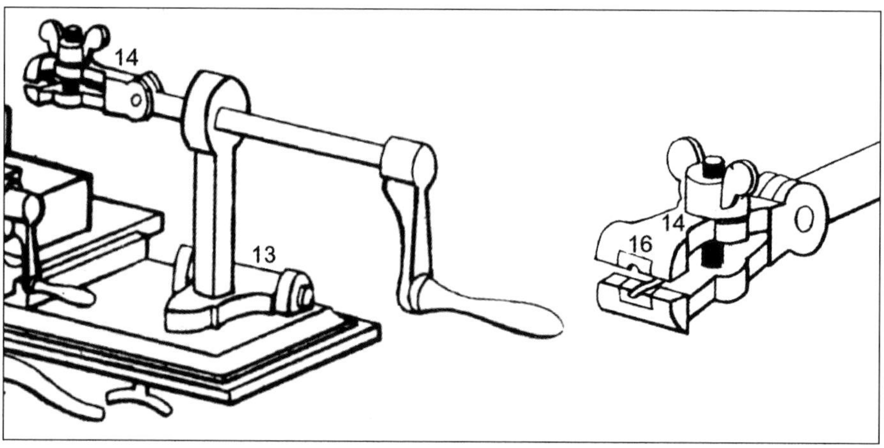

Fig. 2.44. Details showing the 'tailstock' with its hinge, 13, and the 'pin vice', 14, fitted with threading dies, 16. (Gamel, 1826, Fig. XXI)

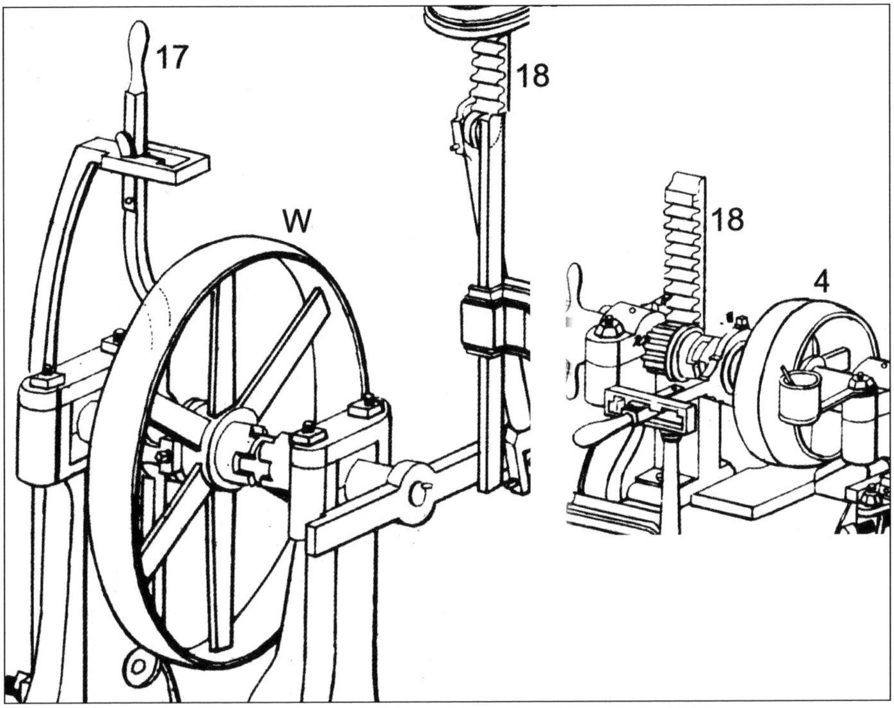

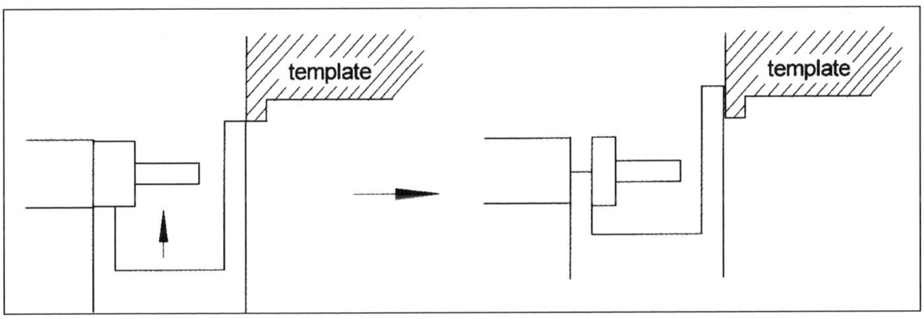

Top: Fig. 2.45. Showing details from, Fig. 2.37. (Gamel, 1826, Fig. XXI)

Above: Fig. 2.46. Cutting off the screw from the bar. (© P. Smithurst)

Right: Fig. 2.47. Cutting off the screw. (Gamel, 1826, Fig. XXI)

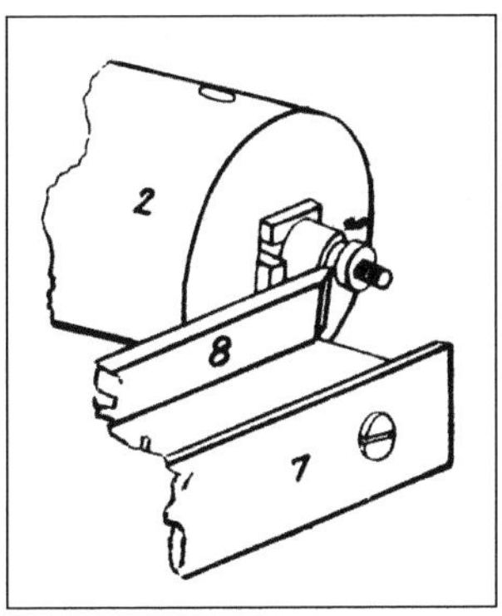

After being cut off, the screws were clamped in wooden jaws in a vice, the flat head filed with a coarse file and the slot cut by a hand saw.

2.14 Grinding and Polishing the blade

These processes followed very much those practiced in France but are described in much less detail. Grinding was carried out using English sandstone grinding wheels 2 arshines (56 inches, 1422mm) in diameter.[17] They were powered by waterwheels via intermediate gearing and line shafting and the shafts on which the grinding wheels were mounted ran on cast iron wheels set in a special bearing box to reduce friction, Fig. 2.48.

The grinder first weighed the bayonet to determine how much metal had to be removed. The edges were then ground to match the gauge. It was then laid across the stone and a shallow 'hollow' formed on the inner face. Using a channel formed in the stone, the back of the blade was ground on each side of the central rib to the required profile. All grinding operations were carried out with a stream of water flowing from a trough mounted on the rear half cover of the stone (not shown). The inner face of the blade adjacent to the neck was ground by a specialist grinder using a stone only 4 vershoks (7 inches / 178mm) diameter.[18]

Polishing was carried out using oak wheels and if the cutlery and edge tool trades in Sheffield are anything to go by, these were around 24 inches in diameter and driven by a water wheel using via overhead line shafting to transmit the power, Fig. 2.49.

The workman sat astride the wheel spindle on a special stool and presented the blade to the wheel rim which was coated with emery powder and hempseed oil. The use of an intermediate coarseness was to remove marks left by grinding.

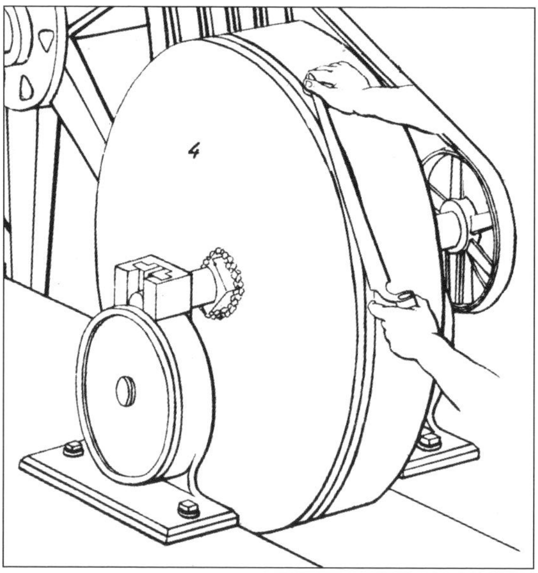

Fig. 2.48. The bayonet grinding wheel with special bearing boxes on either side. (Gamel, 1826 Fig. XXII – part)

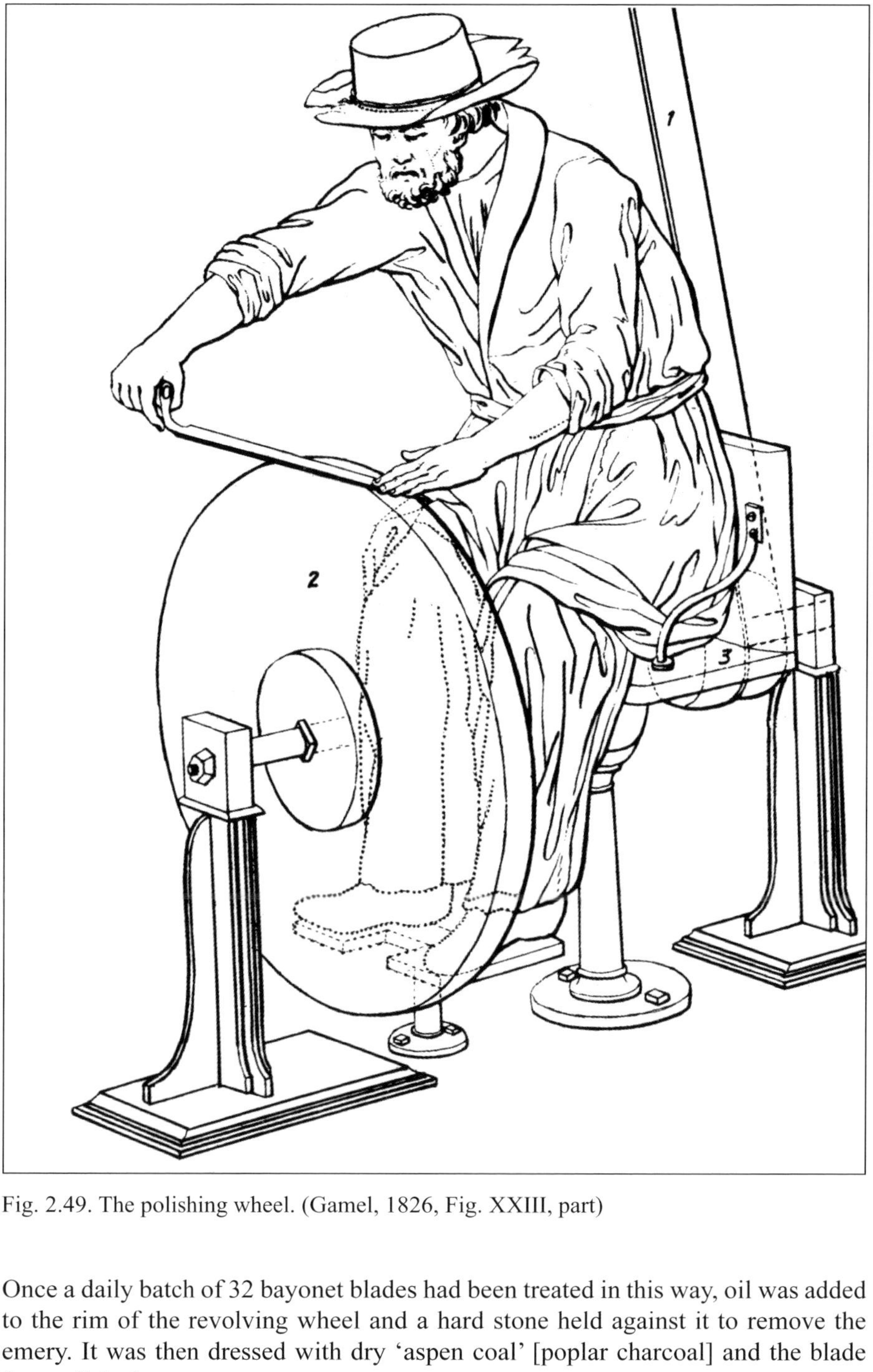

Fig. 2.49. The polishing wheel. (Gamel, 1826, Fig. XXIII, part)

Once a daily batch of 32 bayonet blades had been treated in this way, oil was added to the rim of the revolving wheel and a hard stone held against it to remove the emery. It was then dressed with dry 'aspen coal' [poplar charcoal] and the blade fine-polished.

2.15 Finishing the socket

While a lot of work had already gone into the socket it needed to have the final touches applied which mainly consisted of cleaning all over, including the slots, with a gradation of files followed by polishing with a stick of lime wood and crushed brick or sand. Again, there are parallels with the 'holloware' trades in Sheffield and no doubt elsewhere, in which dies cut out with a hammer and increasingly fine chisels were finished to the very high standards required by use of a pine stick and emery powder.

Similar processes were applied to the locking ring although nowhere is the bending of the forging to form a ring mentioned. Gamel states that *'the inner surface of the sleeve* [ring] *is filed on a mandrel'* which provides a conundrum. A mandrel usually fits *into* a hole and would preclude filing the 'inner surface' so exactly what is meant is rather obscure. At the same time the notch in the bridge of the locking ring was filed. The whole ring was then finished, as with the socket, by polishing with emery paper.[19] This is the earliest mention of emery paper so far encountered, assuming correct translation. The ring was then mounted on the socket and the 'ears' fitted with the screw.

The finished bayonet was reported as weighing 72 zolotniks (10 ounces, 303 grams).

Finally, the bayonet was 'fitted' to the barrel which involved firstly filing the tenon beneath the barrel and the barrel at this point to match a gauge which fitted on the barrel – an identical type of gauge was later used on the Enfield Pattern 1853 bayonet as shown in Chapter 3. The socket was also fitted to a 'reference mandrel' [gauge] and any excess metal removed by filing. The bayonet was then finally fitted to the musket barrel.

Chapter 3

Manufacture of the Enfield Pattern 1853 socket bayonet

3.1 Introduction

The Pattern 1853 series of arms utilised either a 'sword' or 'socket' bayonet. There were various forms of sword bayonets but the most common is that fitted with what is often referred to as the 'yataghan' blade copied from the Turkish short sword of that name; there were others which are an interesting study in their own right but beyond the scope of this publication and which can be found in various published works on British Military Bayonets.

In contrast, the Enfield Pattern 1853 socket bayonet would seem to offer little scope for study beyond cataloguing its various makers prior to its manufacture at the 'new' Royal Small Arms Factory at Enfield in 1857, its modification to fit the 1858/59 'Indian service' musket and later, the Martini-Henry rifle. None of the 'collector' publications appear to stray beyond that remit.

As noted in Chapter 1, it has a distinguished ancestry traced to the French M.1777 bayonet designed by Honoré Blanc for his M.1777 musket and which occupies an important place in the history of bayonets in being the first to introduce an effective method of securing it to the muzzle of the musket by means of the 'locking ring' placed in the middle of the socket, Fig. 3.1.

Its impact is clearly demonstrated by its adoption by Russia in 1808 but, just as the M.1777 musket influenced the design of the Pattern 1853 rifle, it was also to influence the development of the Enfield Pattern 1853 bayonet, Fig. 3.2 (on next page).

The difference in orientation of the blade in relation to the socket is that in both weapons the blade, when fixed, was to the right of the muzzle, but the French

Fig. 3.1. French Model 1777 bayonet. (© P. Smithurst)

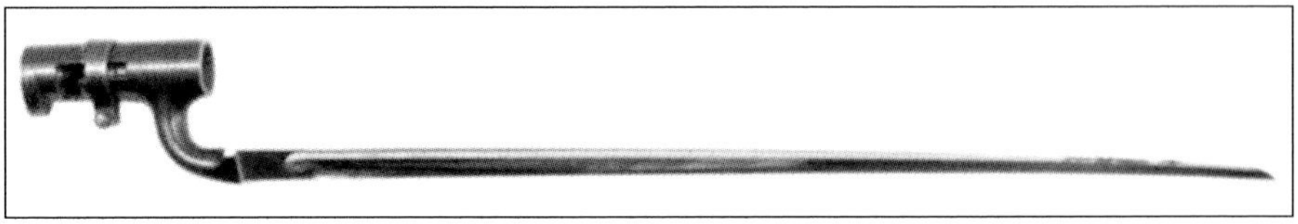

Fig. 3.2. The Enfield Pattern 1853 bayonet. (© P. Smithurst)

musket utilised a bayonet 'stud' or 'tenon' below the muzzle whereas the Enfield rifle utilised the foresight 'bed' as the bayonet stud / tenon. Nevertheless, it can be seen that the Enfield Pattern 1853 bayonet drew heavily upon the French M.1777 bayonet in its conception. Indeed, in various official and other British reports relating to its development, both indirect and direct reference is made to Blanc's locking ring:

> *. . . no general adoption of the "ring" took place until 1852 when it was copied from an arm used on the continent...*[1]

- whichever bayonet was being copied, it owed its origins to the French M.1777. This is reinforced by:

> *The present bayonet ... fitted with the French locking ring...*[2]

Just as with components for the rifle, the bayonet was initially obtained through private contract with various manufacturers and suffered the same problems with regard to provision of patterns and the process of inspection, or 'viewing'.

In his evidence to the Select Committee Thomas Lawrence of the bayonet contractors, Heighington & Lawrence, notes:

> *I would remark, with respect to one pattern bayonet being delivered to seven contractors, that when I returned the pattern into store at the Tower in Birmingham, I asked whether they would be good enough to mark one of my bayonets which they considered equal to the pattern, that I might have a standard pattern to examine by.*
> *. . . they said their instructions were to mark nothing.*

He goes on to note:

> *I can mention one instance in which Mr. Hill, one of the contractors, stated that he was satisfied, and he calls it a good view if out of the number he sends he passes half; he sent down 70, and to his surprise, 69 out of the 70 were passed.*

And when further questioned:

> *Was it within the last fortnight, since Mr. Gunner has been appointed?*

he replied:

> *Yes, certainly.*[3]

From this, and from what Gunner had stated in regard to the issue of patterns etc., it would seem there had been a change in the rigidity of the 'view' and a more pragmatic approach adopted.

Unlike the rifle, the supply of which was primarily shared between contractors in Birmingham and London along with some obtained from Liege and America, Birmingham held a monopoly in bayonet manufacture. But, as with the rifle, at this time of crisis with the Crimean War the government was dissatisfied with their ability to meet contract deadlines. John Anderson, chief engineer at Woolwich Arsenal, in his evidence to the Select Committee on Small Arms, attributes this by inference to a lack of mechanisation. He stated after visiting a number of Birmingham establishments that:

> *. . . engaged in military musket and bayonet work, all of which, however, are in a low mechanical state, and at least 50 years behind most of the other branches of manufacturing industry which we have been examining.*[4]

This is reflected in an article in *The Guardian* in the following year (Appendix 3) which also notes that Birmingham's monopoly had been broken by Francis Preston of Manchester who, through his extensive use of machinery, had been given an order for 8,500 bayonets per month which was *"a larger quantity than any three of the old* [Birmingham] *firms can supply within a given time".* Preston only manufactured bayonets sufficient to meet the needs of the Crimean War but his initiative in adapting his cotton machinery spindle making activity to, and the creation of new machines for, the manufacture of bayonets was undoubtedly another nail in the coffin of the Birmingham contractors for 'government work' and a boost to the establishment of the Royal Small Arms Factory at Enfield. What also makes it an interesting study is that it is the first British bayonet to have its manufacture described in a number of contemporary accounts. Furthermore, its manufacture in Birmingham at least, is represented by an extensive range of specimens held by Birmingham City Museum showing each stage of its production. This is the first time that the collection has been studied in detail and taken alongside the contemporary accounts, it forms the basis of this study.

3.2 Specifications for Manufacture

The only specification for the socket bayonet that has been found is dated 1853 and forms part of Appendix 4 of the Report from the Select Committee on Small Arms of 1854:

> *Specifications for bayonets with locking rings for rifle muskets, Pattern 1853.*

> *The blade and neck also to be entirely of steel, either the best* ***shear or mild cast steel****; soundly welded to the socket which is to be forged of the best clear iron, with a base to support the locking ring, the whole to be free from greys or flaws; the socket itself and base for locking ring to be neatly and accurately turned in a slide lathe. The whole bayonet to be ground, polished and filed up in a workmanlike manner equal to the pattern in every respect, and to weigh, when finished, from 11 to 12 ounces.*
>
> *14th November 1853.*
> *W. Evans.*[5]

It is felt that some explanation of the terms *shear steel* and *mild cast steel* at this point might be appropriate. The basic steel of commerce at the time was what is commonly known as 'Blister steel'. This name arose from the fact that it was made by baking bars of, quite often Swedish, wrought iron at red heat in beds of charcoal in the absence of air. These bars, roughly 3 inches (75mm) wide x ½ inch (12mm) thick and up to 14 feet (4.3 metres) long were packed in stone chests on beds of charcoal, and sealed with a lid made of a thick paste of clay-like consistency from the swarf from grinding wheels, which comprised sandstone and steel particles. Two of these chests were housed within a conical furnace fired from beneath with coke and baked at red heat for up to 7 days. During this process, carbon was absorbed by the iron and reacted with some of the impurities to create gas, and because the iron bars were in a 'plastic state' at the temperatures involved, these gases were able to form bubbles, or 'blisters' on the surface. After allowing to cool, the 'lids' – often referred to as a 'pie-crust', which had become vitrified at the temperatures involved – were broken open and the Blister steel bars extracted. An experienced furnaceman would take a bar and break an end off and, by examining the fracture, could judge what the steel would be useful for. In effect, he was visually judging the carbon content!

Blister steel could be used in its raw state, but it generally underwent further processing. One process entailed it being broken into approximate lengths of 3 feet, several stacked together, heated to a welding heat and welded together under a power hammer. The Blister steel contained all the impurities of the iron bars and treating it in this way would help eject some impurities as slag and consolidate the metal, giving it a degree of, but never complete, homogeneity. For that to be accomplished the Blister steel bars were broken into lengths of around 6 inches and placed in pre-heated crucibles in a coke-fired furnace. Once loaded, the crucibles had a fireclay lid placed on them and the furnace then filled with coke so that the crucibles were surrounded, additional coke being added as melting proceeded, which might take up to 6 hours. When ready, the crucibles were withdrawn, a process requiring great care since the clay from which they were made had become 'plastic' at the high temperatures involved – about 1800ºC – and could tear! Once out of the furnace, the lids were removed, the slag skimmed off, and the molten steel cast into a cast iron mould to produce an ingot. This process also required a high degree of care to ensure the mould filled from the bottom upwards and the stream of molten steel did not touch the sides of the mould as it entered, otherwise a flaw would be formed in the ingot. Bearing in mind the weight of the crucible with its charge of steel would weigh up to 120 pounds (54kg), and the process of removing the crucible from the furnace and the pouring into the ingot mould were done by hand, an exquisite degree of both strength and skill were required. Such steel was very pure and homogeneous and was usually reserved for high quality products, and items made in Britain through to the mid-20th century can be found marked 'Cast Steel' – which refers to the nature of the steel, not the method of making the product!

It has been noted that carbon content determines the nature of the steel whatever its method of production and how this determines its ultimate use. This raises a question in regard to the 'mild steel' referred to in the specification. Today we class mild steel as containing around 0.1% – 0.3% carbon and, like wrought iron, it cannot be hardened by heating and quenching – it is totally unsuitable for bayonet blades. For that purpose, a steel containing up to 1% or more carbon would be more appropriate. So, was the concept of 'mild steel' different at the time those specifications were laid down? So far this question remains unanswered. The Order Books of Thomas Firth and Sons of Sheffield (Appendix 4) show steel supplied for these bayonets and which was clearly favoured by Enfield.

As a prelude to embarking upon a detailed examination of its manufacture, it may be of value to remind readers of the British terminology used for various features.

Little is known of the practices in bayonet manufacture in Britain until this time. Considering John Jones and his son had been recruited from Birmingham in 1817 to improve operations at Tula, bayonet manufacture there might be thought to reflect English practice. However, the Jones' seem to have had little involvement in bayonet manufacture. Both John Anderson's evidence[6] to the Select Committee and *The Guardian* article of 1855 noted earlier, suggest this was not reflected in the Birmingham bayonet making fraternity where little mechanisation was apparent.

So far, the manufacture of the Enfield Pattern 1853 bayonet has only been found to be covered in any detail in two sources, The *Illustrated London News* in 1855 and *The Engineer* in 1859. The first describes manufacture carried out by Francis Preston, the second the

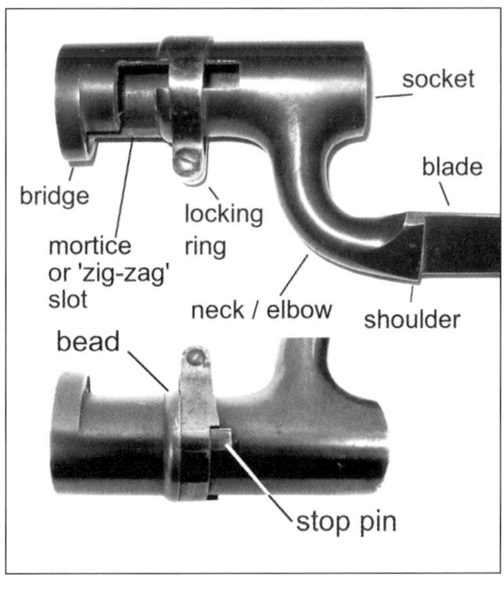

Fig. 3.3. The terminology of the Enfield socket bayonet. (© P. Smithurst)

operations at Enfield. Even combined they offer a very incomplete and disparate picture, but this is probably due to editorial constraints or inaccurate observation, rather than disjointed processes.

Fortunately, there exists in Birmingham City Museums a unique collection showing most, if not all, of the stages in the manufacture of this bayonet, though many are covered in a bitumen-like preservative which precludes assessments made from toolmarks. It seems they were catalogued in 1885 in what is taken to be a numbered sequence of the various processes through which they passed. This sequence will be used but it varies in parts from that recorded in the accounts mentioned:

1 welding the socket and blade
2 socket bridge roughly shaped by hand
3 'drawing' out the blade
4 forming the hollows[7] in the blade
5 socket stamping
6 machining the socket to length
7 socket drilling
8 socket reamed
9 socket turned from neck to ring shoulder
10 centre-hole drilled in squared tip of trimmed blade
11 neck turned in a copying lathe
12 socket behind neck machined
13 edges (corners) of blade milled
14 top face next to elbow planed and shoulders formed on other two faces
15 planing the faces of the blades
16 blade hollows and curved tip milled
17 front of socket turned
18 bending the blade at the neck into its final position
19 socket turned from locking ring buttress to bridge
20 bridge turned in a copying lathe
21 hole drilled for locking ring stop pin
22 locking ring stop pin fitted and squared
23 mortice slots for bayonet stud cut
24 hardening, tempering, grinding and polishing
25 the locking ring

3.3 Welding the socket and blade

It is known from the order books of Thomas Firth & Sons (Appendix 4), and from measurement of one of the Birmingham specimens, Fig. 3.8, that steel bars ¾ inch square were supplied for the blades of these bayonets. On that basis it is estimated that the round iron bar for sockets would have been approximately 1 inch diameter. Having prepared suitable lengths of these, the steel bar had a short length at one end forged round. For this, Preston used a Ryder hammer, Fig. 3.4, invented by William Ryder of Bolton as a means of rapidly forging round spindles used in their thousands in the cotton spinning machinery in Lancashire and patented by him in 1841.[8] It was ideally suited to the task in hand. John Anderson in his evidence before the Select Committee, advocates mechanical improvements at Enfield, including the adoption of Ryder's hammer for certain work on bayonets.[9] So, by the time of the article in *The Engineer*, it is likely that the Ryder hammer was in use, but no evidence has been found to suggest that it was used in Birmingham at that time.

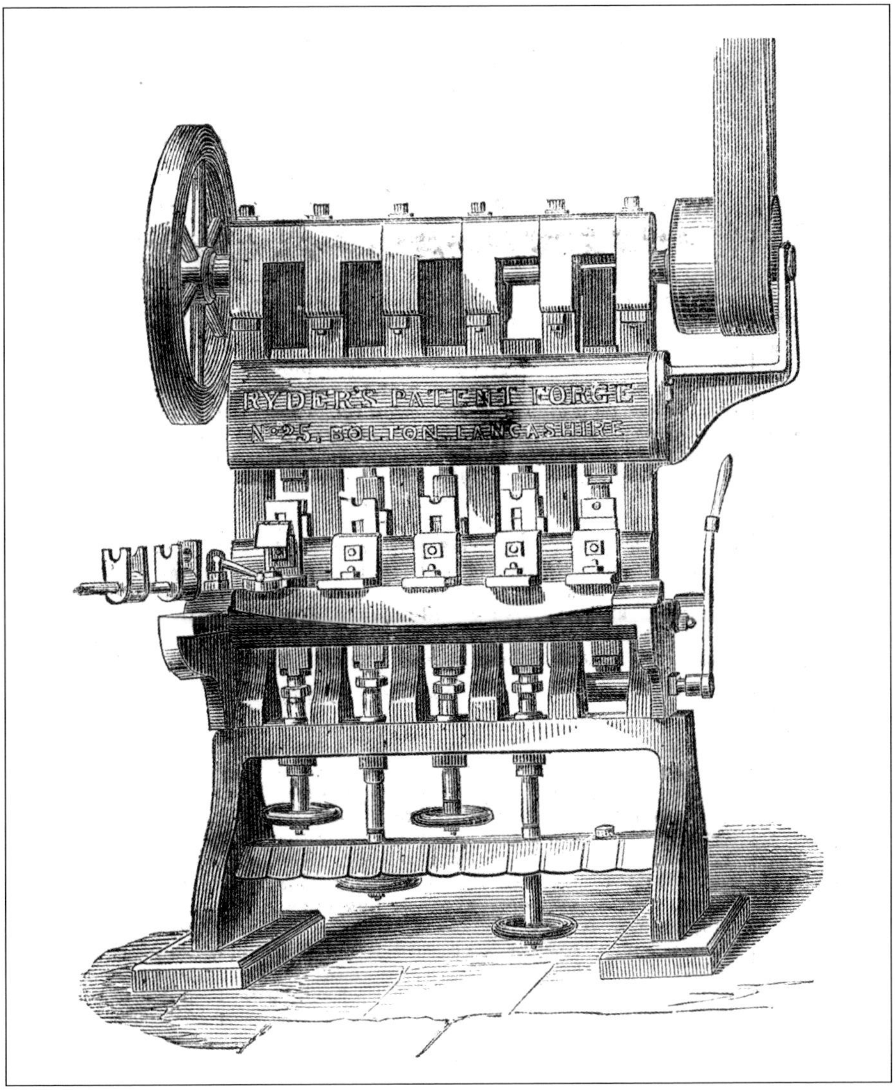

Fig. 3.4. Ryder hammer. (*Illustrated London News*, Supplement, Jan. 26th, 1855, Fig. 1, p.97)

Ryder's hammer consisted of a rapidly rotating overhead camshaft driven by a steam engine. The cams operated on 'pushrods' and these in turn acted on spring-loaded plungers to which a suitably shaped die was fixed, Fig. 3.5.

Thus, the rotation of the camshaft caused the dies to reciprocate vertically at high speed. These dies were matched by dies below them so that when closed together, they formed the required shape, Fig. 3.6.

In the process being considered, the square steel bar would first have had its corners hammered between the flat faces of the dies at the extreme right to create a roughly octagonal section, followed by being forged round in a succession of appropriately sized reducing dies shown to the left. This is more clearly shown in Fig. 3.7.

Having prepared the iron and steel bars, the two were welded together. There was no gas-welding at this date, so the ends of both bars had to be brought to a 'sparkling-white' welding heat in the forge hearth and then welded by hand with a hammer, a highly skilled job.

This weld can be seen in Fig. 3.9 as the junction between the 'bright' iron and 'grey' steel in a polished and etched sectioned socket shown below.

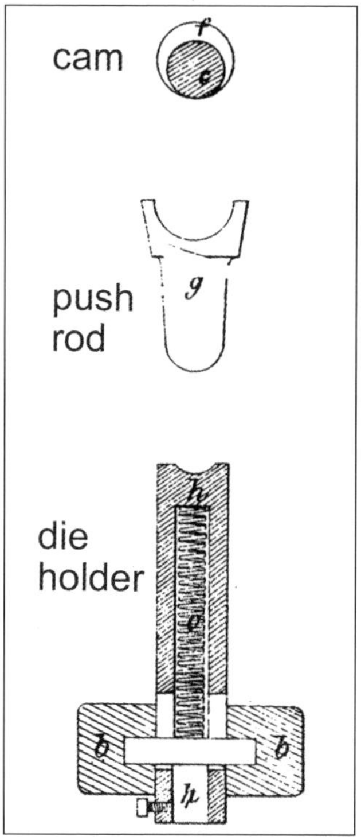

Left: Fig. 3.5. Detail from Ryder's patent showing camshaft, 'push-rod' and die holder.

Below: Fig. 3.6. Detail from Ryder's patent showing the juxtaposed dies or swages, *m*.

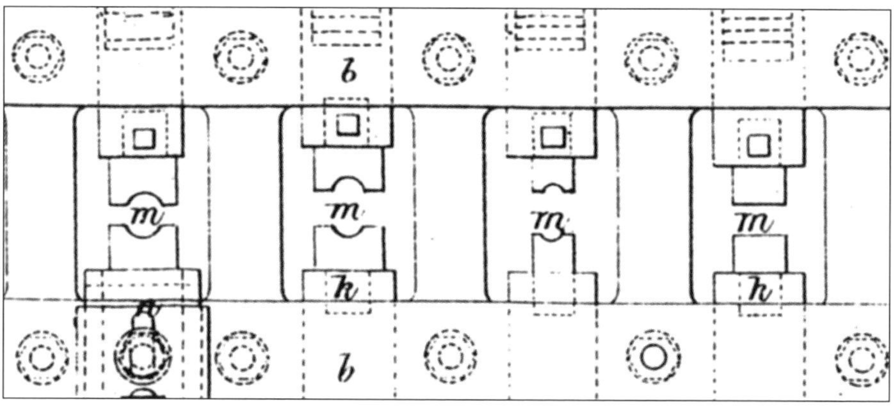

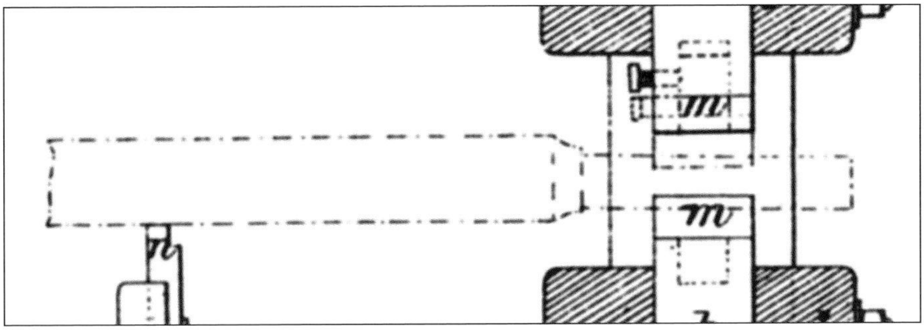

Fig. 3.7. The action of forging a reduced diameter on the end of a bar.

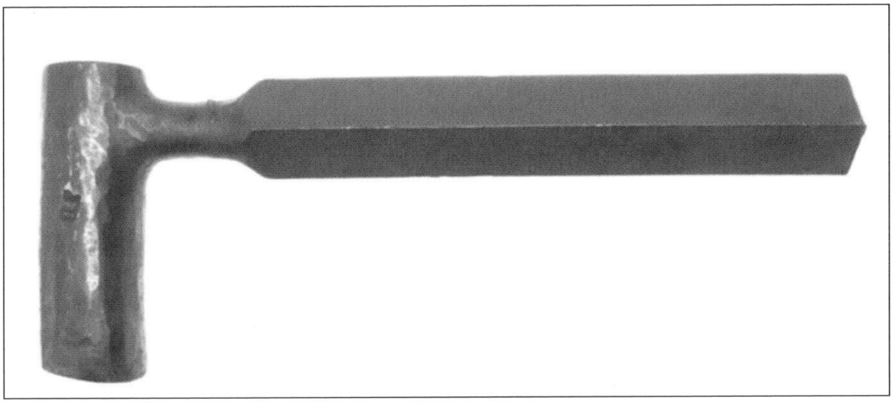

Above: Fig. 3.8. The iron and steel bars welded. (1885S00609.00001, courtesy Birmingham Museum Trust)

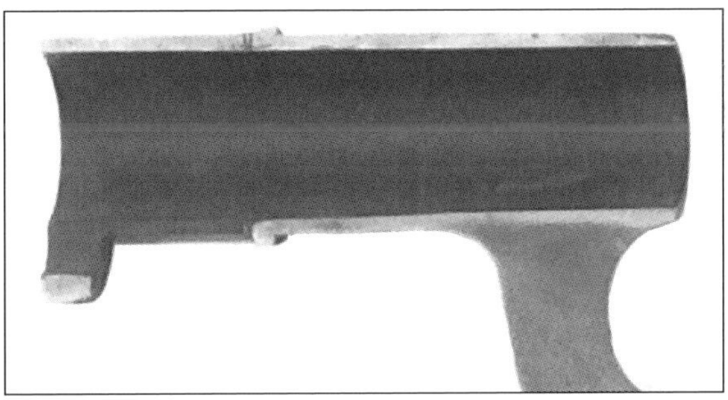

Right: Fig. 3.9. The junction of the welded iron socket and steel elbow. (© P. Smithurst)

3.4 Socket bridge roughly shaped by hand forging

It would appear from the Birmingham Museum specimens, Fig. 3.10 (on next page), that at this point the socket body was roughly formed to create a vestigial 'bridge' by hand-forging.

However, this operation is not alluded to in the operations by Preston,[10] or at Enfield,[11] but may simply have been part of the 'smithing' work referred to in these accounts before commencing their more detailed descriptions of later stages.

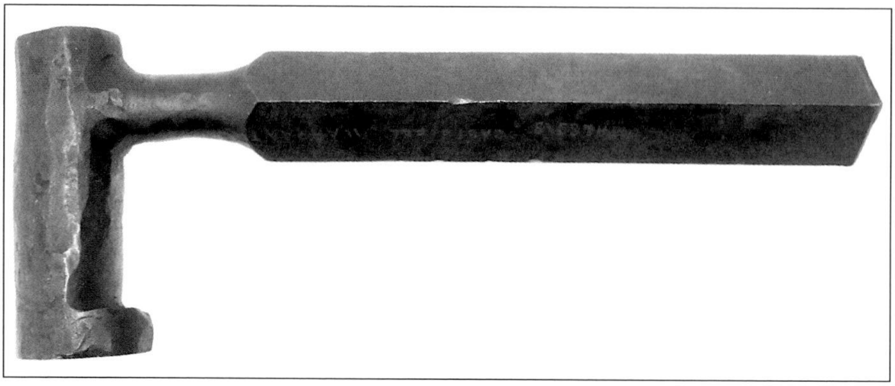

Fig. 3.10. The socket body and bridge roughly formed. (1885S00609.00002, courtesy Birmingham Museum Trust)

Fig. 3.11. Marking on the steel bar which would become the blade. (1885S00609.00002, courtesy Birmingham Museum Trust)

An additionally informative feature of this specimen is the marking on the steel bar, "Thomas Firth & Sons", "Cast Steel", "Warranted", Fig. 3.11.

Thomas Firth & Sons, one of the Sheffield steelmakers, were well known suppliers of high quality steel to both the private small arms manufacturers and Enfield and their activities in this field have been detailed elsewhere.[12]

3.5 'Drawing-out' the blade

The square bar which formed the blade was heated and 'drawn out' in stages to 18 inches long, at the same time being converted into a roughly triangular section, Fig. 3.12.

In his 1854 patent[13] Preston proposed performing this operation using a Ryder hammer. This is confirmed in the statement that in this case the descent of the 'hammers', or more correctly upper die blocks, was gradually reduced in sequence and the transfer of the 'blade' to each in succession enabled a taper to be more easily produced.[14] However, while Preston used the Ryder hammer with such dies for this purpose, he withdrew it from his patent specification as he had discovered it to be in use elsewhere. Since Anderson's comments suggest Ryder hammers were not used at this early date, this may be an oblique reference to Lawrence's patent noted below.

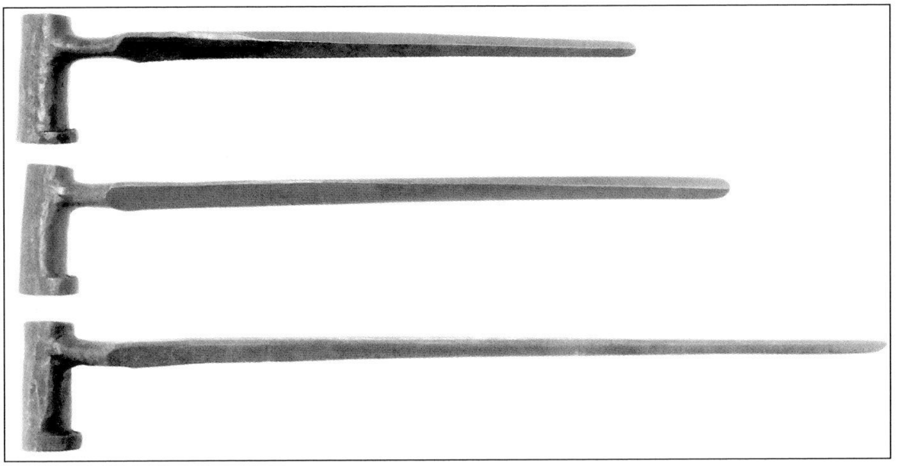

Fig. 3.12. Blade drawn out to 12, 14 and 18 inches and given a roughly triangular section. (Courtesy Birmingham Museum Trust, 1885S00609.00004, .00005 and .00006 respectively)

3.6 Forming the hollows in the blade

One of the Birmingham museum specimens clearly shows this stage, Fig. 3.13, but unfortunately the hollows are not so clear in the photograph.

Examination of this specimen fails to reveal how these hollows were formed but they have a consistent taper without any steps which suggests the use of a fullering tool. Alternatively, it may indicate application of a patent granted to Thomas Lawrence, (presumed to be the Lawrence of Heighington & Lawrence, one of the Birmingham bayonet contractors) in 1854 in which he states:

> *In the bed of the anvil block of a tilt or forge hammer (... working by perpendicular action and commonly known as Froming's Patent) I sink a mould or groove of a V form, its two sides presenting convexities exactly corresponding with the concavities required in the* [outer] *sides of the bayonet blade, and on the face of the hammer block I form a projecting rib or die of precisely the same convexity which is intended to shape the groove on the third* [inner] *side of*

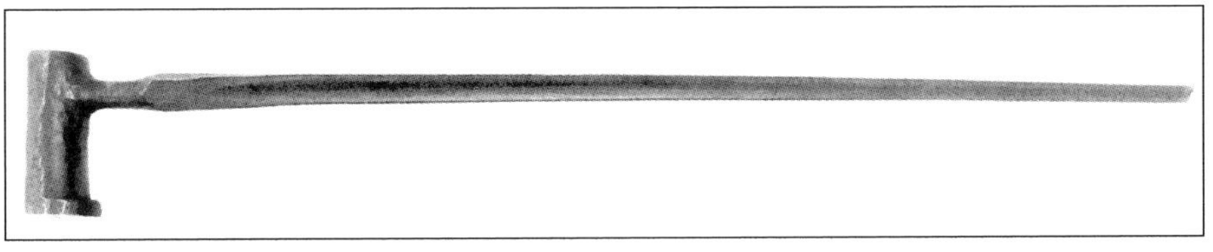

Fig. 3.13. Stage 7, hollows forged in blade. (1885S00609.00007, courtesy Birmingham Museum Trust)

the blade. The blade in its rough state, of a triangular or what is generally termed in the trade a three square section, each side being perfectly flat, is laid in the groove of the anvil block, and by repeated descents of the hammer is shaped into the requisite form.[15]

However, no definite record of the application of Lawrence's patent has been found.

On the other hand, Preston created the hollows by means of tapering rolls to produce the 'inner' hollow, that is, the one facing the barrel when the bayonet is fitted, at the same time forming the 'outer' hollows by the roll pressing the blade into a tapered die having convex inner faces. In this, some similarity with Lawrence's patent is apparent.

Additional illustrations of this machine are shown in Figs. 3.15 and 3.16.

However, a few more constructional details are revealed in his patent drawings of 1854, Figs. 3.17 and 3.18.

The table, *n*, slid in dovetail grooves and was linked to the crankshaft by means of a connecting rod. Thus, as the crankshaft rotated, the table, *n*, moved backwards and forwards. The table was fitted with two blocks, *o*, each fitted with a die, *p*. The table also had a rack, *q*, which engaged with a pinion on the shaft, *r*. This shaft carried what are referred to as two steel 'bosses' but are more correctly termed rolls, *s*. These rolls each had grooves tapered at the sides and with a convex rib at the bottom. The tapered groove and rib of the rolls and the cavity in the dies

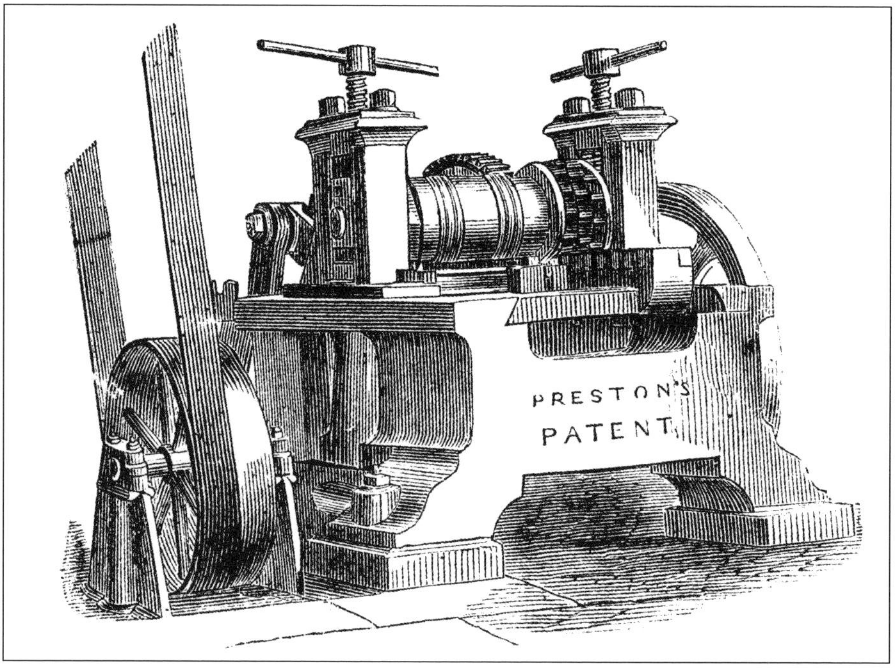

Fig. 3.14. Preston's blade 'fullering' rolls. (*Illustrated London News*, Supplement, Jan. 26th, 1855, p.97, Fig. 3)

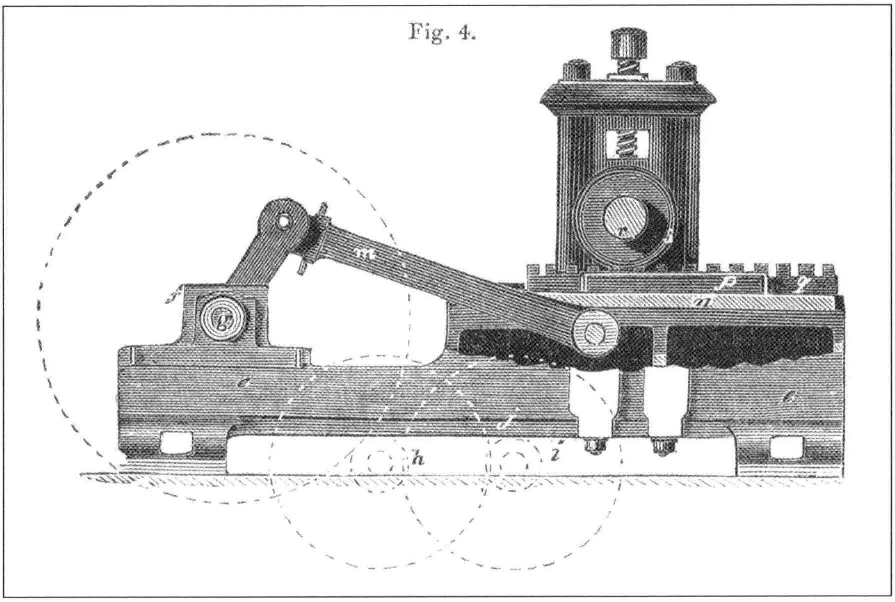

Fig. 3.15, Preston's blade rolling mill, side view. (*Mechanics Magazine*, Vol. LXIII, Sept. 8, 1855, Fig. 4, p.217)

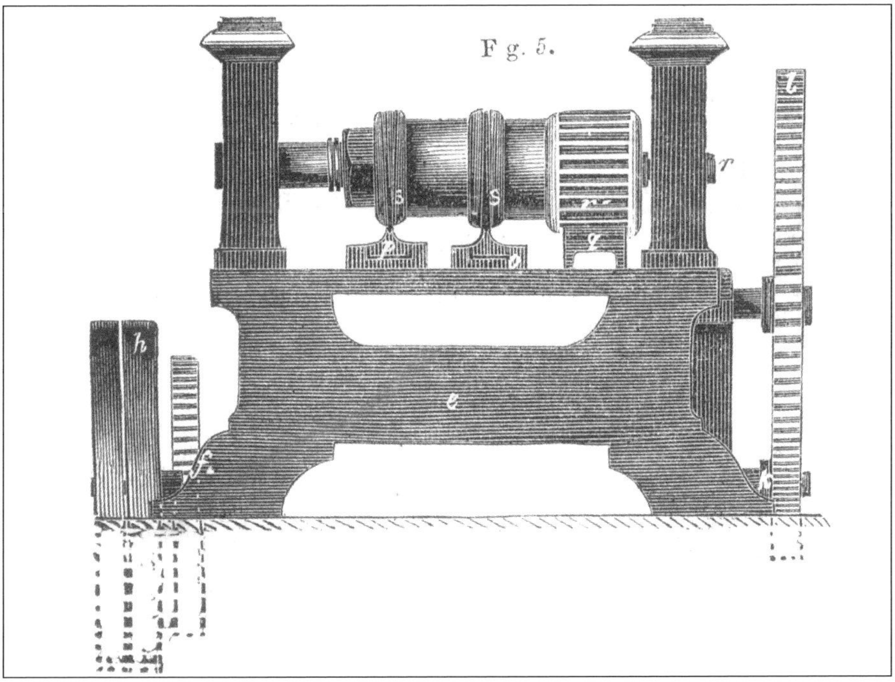

Fig. 3.16, Preston's blade rolling mill, end view.

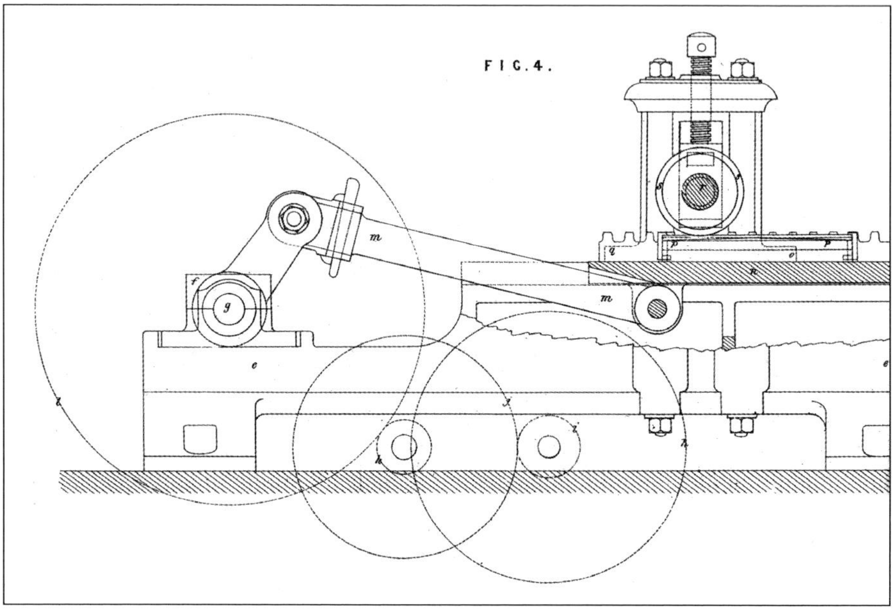

Fig. 3.17. Side view of Preston's rolling mill for producing the hollows on triangular bayonet blades, from his patent of 1854.

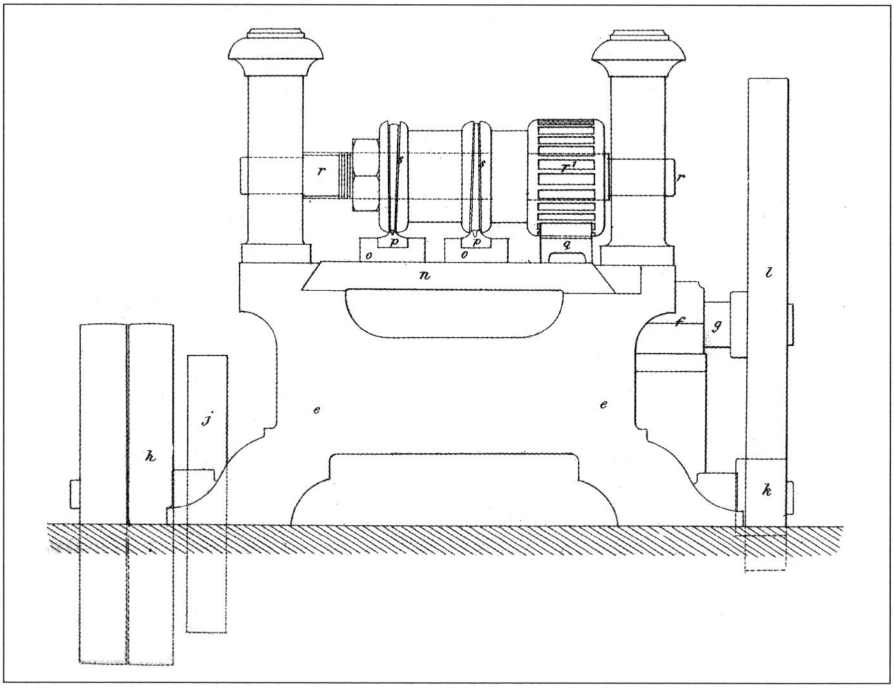

Fig. 3.18. End view of Preston's bayonet blade rolling mill.

corresponded to the taper and 'hollows', or fullers, of the bayonet blade. Details of these features are shown in Figs. 3.19 and 3.20.

A very ingenious feature was that the sides of the grooves in the rolls were made to overlap the top edges of the dies in such a way as to act as shears and trim off any excess metal – 'fins' – exuded from the dies in the process.

The mode of operation was to take a bayonet forging with the blade at right angles to the socket, heat it to correct forging temperature and lay the blade with the 'inner' face uppermost in one of the dies, *p*. The machine was then set in motion. One half revolution of the crankshaft moved the table and, by means of the rack fitted to it, the roll also, so that the forging had the inner hollow formed and was pressed into the dies to form the outer hollows. This only occupied one half revolution of the crank – a second bayonet forging was placed likewise in the second die to be operated upon during the second half of the rotation when the motion of the table was reversed.

A further patent by Preston of 1856[16] was basically an improvement of the mechanics of his first blade rolling machine but it contains a plan view of the forging

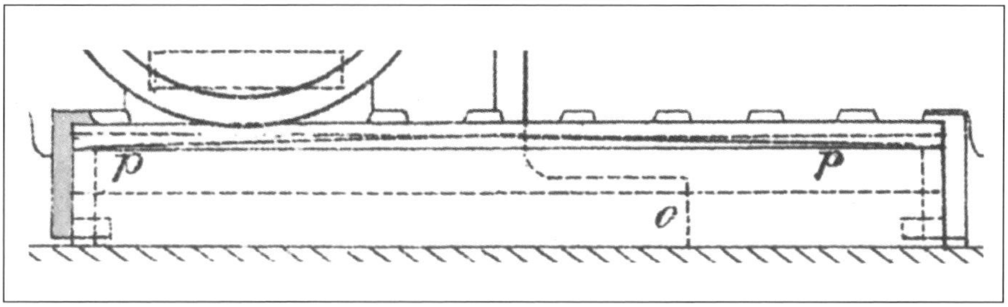

Fig. 3.19. Detailed side view of Preston's rolling mill showing the rolls and the dies – the visible portion of the socket of a bayonet forging is shown in solid grey.

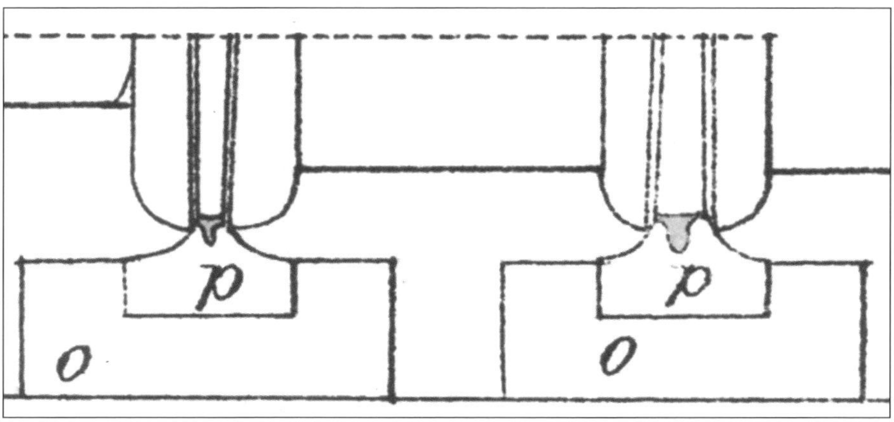

Fig. 3.20. Detailed end view of Preston's rolling mill showing the rolls and the dies working the blade forging shown in solid grey.

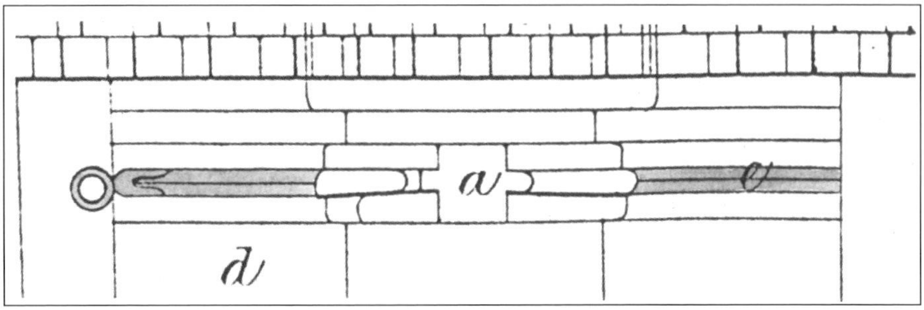

Fig. 3.21. Detail from a plan view of Preston's rolling mill in his 1856 patent showing the rolls and the die working the blade forging shown in solid grey.

in the die and being acted upon by the roll, Fig. 3.21. However, it gives the impression that the 'outer' hollows were uppermost which, of course, they were not! The roll seems also to have lost its capacity for trimming excess metal exuded in the process but that may, again, be an error in the illustration.

At Enfield there is no mention of the grooves being formed by forging or rolling in the account in *The Engineer*, but it is considered that this is probably an oversight in the description; pre-formed grooves would ease later operations and avoid wastage of steel which was an expensive commodity.

3.7 Stamping the socket

The only known illustration of this process is that showing Preston's operations and whilst simplistic, it gives an indication of the type of equipment needed, Fig. 3.22.

The falling hammer, or *tup*, is fitted with a die which is a replica of that on the base, and it goes without saying that each die had to be exactly the same and, when the two were in contact, they mated perfectly. Everything needed to be of substantial proportions, especially the foundations, since the *tup* weighed between 4 and 5 hundredweight (approximately 200 – 250 kg). It was raised by steam power and allowed to free-fall onto the bottom die into which had been placed the white-hot

Fig. 3.22. Preston's socket stamping machine. (*Illustrated London News*, 1855, Supplement, Jan. 26th, p.97, Fig. 2)

roughly formed iron socket. Two or three such blows may have been needed to properly shape the socket so that it filled the die, any excess metal being squeezed out as a 'fin' between the die faces. A detail of the bottom die is shown in Fig. 3.23.

Stamping took place in two stages. The first brought it close to its finished form, Fig. 3.24.

The second stamping formed the socket to its final shape preparatory to machining – particularly noticeable are the 'bead' that will form the 'base' for the locking ring and the 'fins', Fig. 3.25.

Fig. 2.

Fig. 3.23. Detail of Preston's socket stamping machine.

Right: Fig. 3.24. Detail of socket after first stamping – note the small 'fins' and vestigial 'bead'. (1885S00609.00008, courtesy Birmingham Museum Trust)

Far right: Fig. 3.25. Detail of socket after second stamping – note the correctly formed bead and larger 'fins'. (1885S00609.00009, courtesy Birmingham Museum Trust)

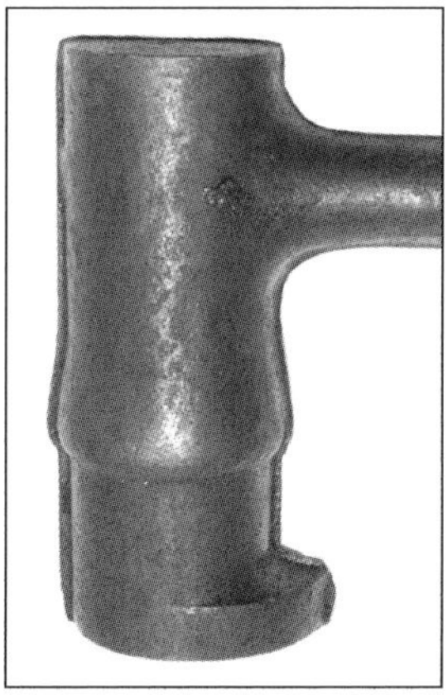

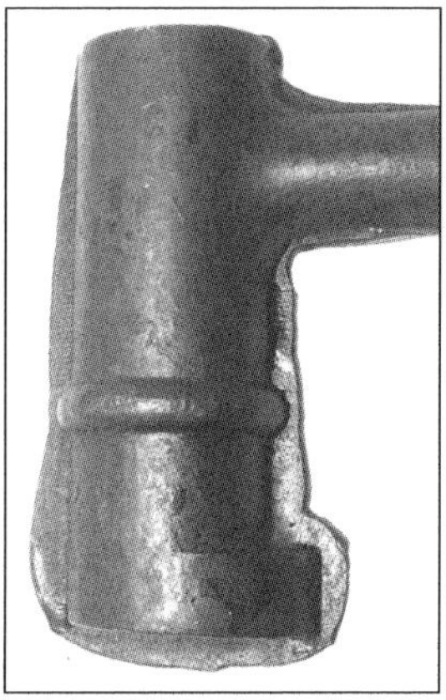

It has to be presumed that this was followed by a third operation, trimming off the fins by pressing through an appropriately shaped trimming die. As will be discussed later, the socket forging produced by Preston would have differed slightly from those shown here because, unlike the bayonets produced at Enfield or in Birmingham, the socket of Preston's bayonet had an integral 'stop pin'.

3.8 Machining the socket to length

There is no mention of this stage in the account regarding Preston's operations, but it would of course have been necessary. At Enfield it is described as taking place after the blade had been drawn to length and the socket (presumably stamped) was still solid and each end of the socket was milled. No illustration of this has been found but it is clear that this could have been achieved simply by passing it between two correctly spaced rotating cutters, one at each end. The ends of the machined socket would each need to be in the required juxtaposition to the elbow and this would have been achieved by clamping in a suitable fixture on a milling machine so that its two ends could be presented to the two cutters in the required position. This is illustrated in Fig. 3.26.

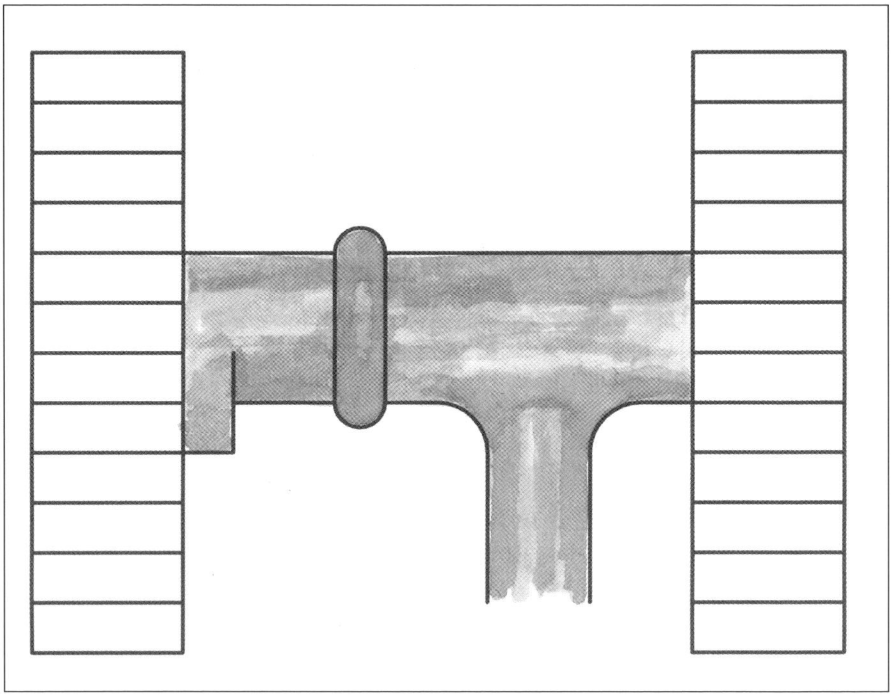

Fig. 3.26. Sketch suggesting the method of milling the socket to length by fitting it in an accurately shaped and positioned fixture on the milling machine table and passing it between two rotating cutters. (© P. Smithurst)

This stage is represented in the Birmingham Museum specimens, Fig. 3.27.

There is no information as to how this was achieved in Birmingham, but it is difficult to imagine a simpler method than that described to achieve the necessary result. Given Preston's mechanical aptitude he probably employed a similar method.

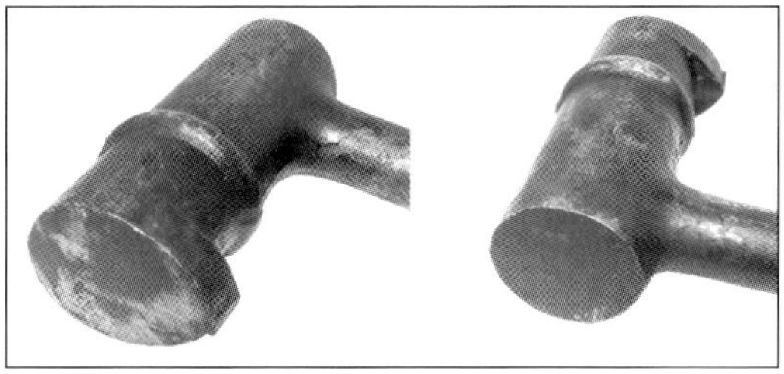

Fig. 3.27. The socket trimmed to length. (1885S00609.00011, courtesy Birmingham Museum Trust)

3.9 Socket drilling

The Birmingham specimens show this as two stages, but how they were carried out is not recorded. The first specimen reveals a hole positioned centrally in the socket body and a substantial amount of metal left for subsequent operations on the bore and outer circumference, Fig. 3.28.

The account of Preston's operations states that the socket was simply drilled *in an ordinary drilling machine* and was carried out before the blade had been drawn out and the hollows formed.[17] It implies only one operation. Considering the accuracy with which this needed to be done for the bayonet to be a close fit on the muzzle of the rifle, this raises serious questions about the nature of the drills and drilling machines used. It is worth remembering perhaps that the twist drill invented by Morse did not appear until 1863,[18] so the common drills available would have been the so-called 'spade' drills, an example of which is shown in Fig. 3.29.

Right: Fig. 3.28. The first drilling of the socket. (1885S00609.00012, courtesy Birmingham Museum Trust)

Below: Fig. 3.29. A typical 'spade drill' of 0.4 inches diameter. (© P. Smithurst)

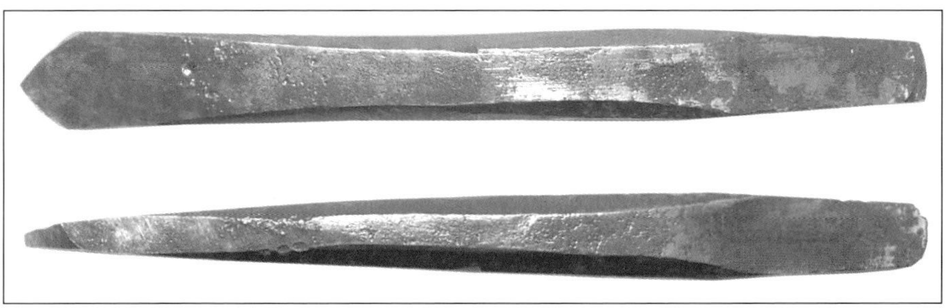

Such drills were hand-forged, and to ensure the square pyramidal ends were equal in every respect and concentric with the centre line of the drill and its point, they would have required extensive ‘fine finishing’. While drilling would have been a necessary precursor to producing an accurate and finely finished hole by boring, to accept the drilled hole as ‘finished’ runs counter to the quality expected. At Enfield too, the hole was also reportedly drilled in a vertical drilling machine. Close examination of the socket on a bayonet made by any of the manufacturers shows a finely finished bore and it is suggested, therefore, that the recorder of the operations by Preston probably referred to the first drilling.

None of these accounts mention the obvious – that the bayonet socket would need to have been held in a truly upright position, otherwise the drilled hole would not follow the centre-line of the socket. For this some form of simple fixture would have been required into which the socket could be accurately fitted and held securely.

A second Birmingham specimen below, Fig. 3.30, shows the hole enlarged.

The only account of this operation is in the descriptions of work at Enfield where the the machine shown in Fig. 3.31 was used.

This is an inadequate illustration of a machine of some complexity. It was ‘self-acting’ inasmuch as the boring tool/drilling bit was fed automatically into the existing hole in the socket. Even an enlarged portion, Fig. 3.32, only provides minimal additional detail.

The bayonet was clamped by its blade on a large faceplate. Machine faceplates by their nature are flat and square to their axis of rotation which is coaxial with that of the machine. The bayonet forging had to be mounted on the faceplate so that the hole in the socket was coaxial with the axis of the faceplate. This imposed certain requirements of the forging; the blade had to be straight; it had to be flat on its ‘inner face’ which also had to be at 90° to the axis of the hole in the socket in two planes at 90°.

Fig. 3.30. The second drilling of the socket. (1885S00609.00013, courtesy Birmingham Museum Trust)

Fig. 3.31. The machine for second drilling of the socket at Enfield. (*The Engineer*, 1859, p.384)

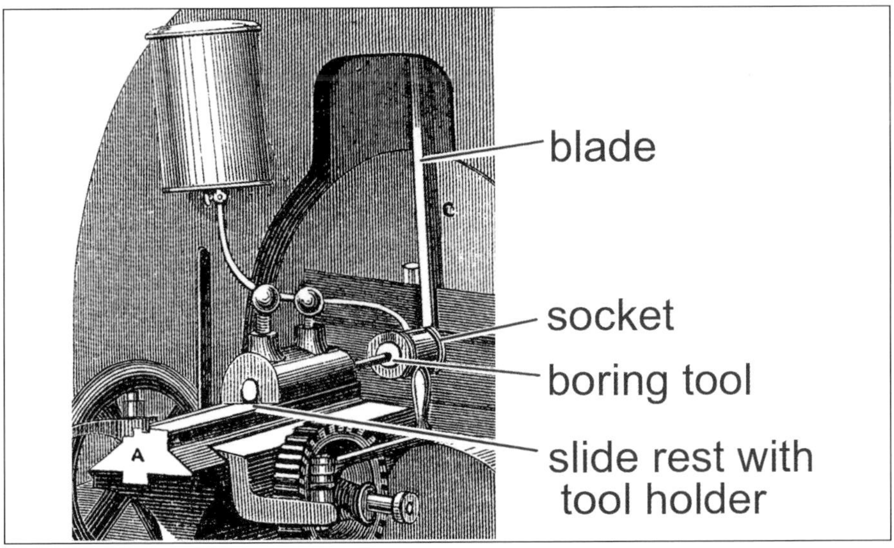

Fig. 3.32. Detail of the machine for second drilling of the socket at Enfield.

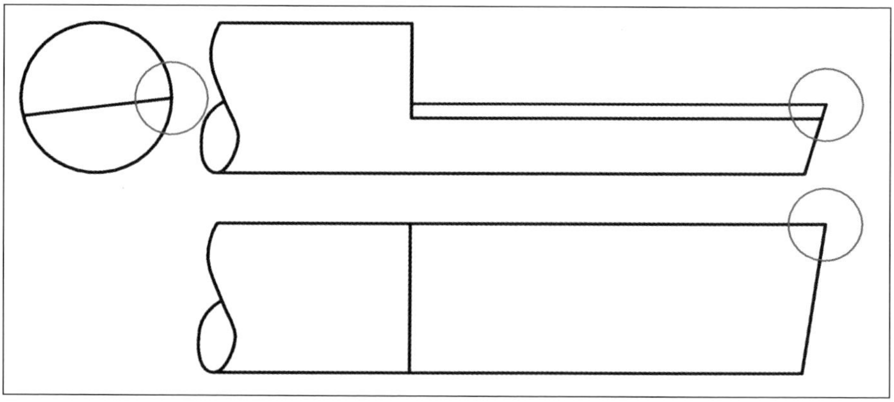

Fig. 3.33. Sketch showing the features of a D-bit with its cutting point circled. (© P. Smithurst)

However, the author of the account in *The Engineer* states that only after turning the socket from elbow to base ring, stage 10, was the blade:

> *straightened and set preparatory to the blade being cut off to the right length . . .*

It is inconceivable that this was not performed to enable this second stage enlarging the hole in the socket to be carried out. To attempt to mount a deformed blade/socket on the faceplate such that the hole of the socket was coaxial with the spindle would have been at least very time consuming, if not futile. It has to be presumed therefore that the sequence of events in this instance is incorrectly recorded.

A sheet iron cover surrounded the faceplate to prevent injury from the rotating bayonet blade. Then, with bayonet revolving, the boring bit was automatically fed into the hole to enlarge it to the required size. This bit is described as 'half-round', and is commonly referred to, understandably, as a 'D-bit', Fig. 3.33.

D-bits were formed from a solid bar whose diameter was very close to, if not the same as, the hole it was intended to produce. The 'D' portion tended to be, again, the same length or slightly longer than the hole they produced. This gave them far greater rigidity than the 'spade drills' commonly in use at that time. D-bits cut on a front corner, which was made an acute angle through providing what is known as 'rake' by inclining the top face and 'relieving' the front face by grinding after hardening and tempering. This creation of a point allowed them to work on a smaller diameter hole. If the D-bit was the same diameter as the hole, the straight, hardened edge behind the point could also act as a reamer and give the hole a finer finish.

3.10 Socket reamed

A curious point is raised in the article in *The Engineer* where it states the hole was then *finished off with a slightly coned rimer* [reamer], *to give it the same taper as the barrel*. Measurements of a small group of Pattern 1853 Enfield rifle barrels spanning the dates 1854-1869 (Appendix 5) show that in the post-1857 Enfield-made barrels the largest variation between these two diameters is 0.009 inches (0.23mm). The largest variation is 0.015 inches on diameter, or .0075 inches (0.19mm) on the radius over a length of 2 inches and it is argued that for all practical purposes, this is not tapered at all and is simply inherent inaccuracy due to tool or machine bearing wear, and that the muzzle portion of the barrel was effectively cylindrical to accept a bayonet with a cylindrical bore in the socket. Nevertheless, it does raise the question of tolerances permitted during inspection and is obviously an area for further research to confirm or refute these conclusions. Petrie[19] notes that in the case of non-interchangeable arms, when being packed for transport *the proper bayonet belonging to each musket is to be attached to the guard swivel by a piece of string and it must not be separated without precautions being taken for its re-appropriation to the right musket. This is not necessary for interchangeable muskets as their bayonets fit universally.* This raises a further interesting question: were the bores of the bayonet sockets so consistently uniform that they would fit an interchangeable rifle better than they would a non-interchangeable one? A more likely answer would be that only the bayonets made at Enfield were endowed with such characteristics.

This is supported by the fact that at Enfield, the bore of the socket was finished by broaching – the forcing through the bore of a tool-steel cutter of the correct size having circular cutting edges designed to remove a very small amount of metal, Fig. 3.34.

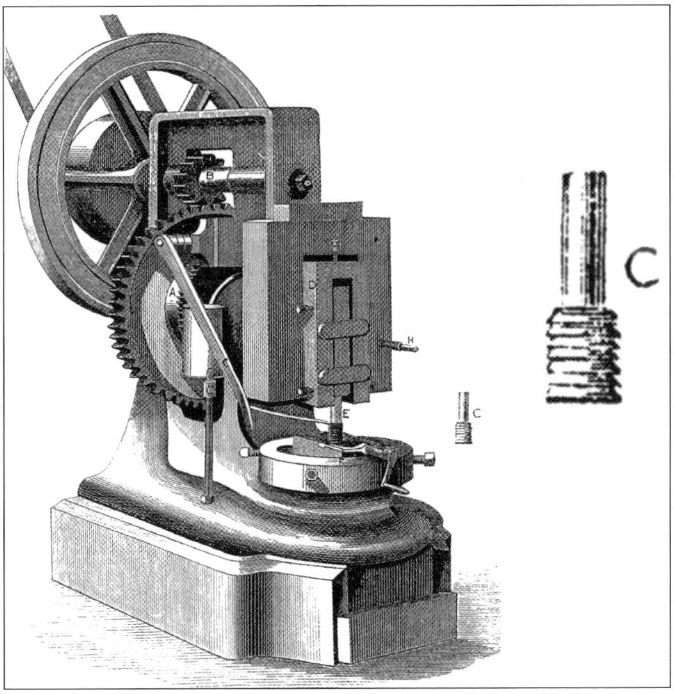

Fig. 3.34. The broaching machine used at Enfield and the broach, C. (*The Engineer*, 1859, p.384)

The accuracy of this method is supported by an Enfield-made bayonet in near pristine condition in the author's possession which has a socket with diameters of socket openings which only vary by 0.001 inches. A similar bayonet by Preston has a socket with the same variation.

3.11 Socket turned from neck to ring bead

This stage is again represented in the Birmingham Museum specimens, Fig. 3.35.

The account in *The Engineer*[20] simply notes this was performed in a large lathe. It will be seen from Fig. 3.35 that, in the Birmingham specimen at least, the top face of the locking ring bead, originally rounded from the die-stamping operation, has also been turned so that it is square with the socket body. It clearly underwent a second turning operation, not seen specifically commented on, since on finished bayonets this has a quadrant profile. On purely practical grounds this was undoubtedly the case with Preston's and Enfield-made bayonets also – to perform that operation separately would have been wasteful of time and require an additional machine.

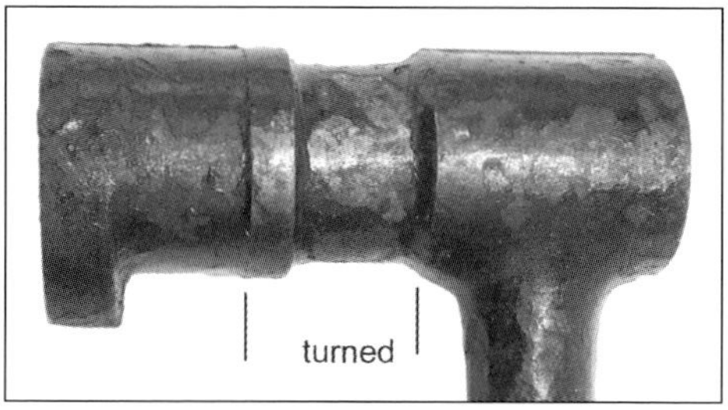

Fig. 3.35. The socket turned from elbow to lower end of ring bead. (1885S00609.00015, courtesy Birmingham Museum Trust)

3.12 Centre-hole drilled in squared tip of trimmed blade

This was simply a prerequisite of stage 13 and the centre hole is shown in Fig. 3.36.

Whilst simple-looking, this had to be performed with great care to ensure it was central on the tip of the blade and would have required an accurately positioned holding device on the drilling machine. Although not stated, it is clear the blade at this stage would need to be longer than the finished blade, so no trace of this hole remained when the tip was correctly formed.

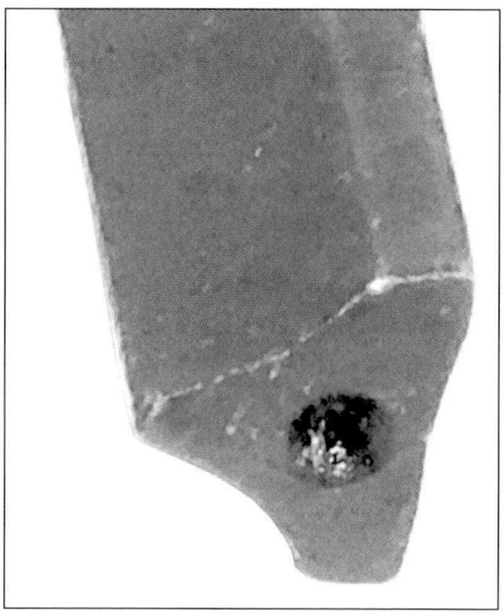

Fig. 3.36. The centre hole in tip of blade. (1885S00609.00016, courtesy Birmingham Museum Trust)

3.13 Neck turned in a copying lathe

The naming of this stage might give the impression of it being a straightforward operation, but reflection will show several important requirements had to be met. The centre axes of blade and the bore of the socket had to be at 90°; the blade-elbow axis also had to be at 90° to the centre-line of the bridge. The order books of Greenwood & Batley of Leeds[21] show that a machine for this purpose was supplied in 1859:

Col Dixon, Enfield *28th September 1859*
810 *2 copying lathes for turning neck of bayonet,* *£50*
special, to stand on ordnance bed same as before.

3.14 Socket behind neck machined

It will be apparent from consideration of the form of the bayonet and from Fig. 3.37 that this portion of the socket could not be turned in a lathe since rotation would be prevented by the projecting neck and blade. The description of operations at Enfield has already been noted as being very scant with regard to the bayonet but states that this procedure was accomplished by 'milling'[22] and offers no further information. Those familiar with machine tool practice will know that there are basically two types of milling operations – 'horizontal' milling and 'vertical' or 'end' milling. In the first, the milling cutter takes the form of a disc or cylinder of tool steel with teeth on its circumference and sometimes extending a small distance radially inwards. In use it revolves with its axis horizontal so the plane of the cutter is vertical. Sometimes the edge was suitably formed to create a profile, but in the absence of precision grinding machines at the time, resharpening would have been a very difficult undertaking and would have resulted in a change of size and a loss of accuracy. They were generally of relatively large diameter so considering the relatively confined space which had been turned between the 'bead' against which the locking ring abuts and the 'elbow', size would have precluded their use.

Conversely, a 'vertical' or 'end milling' cutter is essentially a cylinder of tool steel of relatively small diameter with teeth formed on its end face and for a suitable length on its periphery. This allows it to cut on its end face and its periphery, its peripheral teeth allowing it to make a deeper cut; when rotating in a vertical position on its axis at high speed and the workpiece is presented to it, it will remove metal easily. Its smaller size than a horizontal milling cutter suggests it being more suited to the operation under consideration.

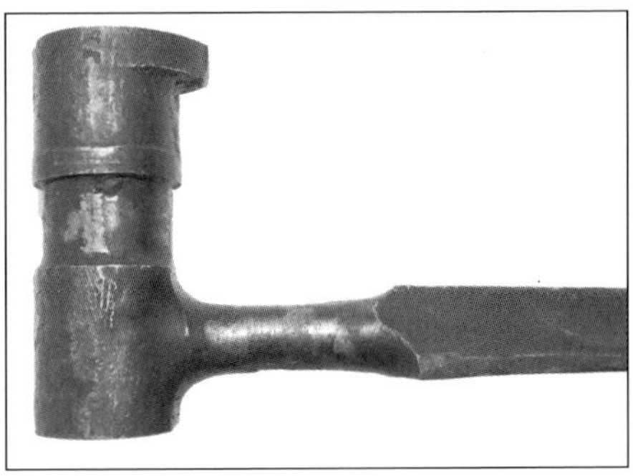

Fig. 3.37. The neck/elbow after turning. (1885S00609.00017, courtesy Birmingham Museum Trust)

A machine can be envisaged which has a suitable mandrel upon which the socket can be securely fixed, and which is capable of rotation between pre-set limits below the vertically rotating cutter whose position can be adjusted both vertically and horizontally, parallel to the socket on its mandrel, Fig. 3.38.

It is envisaged that with the socket rotated against one of its limiting 'stops', the rotating end mill would be fed longitudinally into the metal to be removed by, say, half its depth. In that position, the socket would be rotated until it came into contact with its opposite limiting stop. The cutter would be advanced again at its full depth and the socket rotated in the opposite direction, and this sequence would be followed until the surplus metal had been removed and this area was flush with the turned portion of the socket. By using this sequence and rotating the socket against the milling cutter, its surface would be finished smooth. If the opposite method, i.e., moving the cutter longitudinally for the full length of the cut, then rotating the socket and moving it in the opposite direction was employed, it would have resulted in a series of flat striations as opposed to a truly curved finish.

However, the method suggested would have resulted in a series of 'scallops' along the shoulder of the junction with the elbow, as shown in Fig. 3.39 which shows the milled area 'flattened out'.

These could easily be removed by fully traversing the cutter along these edges at the end of the process.

In contrast, Francis Preston performed this operation using a 'planing' or 'shaping' machine, Fig. 3.40.

It is clear from the description of Preston's operations and a study of Fig. 3.40 that he followed a different sequence from that represented by the Birmingham contractors specimens and at Enfield as reported by *The Engineer*, insofar as the blade of the bayonet has been finished to size and shape and bent to its finished position, the socket body has been turned and the mortice slots for the foresight formed.

If we take the *Illustrated London News* account at face value, the bayonet was securely mounted by its socket on a close-fitting stud projecting from the front

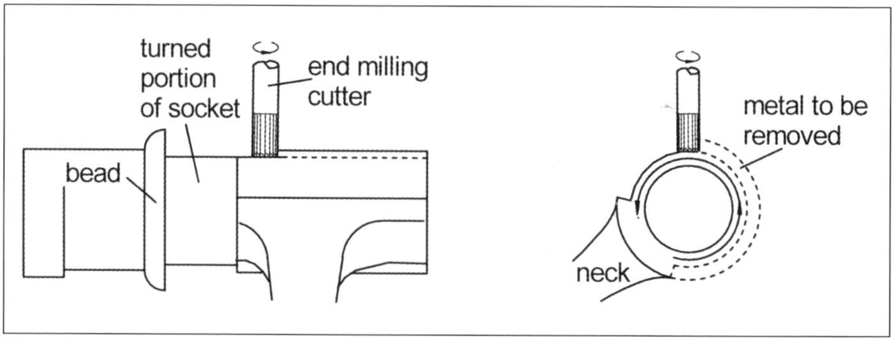

Fig. 3.38. Sketch showing the suggested nature of the milling operation on the socket behind the elbow. (© P. Smithurst)

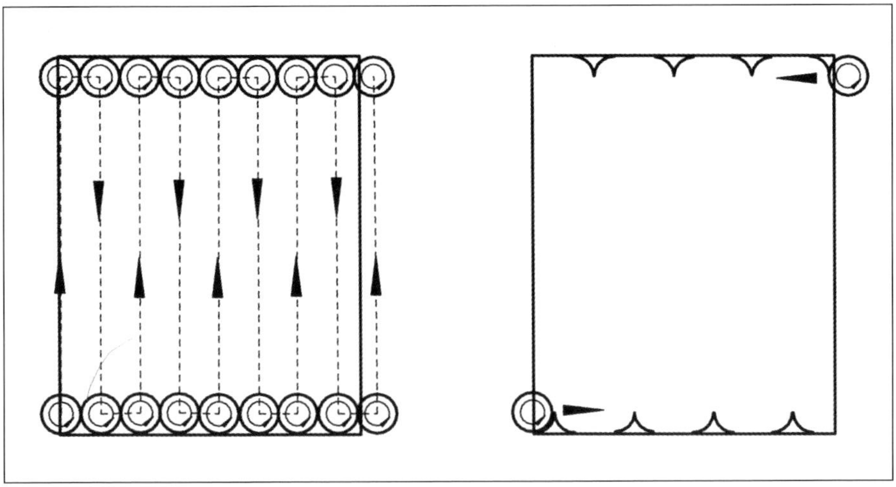

Fig. 3.39. Sketch showing the ‘scallops’ created in the shoulder of the elbow abutment due to only partially traversing the milling cutter along these edges. (© P. Smithurst)

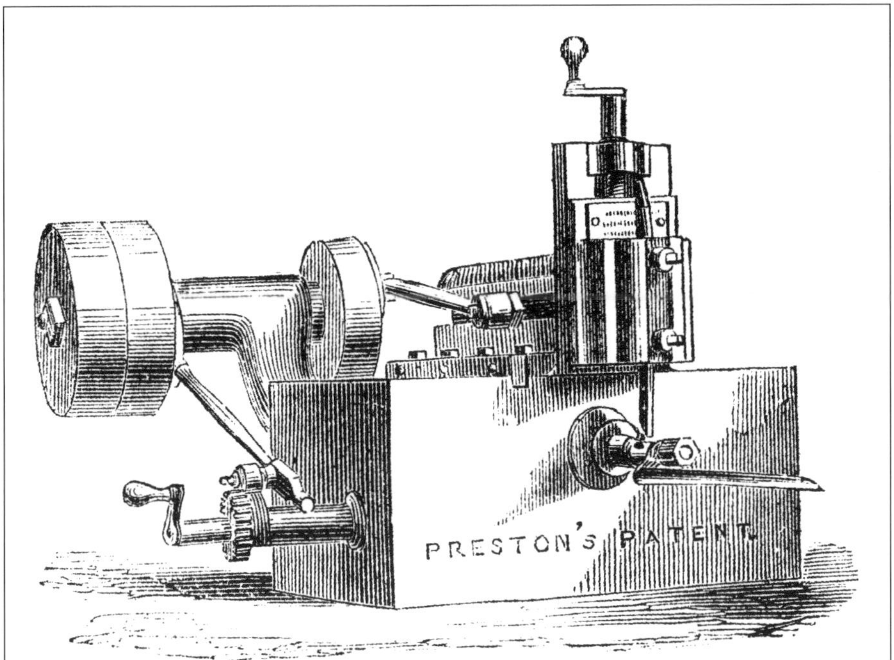

Fig. 4

Fig. 3.40. Preston’s socket planing machine. (*Illustrated London News*, 1855, Supplement, Jan. 26th, p.97, Fig. 4)

of the machine below the reciprocating 'ram' which carried a cutting tool. With everything ready, the machine was set in motion: with each stroke of the ram, the stud on which the bayonet was mounted was automatically rotated incrementally and the machine automatically disengaged when the required degree of rotation had been achieved, Fig. 3.41.

It was then rotated manually to its starting point, the cutting tool adjusted to remove more metal and the machine set in motion again and the process repeated until finished. The planing tool marks are just visible on the socket of the Preston bayonet in Fig. 3.42 where they appear as very narrow longitudinal striations.

However, one aspect of Preston's approach presents something of a conundrum. He contrived during this planing operation to leave a small portion un-machined to become the 'stop pin' for the locking ring. It will be seen from Fig. 3.43 that this lies in the middle of the turned portion.

This could not have been accomplished using the over-simplified description in the *Illustrated London News* article; Preston would have needed to have left an unmachined portion as a belt or rib during turning, Fig. 3.44.

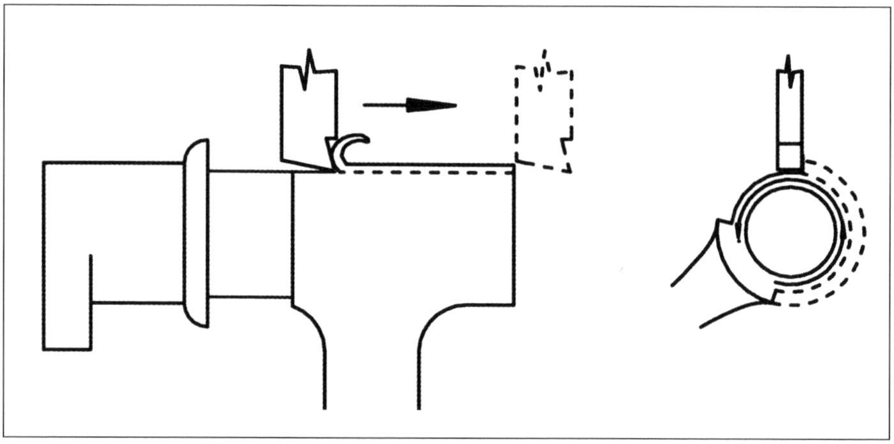

Above: Fig. 3.41. Diagrammatic representation of the operations of Preston's planing machine. (© P. Smithurst)

Left: Fig. 3.42. Toolmarks on a Preston bayonet. (© P. Smithurst)

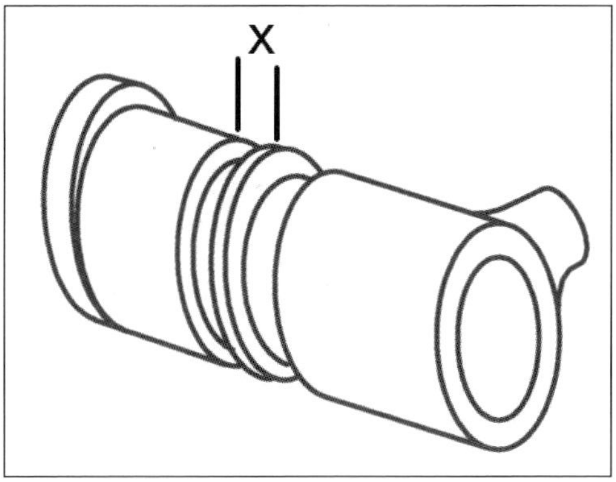

Above left: Fig. 3.43. Comparison of finished socket, bottom, with the socket turned between bead and elbow, top. (1885S00609.00015, courtesy Birmingham Museum trust)

Above right: Fig. 3.44. Sketch showing the band needed to be able to form an integral 'stop pin'. 'X' is the distance between the front face of the bead and the face of the stop pin in contact with the locking ring.

Considering that on a bayonet made by Preston, the distance 'X' between the bead and the stop pin is only just over 0.2 inches, this would have required a very narrow cutting tool to enable it to be inserted in that space. Planing tools need to be substantial to resist the forces experienced during use and such a small tool would only have enabled very shallow cuts to be taken, Fig. 3.45, making it a lengthy process.

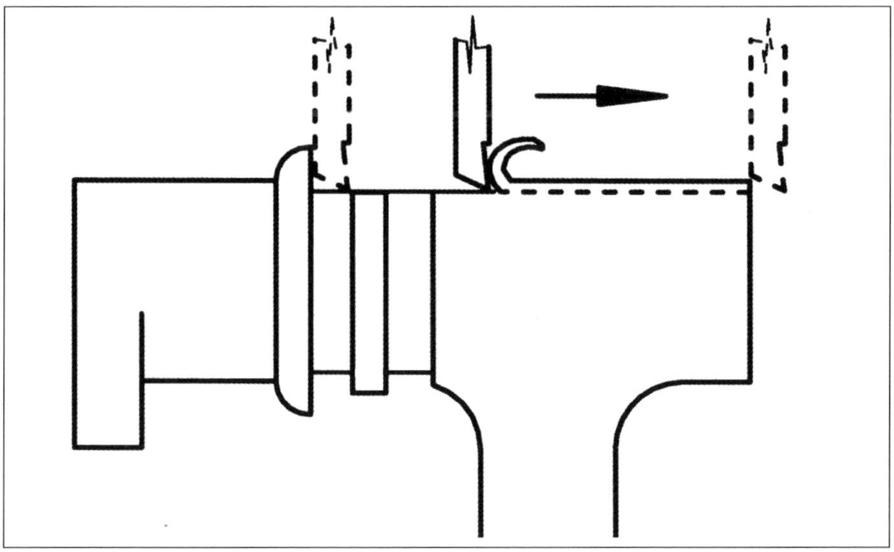

Fig. 3.45. A planing cutter of significantly reduced size to fit in the gap 'X' in Fig. 3.52. (© P. Smithurst)

A little consideration will also show that a long, un-planed portion had to be retained for subsequent formation of the stop, Fig. 3.46.

This rib would then need to be removed; only part could be removed by turning so it was a combined turning and planing operation, Fig. 3.47.

The desire to create an 'integral stop' therefore required several operations and machines and would have added to cost. Had Preston not bent the blade into its finished position, which presumably meant it could not be reversed on its mounting in the planing machine, these operations might have been accomplished more easily.

The planing tool marks left on Preston's bayonets are not visible on Enfield or Birmingham-made bayonets that have been examined and may suggest an alternative method was used for this operation, as is noted earlier. It might also have resulted from extra care in finishing since, although not mentioned in any narrative examined, the socket still needed filing to remove the steps adjacent to the elbow-socket junction created by these operations, Fig. 3.48.

It might also suggest that Preston's bayonets were subject to a possible relaxation of inspection criteria for something that was purely cosmetic at a time of desperate need.

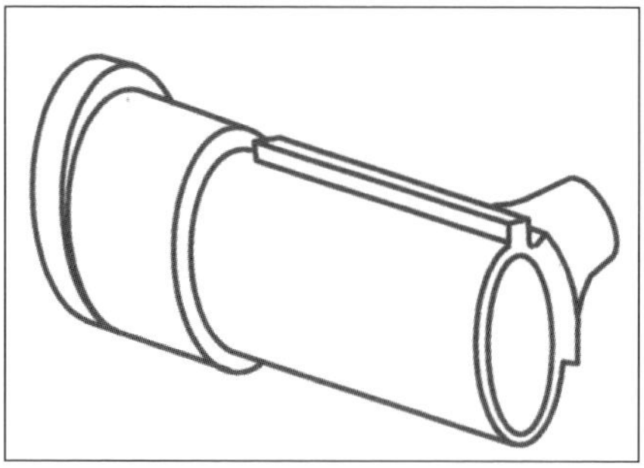

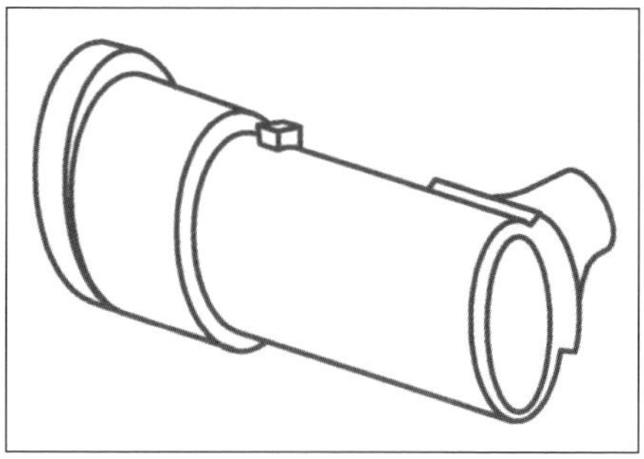

Above left: Fig. 3.46. The un-planed rib. (© P. Smithurst)

Above right: Fig. 3.47. The excess metal of the rib removed to leave the stop. (© P. Smithurst)

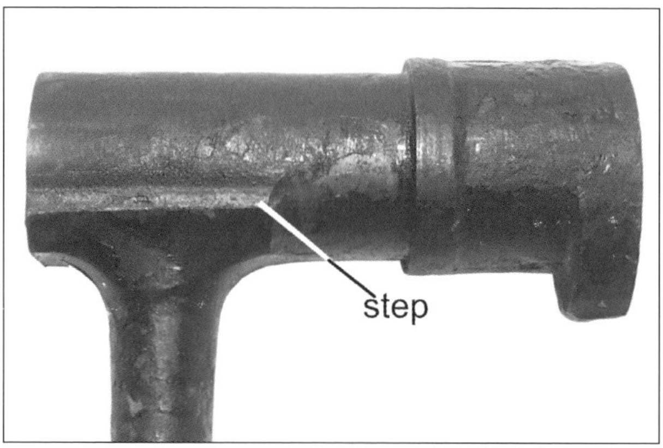

Fig. 3.48. The result of 'machining behind the neck' (1885S00609.00018, courtesy Birmingham Museum Trust)

3.15 Machining the blade

The bayonet may seem a simple item but consideration of the geometry of the blade and its relationship with the socket reveals a degree of complexity in applying mechanisation to its manufacture and the fixing of the bayonet in the various machines. While the machines were straightforward, fixing the bayonet required careful planning for each stage in the manufacturing process to achieve the desired outcome. Unfortunately, the Birmingham Museum specimens examined lacked examples showing some stages of work on the blade and likewise *The Engineer* lacks fine detail in its commentary so much has had to be deduced/conjectured from an engineering standpoint. Furthermore, all of the operations relied upon the blade being properly straightened in a previous operation and being sufficiently oversized to allow it to be brought to finished dimensions.

3.16 Edges (corners) of blade milled

Once again, *The Engineer* account provides limited information: the bayonet was *fixed upon a plate worked backwards and forwards by means of a screw with a revolving cutter block placed above; and thus, the three angles of the blade are faced true. This is effected by the aid of three different machines.*

In the light of a later statement, this has been interpreted as relating to the edges of the blade. i.e., the corners of the blade, and amongst the Birmingham Museum specimens examined, there is one which reflects this, Fig. 3.49.

A machine as shown in Fig. 3.50 (on next page), used in a later stage for milling the 'hollows' of the blade, is illustrated in *The Engineer* and is taken to be representative of the milling machines used.

This machine is very much in the nature of the machine manufactured by George S. Lincoln around 1855 to the design of F. A. Pratt,[23] one of the founders of the Pratt & Whitney Company and who were still supplying descendants of this machine in 1917.[24]

The machines used at Enfield were reportedly made by Fairbairn of Leeds[25] but evidence of the Greenwood & Batley order books shows an order placed on 28th September 1859:

824	*3 straight milling machines, one set for milling the edges of blades of bayonets.*	*£105*

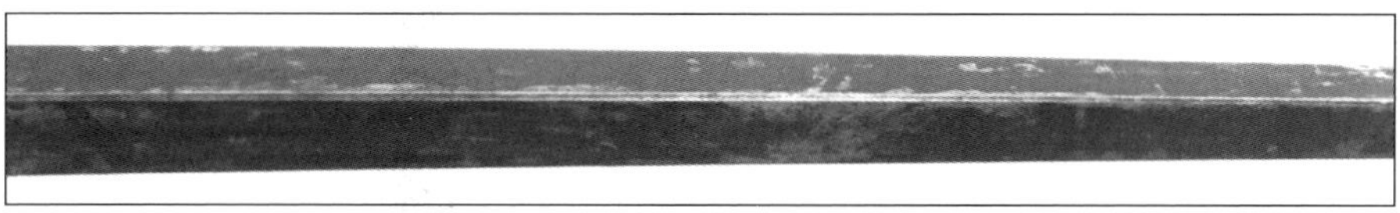

Fig. 3.49. Blade with edges/corners milled. (1885S00609.00019, courtesy Birmingham Museum Trust)

Fig. 3.50. Machine for milling the blade edges. (*The Engineer*, 1859, p.384)

indicating they were the suppliers. The top face (inside face when fitted to the rifle) of the blade needed to be in the form of a truncated equilateral triangle with its centreline passing at 90 degrees in two planes through the centreline of the socket, Fig. 3.51.

Therefore, when fixed in the milling machine, the socket was mounted on a suitable horizontal spigot allowing rotation about the socket axis to bring one edge horizontal and the hole in its tip engaging with a suitable 'centre point', Fig. 3.52, as a means of alignment before being securely fixed.

After milling one edge, the bayonet was removed, rotated 180 degrees about the blade axis to re-orientate and bring the opposite edge into position and fitted into a second milling machine in the same manner as before. What might be called the back edge – the apex of the triangular cross-section – required the socket axis to be angled in the vertical plane to bring this edge horizontal, Fig. 3.53.

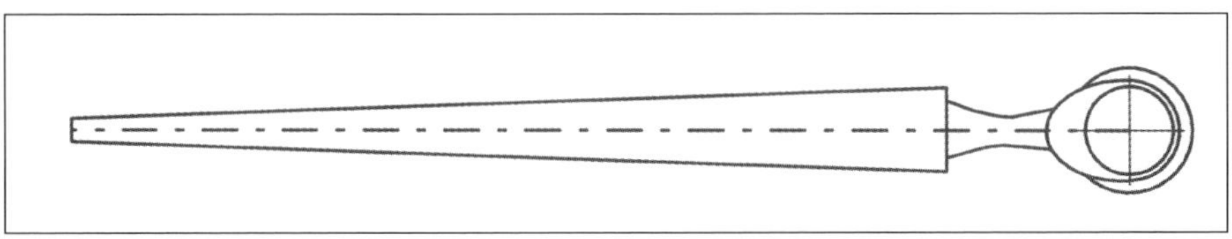

Fig. 3.51. The finished form of the top face after edge milling. (© P. Smithurst)

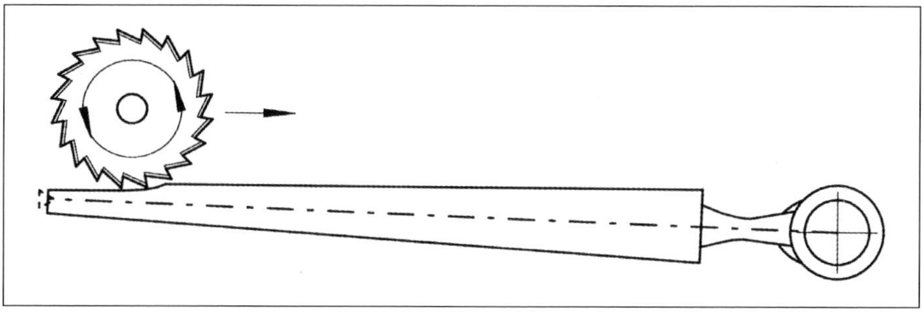

Fig, 3.52. Bayonet fixed in milling machine for milling one edge. (© P. Smithurst)

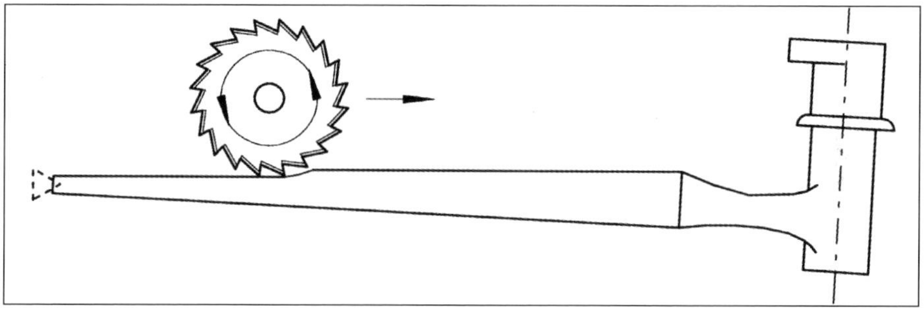

Fig. 3.53. Milling the 'back' edge. (© P. Smithurst)

3.17 Top face next to elbow planed and shoulders formed on other two faces

After the edges had been milled, *The Engineer* tells us *then, by means of a little cross-cut shaping machine, the broad side of the bayonet* [blade] *is flattened down for a small portion of its length.* For those not familiar with machine tools, what is referred to as a planing machine in Fig. 3.50 is often referred to as a 'shaping machine' – both operate on the same principles but differ in construction – in which metal is removed by a cutting tool reciprocating longitudinally which on each stroke 'pares' away some metal and is automatically moved incrementally sideways.

There is a specimen in Birmingham Museum which has undergone this operation, Fig. 3.54:

Fig. 3.54. Bayonet with a short portion of the blade machined flat. (1885S00609.00019, courtesy Birmingham Museum Trust)

Fig. 3.55. A finished bayonet showing the shoulders on the side faces. (© P. Smithurst)

Following this, the angle and shoulders on the remaining sides were shaped, presumably by the same means, as shown in a finished bayonet, Fig. 3.55.

3.18 Planing the faces of the blades

This is the point at which machining of the faces of the blades began and the simple statement in *The Engineer* – *it is finally fixed three consecutive times so as to be planed to truth the whole of its length* – belies the additional complications which had to be overcome to mount the blade correctly in the machines.

To maintain correct overall geometry, the bayonet had to be mounted so that the blade projected with each face at right angles to the socket and in the same horizontal plane as the traversing of the cutter. It would also need support along its length to avoid any flexing under the pressure of the cutter as it passed over the length of the blade. And all of those criteria would have to be met by all three machines.

Placing the bayonet so that the 'inner' face – that which faces the bore when fitted to the rifle – was in the correct position was simply a matter of mounting the socket on a vertical spigot, Fig. 3.56, and correctly locating it by a centre-point being inserted in the centre hole at its tip, before being securely fixed.

The remaining faces clearly required the socket to be angled such as is shown in Fig. 3.57.

However, as shown on the left in Fig. 3.57, the small triangular tip of the blade with its centre hole indicates the plane of these faces angles downwards away from the socket; it therefore needed to be rotated about the socket axis to bring the appropriate plane to the horizontal – one such is shown on the right in Fig. 3.57.

While this setting would allow the task of planing the faces to be accomplished, it is not

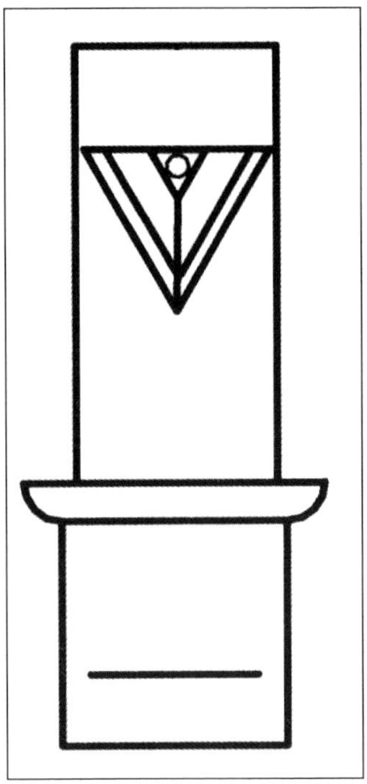

Fig. 3.56. Sketch to show first orientation of socket/ blade for planing the inner face flat. (© P. Smithurst)

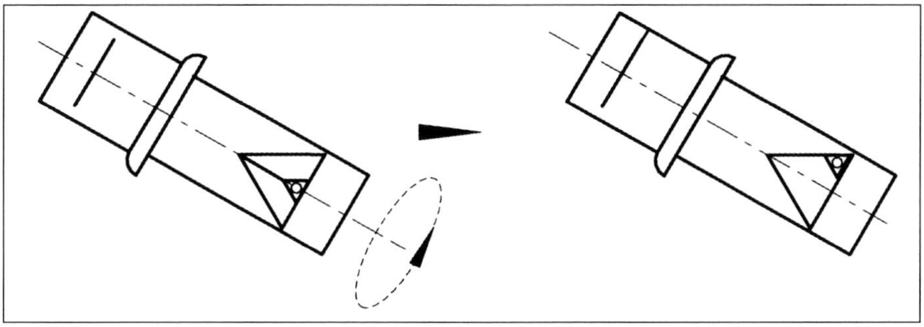

Fig. 3.57. Sketch showing the angling of the socket for planing the side faces. (© P. Smithurst)

perfect and would have been better if the tip of the blade was placed so that the centrelines of the faces were coplanar with the path taken by the cutter as it traversed the length of the blade. For that, the socket needed also to be rotated about a perpendicular axis passing through the centre line of the blade, Fig. 3.58, to create the position shown in Fig. 3.59 and in which the tip of the blade could be accurately located by means of the centre-hole in its tip.

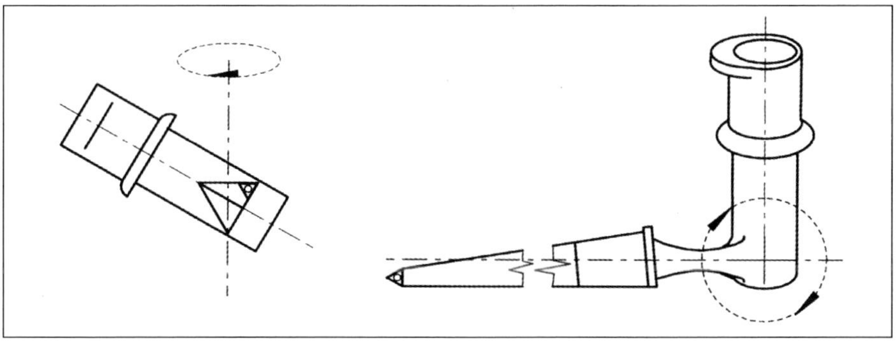

Fig. 3.58. Sketch showing end elevation (left) and plan view prior to rotation. (© P. Smithurst)

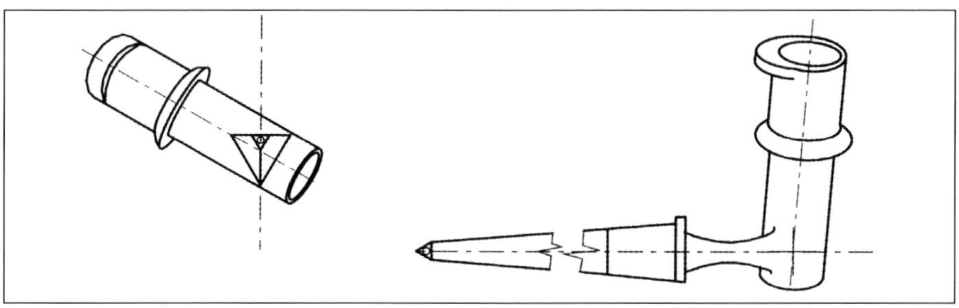

Fig. 3.59. Sketch showing end elevation (left) and plan view of correct alignment ready for planing one side-face of the blade. (© P. Smithurst)

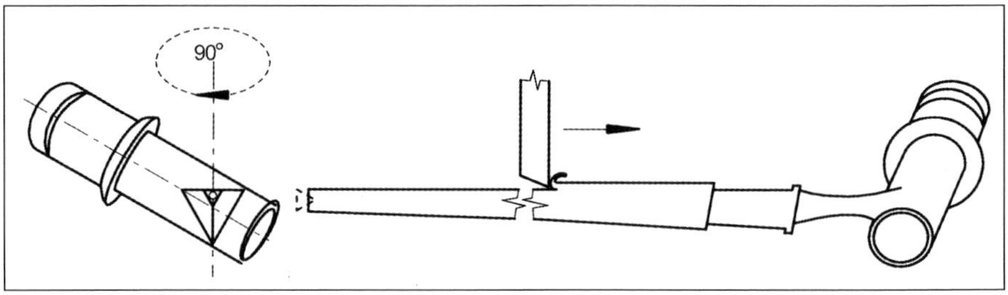

Fig. 3.60. Sketch showing the planing of one of the side faces. (© P. Smithurst)

A perspective sketch, Fig. 3.60, shows the planing operation on one of the side faces and reveals the value of the 'cross-planing' of a short section of each face mentioned earlier. On all faces these would possibly act as a datum for removal of the correct amount of metal. Identical settings of the bayonet in the machines would have been necessary for the cross-planing operation and certainly for the milling of the hollows in the blade.

3.19 Blade hollows and curved tip milled

In the case of milling the hollows, the only difference from planing the faces would have been the use of a milling machine similar to that shown in Fig. 3.50. The order books of Greenwood & Batley of Leeds, showed that once again, the Enfield machines were ordered from them:

28th September 1859

823 *3 straight milling machines, comprising one set for milling flutes in blade of bayonet, special, same as m/c at Enfield* *£90*

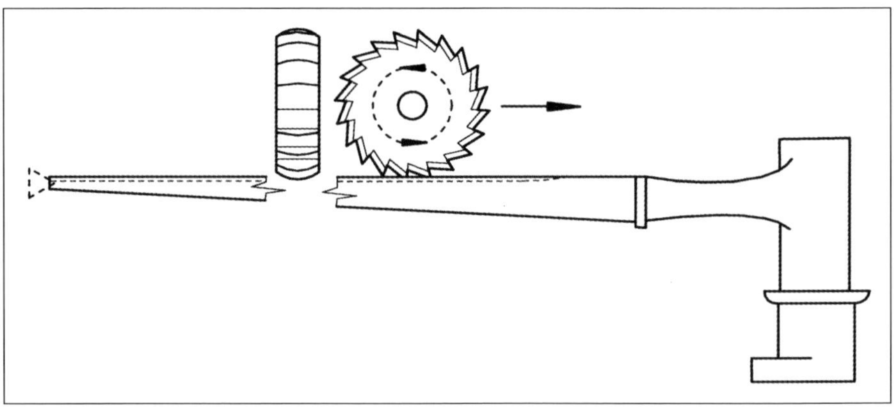

Fig. 3.61. Milling the hollows. (© P. Smithurst)

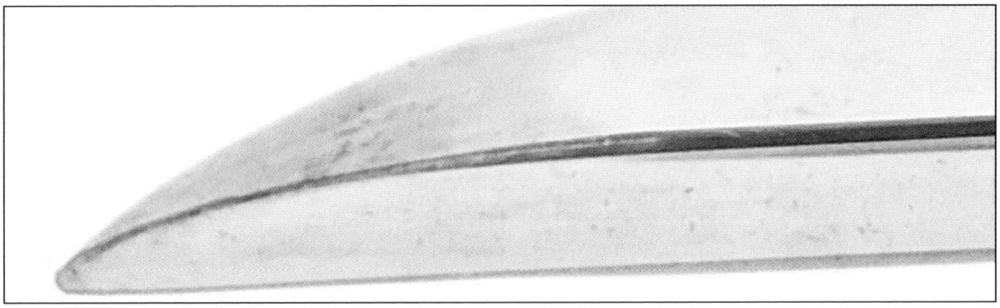

Fig. 3.62. The tip of a finished blade. (© P. Smithurst)

These machines were fitted with a rotary cutter having a convex edge of the correct size and form, Fig. 3.61, – the radius is close to that of a £2 coin.

After milling the hollows, the tip was milled to its curved form which apart from creating a sharp point, also removed the centre hole, Fig. 3.62.

3.20 Front of socket turned

The next stage was to turn the accessible portion of the front of the socket, Fig. 3.63.

At some stage, the excess metal left behind at the junction of socket and neck after various machining operations had to be removed and the two features blended in. Whilst this might be achieved by filing, there is an intriguing entry in the Greenwood & Batley order books:

7th December 1859

917 2 edge-milling machines, double for copying, milling part of neck and socket of bayonet £220

The use of such a machine has not been mentioned in any of the accounts studied. Considering the nature of this junction, Fig. 3.64, suggests a machine similar to that

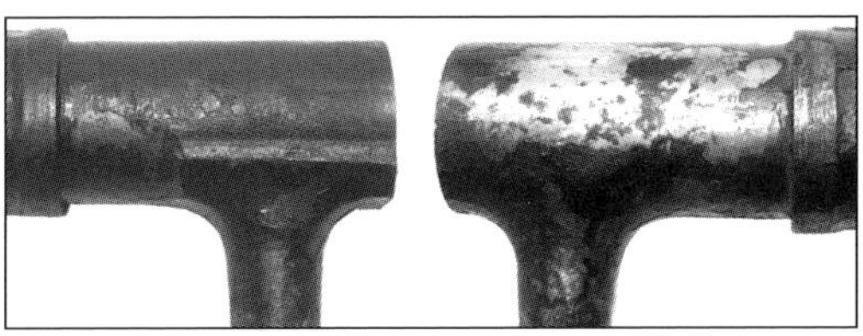

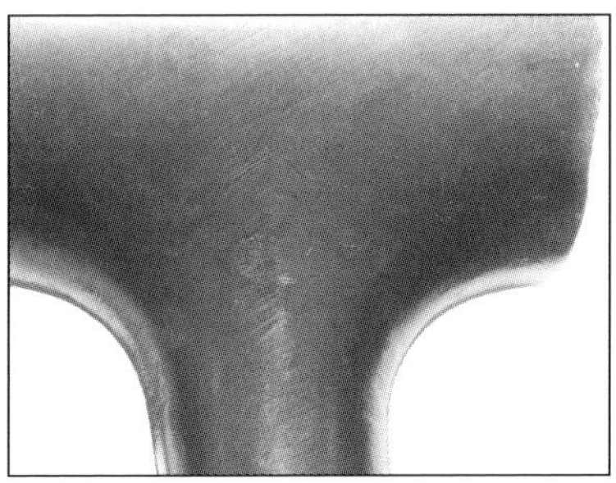

Above left: Fig. 3.63. On the left, the un-turned socket; right, the socket has had a small portion at the front removed by turning. (1885S00609.00018 and 1885S00609.00027 respectively; courtesy Birmingham Museum Trust)

Above right: Fig. 3.64, Detail of the finished elbow-socket junction. (© P. Smithurst)

used for milling the nipple bolster on the rifle barrel, or as noted in the order book, a copy milling machine using a master pattern similar to the machining of the rifle hammer. Whatever the nature of the machine, the junction was finished by use of fine files evidenced by the toolmarks visible in this enlarged image.

3.21 Bending the blade at the neck into its final position

When the machining operations on the blade were finished and those on the socket up to this point, the blade was bent into its finished position. *The Engineer* account simply states that the neck/elbow was bent in a 'lever mould'. In contrast, another account[26] notes that the elbow portion was heated in a furnace:

> *and when sufficiently hot, the bayonet socket is placed over a stud, which fits it and is there held until a slide advances, catches the blade, and turns it forcibly forward, the neck coming into contact with another stud, which it closely embraces and gets therefrom its due curve... After cooling, the neck is struck forcibly across an anvil to test its soundness and the indent thus made is never removed.*

This indent is very slight but can be discerned in the correct light close to the junction with the blade.

Again, the Greenwood & Batley archives holds a drawing, No 736, of a machine for this purpose, Fig. 3.65:

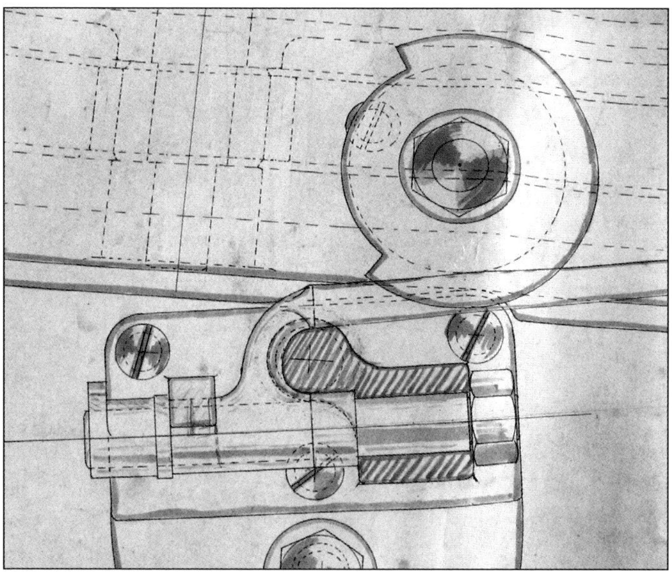

Fig. 3.65. Detail from a workshop drawing of a bayonet bending machine supplied by Greenwood & Batley of Leeds. (Drawing 736-1, courtesy West Yorkshire Archives)

What is worth noting is that after bending, the blade is slightly angled away from the centre line of the socket/barrel, believed to be a sensible precaution against injury to the soldier's hand when loading with the bayonet 'fixed'. It is a common feature of bayonets used with muzzle-loading firearms.

3.22 Socket turned from locking ring bead to bridge

With the blade in its final position, the socket was then turned between the ring bead and the bridge, shown on one of the Birmingham Museum specimens, Fig. 3.66.

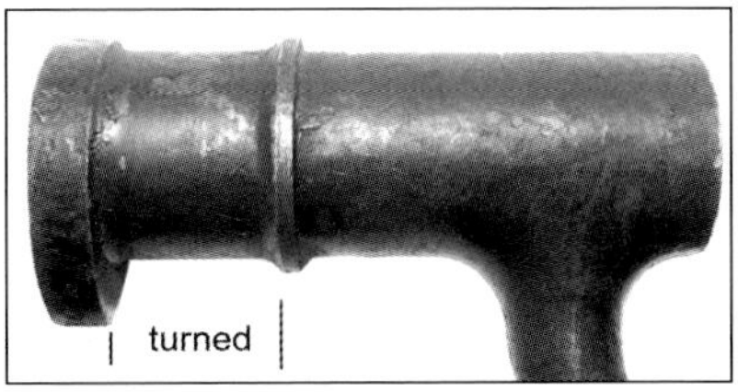

Fig. 3.66. Showing the socket after turning between bead and bridge. (1885S00609.00033, courtesy Birmingham Museums Trust)

3.23 Bridge turned in a copying lathe

The bridge is a simple geometric form and ideal for turning in a simple copying lathe.

Even simple copying lathes were sophisticated machines and for those not familiar with them some sketches have been prepared to outline their functional elements. These focus on the principal features of the lathe and how it functioned – other features have been omitted for clarity. A simple copying lathe could be set up in the following manner.

A mandrel on which is fixed a pattern of exact size and form of the bridge on the socket is fitted in the lathe, Fig, 3.67.

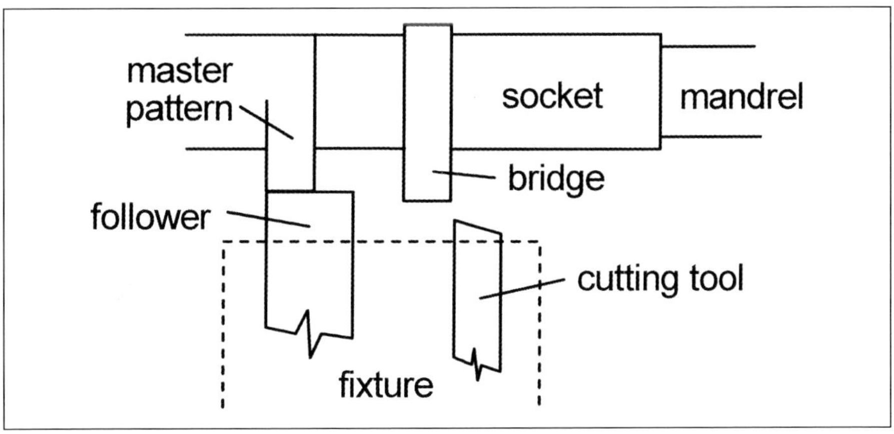

Fig. 3.67. Sketch giving a plan-view showing the principal features of the copying lathe used to machine the bridge – the bayonet fitted on the mandrel and the follower put into contact with the pattern bridge. (© P. Smithurst)

The bayonet is fitted with its socket on the mandrel so that the over-sized bridge is exactly aligned with the 'pattern' bridge – none of the accounts studied state how this was accomplished. Had the slot for the bayonet stud on the barrel, i.e., the foresight bed, been formed, this could have engaged with a stud on the mandrel. The lathe is fitted with a 'follower', a hardened steel bar with a polished tip aligned with the pattern and adjusted in its fixture on the lathe so that its tip is in contact with the pattern as shown in Fig. 3.67. Having set the follower and locked it in position, the fixture is moved longitudinally so that the tip of the cutting tool can be adjusted so that it also is in contact with the pattern and is then locked into position, Fig. 3.68.

The fixture, which can be moved radially as well as longitudinally, is then returned to its original position so that the follower is in contact with the master pattern and the tip of the cutting tool is ready to remove excess metal from the bridge of the socket when the lathe is set in motion, Fig. 3.69.

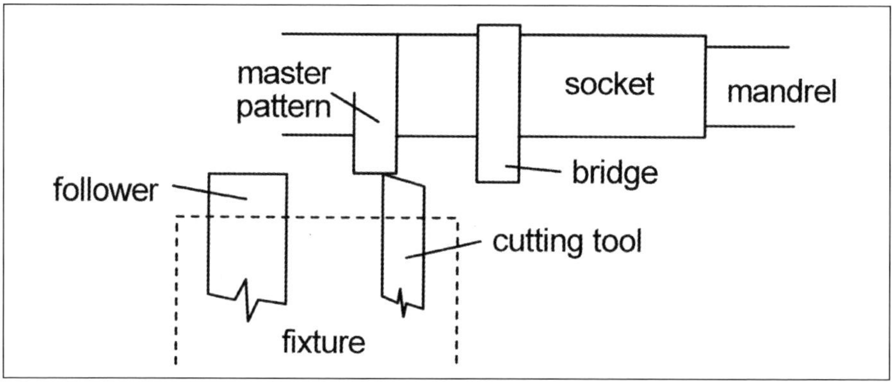

Fig. 3.68. The fixture has been moved longitudinally and parallel to the axis of the lathe to allow the cutting tool to be adjusted so that its tip is in contact with the master pattern. (© P. Smithurst)

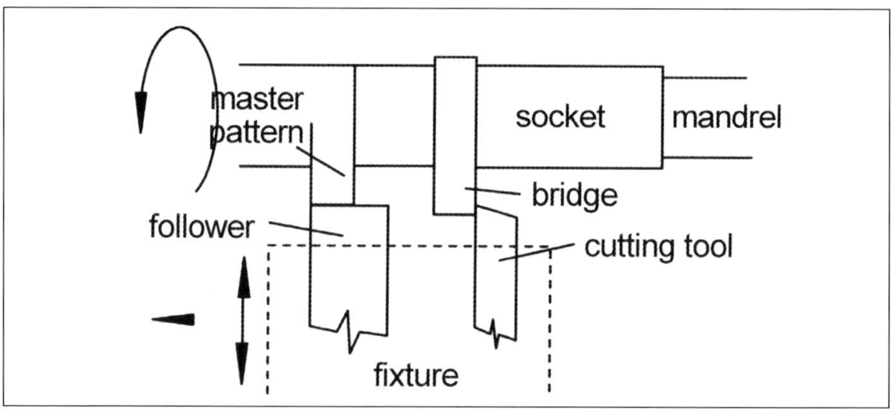

Fig. 3.69. The follower is in contact with the master pattern and the tip of the cutting tool ready to commence removing metal when the lathe is set in motion. (© P. Smithurst)

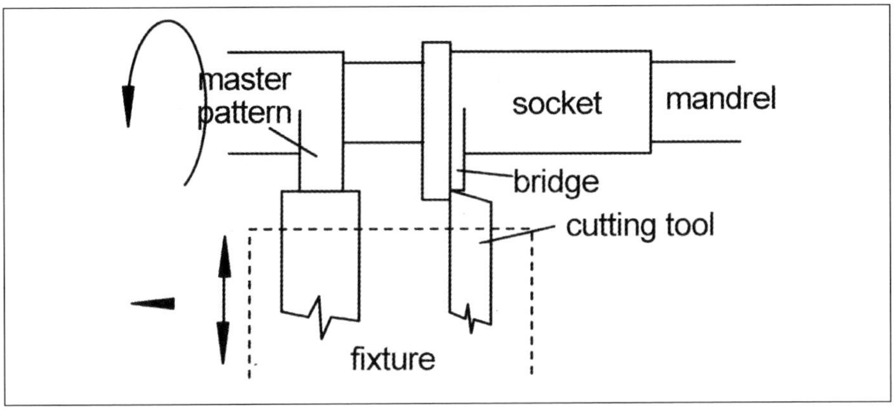

Fig. 3.70. The follower is in contact with the master pattern and when the lathe is set in motion, the fixture is traversed to the left and the cutting tool removes excess metal from the bridge on the socket. (© P. Smithurst)

The fixture is pulled inwards radially by springs so that the contact between follower and master pattern is maintained – since the master pattern has a lobe corresponding to the bridge, during rotation these springs allow the fixture to move radially backwards and forwards and thus the cutting tool also copies that motion; if the fixture is at the same time moved longitudinally, the shape of the master pattern is transferred to the bridge on the socket, Fig. 3.70.

Again, there is evidence to show that such machines were supplied by Greenwood & Batley of Leeds:

28th September 1859

811 *2 copying lathes for turning the bridge of bayonet, special, to stand on Ordnance bed same as before* £70

3.24 Hole drilled for locking ring stop pin

It has already been noted that an important aspect of Preston's machining operation was that it left a portion un-machined which forms the stop pin of the locking ring and was therefore integral with the socket, unlike those produced elsewhere in which a stop pin was fitted separately. On very clean examples of the Enfield and Birmingham made bayonets, the underside of this stop pin can be seen inside the socket, Fig. 3.71.

Fig. 3.71. The end of the stop pin seen within the socket. (© P. Smithurst)

3.25 Locking ring stop pin fitted and squared

This seems to imply that the stop pin was simply a round bar threaded for a short distance approximating to the thickness of the socket walls, screwed in tightly and cut off to the required length/height. This would have been distinctly easier than using a threaded piece of square bar – with a randomly threaded hole it would have been almost impossible for the stop pin to be correctly aligned when tightened in the threaded hole. Even so, subsequent 'squaring' of the pin and adjusting its height after fitting, whether by filing or by machine, would have required a lot of care to obtain the correct size in addition to avoiding damage to the socket. Unfortunately, no account studied has any comment on this small but important operation.

3.26 Mortice slots cut

This was carried out in three stages. First to be cut was the transverse slot and could have been done either by a milling machine or by a shaping/planing machine using cutters of correct width. Correctly placing the socket on the machine was crucial, as was the depth of cut, to produce a slot whose ends coincided with the ends of the two longitudinal slots. The Birmingham Museum specimens show that the next slot to be cut was the one at the front, i.e., the muzzle end of the socket, followed by the rear slot, Fig. 3.72.

The only contemporary illustration so far found is that accompanying the article[27] describing Preston's manufacture of this bayonet and shows the cutting of the rear mortice slot through the bridge, Fig. 3.73 – a slightly different view of the same machine appears in another article.[28]

It is presumed that the bayonet was inserted into a triangular hole matching the root of the blade and resting on the blade shoulders – this would have created the correct orientation assuming all

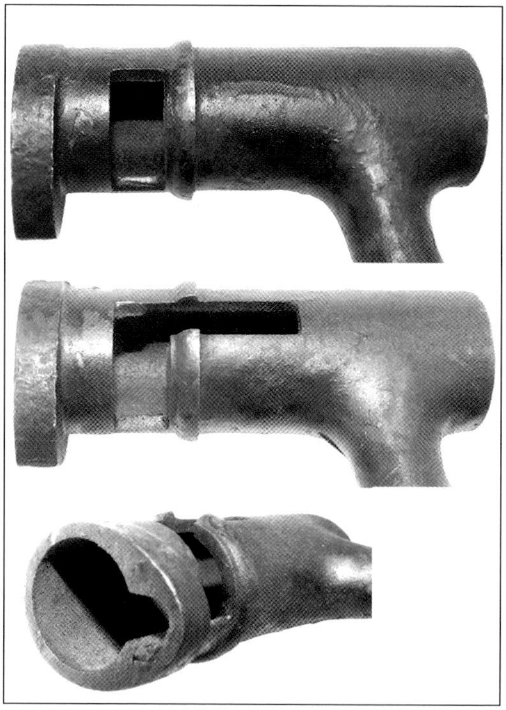

Fig. 3.72. Specimens showing the sequence of cutting the mortice slots. (From top to bottom, 1885S00609.0035, .0036 and .0037 respectively, courtesy Birmingham Museums Trust)

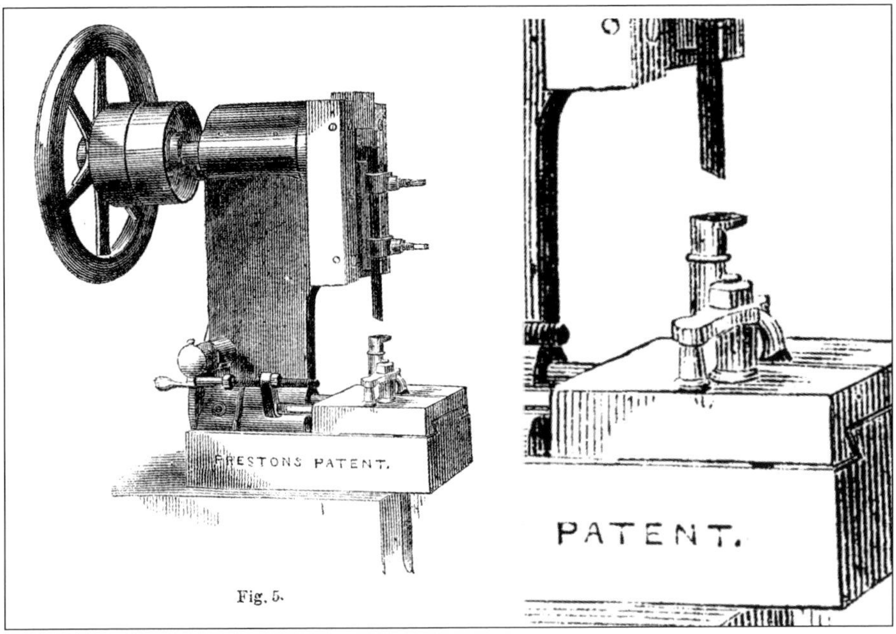

Fig. 3.73. Preston's machine for producing the rear mortice (*Illustrated London News*, Supplement, Jan. 26th, 1855, Fig. 4, p.97)

the preceding operations had been carried out accurately – and was clamped in place by the device bearing down upon the neck. The machine also had the facility of moving the socket towards the vertically reciprocating cutter so that when the rear slot had been cut, the machine would then cut deeper into the bridge to allow the passage of the foresight. It cannot be imagined that the process carried out at Enfield, and possibly by the Birmingham contractors, would have been significantly different although no details of any machines used by the latter have been found.

3.27 Hardening, tempering, grinding and polishing

There is some discrepancy in published accounts as to when hardening and tempering were carried out, some stating it was before the mortices were cut,[29] another states it was after bending the neck[30] while a third[31] states it was done after cutting the mortice slots! Nor is there any indication of the temperatures used – while they were not able to measure the temperature, the blade might have been quenched in water, or oil, at a dull red, a cherry red or a bright red heat. Likewise, 'tempering colours' are not recorded. The blade was then tested for strength and flexibility in the same manner as for the French and Russian bayonets by anchoring the point and bending across a block.

The blade was now ready for grinding, and in the absence of any mention of machines it has to be presumed this was done by hand in a similar fashion to that

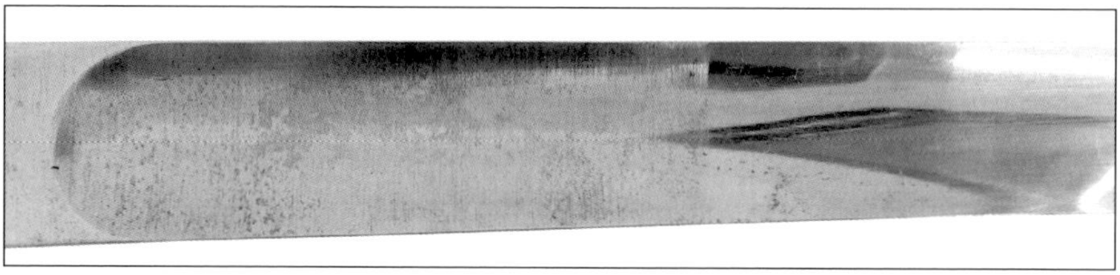

Fig. 3.74. Demarcation between the crosswise and longitudinal polishing – which acts as a curved mirror. (© P. Smithurst)

applied to the French and Russian bayonets previously discussed. If the traditional practice of the Sheffield cutlery trades was followed there would have been at least three stages. First, grinding proper to remove tool marks, done on a sandstone wheel fed with water. Then came 'glazing', to remove grinding marks, which was carried out on the edge of a built-up wooden wheel to whose periphery was attached a strip of 'bull-neck' or buffalo leather shaped to match the grooves, a coating of 'animal glue' applied and dressed with emery powder. This may have involved more than one stage with different grades of emery to obtain a finer finish – and may have given rise to the terms 'bulling' or 'buffing'. Finally, it would be polished with a similar wheel to glazing but dressed with 'crocus powder' – or 'rouge' – a very fine iron oxide but without using glue. And as with the French and Russian bayonets, because of the socket, the inner face could only be ground for a certain length longitudinally and the lower portion was ground and polished crosswise – referred to as 'crossing' in the Sheffield cutlery trades, Fig. 3.74.

3.28 The locking ring

In many respects the locking ring centrally placed on the socket was the crucial feature which made bayonets of this type so successful, yet all the accounts of the manufacture of this bayonet give it scant attention. The only comment worthy of mention is the simple statement that:

> *The locking ring for securing it to the barrel is struck into shape while hot, between dies, and under one of Colt's patent screw drops – in fact, it is coined, and then finished off by machines.*[32]

Its important features are shown in Fig. 3.75.

The terminology shown is not the official version as far as is known – it is purely for convenience. When the bayonet is fitted to the rifle, the foresight passes through the bridge on the socket and the locking ring and is slid to the end of the rear mortice; on rotating the socket, the sight bed moves along the cross mortice and is brought into line with the front mortice; the bayonet can then by slid further onto the muzzle until the sight bed reaches the end of the front mortice. Fig. 3.74 gives a side view of

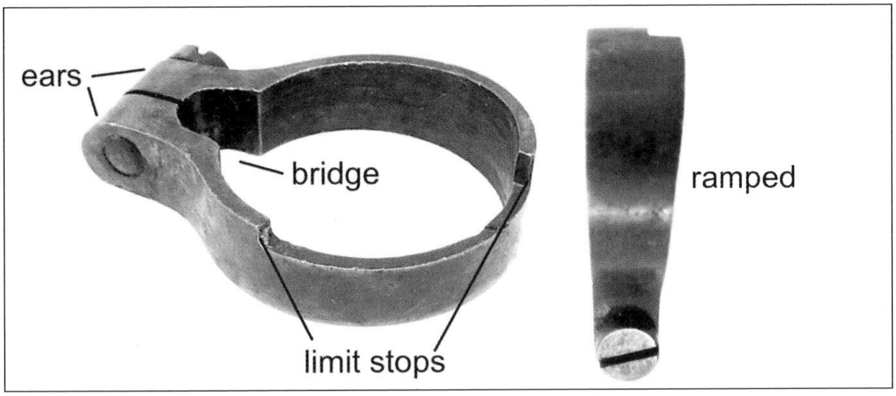

Fig. 3.75. Features of the locking ring. (© P. Smithurst)

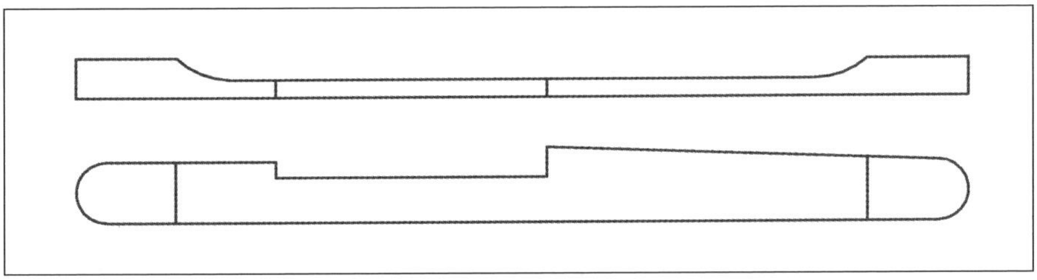

Fig. 3.76. the 'developed' locking ring. (© P. Smithurst)

the ring and it can be seen the forward edge is distinctly 'ramped'. Thus, when the bayonet is in place, the ring is rotated and this ramp bears upon the foresight bed and the bayonet is secured. The rotation of the ring is restricted by the limit stops.

If we imagine the ring opened out flat – a 'development' in engineering drawing terms, Fig. 3.76 – it resolves into a very simple shape eminently suited to a die forging operation.

However, as to the processing of the forging into the finished ring and fitting it to the socket, there is no record; any guesswork will be left to the reader but a consideration of the manufacturing details in Chapter 1 might be of value.

3.29 Inspection and proof

This stage is best expressed in the official documentation:

> *The bayonets will be examined by the plug, and must fit exactly; they will be struck on a stake at the bend of the neck, the blade bent over a block in the usual manner, the locking ring will be closely inspected to see that it is neatly and accurately adjusted to its base, and to the*

> *socket, so as to act smoothly and without friction. The blade will be gauged in three places, and examined to see that the grinding and polishing has been properly executed.*
>
> *14th November 1853.*
> *W. Evans.*[33]

It is suggested in an official but unsourced document that the block was 5/8″ high and placed at the centre of the blade.

After they had passed muster, the inspectors would stamp the ricasso. These stamps were all of a similar form consisting of a crown, above or below which was a capital letter which identified where the bayonet had been made and below that, a number identifying the inspector. Thus, Enfield would have the letter E; Birmingham the letter B but in addition to the inspector's stamp, Birmingham-made ones usually had the name of the contractor, as did those made by Francis Preston. However, in this particular instance, Fig. 3.77, the Preston bayonet lacks the inspector's stamp, possibly because the blade broke during the bending test.

From a collector's perspective, foreign-made bayonets are the scarcest and I am indebted to Graham Priest for images of the various European contractors' inspectors stamps to be found, Fig. 3.78.

Fig. 3.77. Marking on a Preston bayonet. (© P. Smithurst)

Fig. 3.78. Marks to be found on European contractors' bayonets; *left*, Kirchbaum, Solingen: *centre*, Escoffier, France: *right*, Liege. (Courtesy Graham Priest)

However, undoubtedly the rarest of all these bayonets are those produced in America at the time of the Robbins & Lawrence contract to supply Pattern 1853 rifles and these appear to have been first reported by Priest in 1996,[34] Fig. 3.79.

Fig. 3.79. Bayonet made alongside the Robbins & Lawrence manufactured rifles. (Courtesy Graham Priest)

Conclusions

It is clear that in the space of around 80 years there was a gradual transition from hand-craft to mechanised manufacture of bayonets. This first becomes apparent in Gamel's descriptions of operations at the Tula factory in Russia and, because they were manufacturing the same weapon, his account provides a contrast with the methods employed in France as detailed by Rauch 30 years earlier in the closing years of the 18th century.

Another 30 years later the Enfield Pattern 1853 bayonet, which copied many features of the French Model 1777 bayonet, was being manufactured in Britain at the Royal Small Arms Factory at Enfield and by private contractors at home and abroad. New levels of mechanisation had been achieved, notably at Enfield and by Francis Preston for whom it appears this was his only venture into arms manufacture. While some practices reflected those in use at Tula, the socket was now formed by die stamping followed by numerous machine operations to bring it to its final form and likewise, the blade was being shaped by machines. Hand work was largely restricted to the welding of a piece of steel for the blade to a piece of wrought iron for the socket and in the finishing operations of grinding and polishing the blade. This transition from hand-craft to mechanisation in bayonet manufacture, as with the firearms they were intended to be used with, transformed the simple bayonet from a 'work of art' into an engineered product. Each of these bayonets represent milestones in this evolutionary process.

Appendix 1

Weights and Measures

English Measures

The basic length standard for many years was the yard.

1 yard (yd.) = 36 inches
1 foot (ft. or the number followed by ′) = 12 inches
1 inch (in. or the number followed by ″) = 25.4mm (approximately)
(thus, 1 foot 3 inches could be written as 1 ft. 3ins. or 1′ 3″)

The inch was subdivided into 1/8, 1/16, 1/32, 1/64.

Pound (lb.) = 16 ounces (oz.) = 453 grams (approximately)
Ounce = 28.34 grams (approximately)

French measures

1 point	= 0.188mm
1 ligne/line = 12 points	= 2.256mm
1 pouce (Paris inch)	= 12 lignes = 27.07mm = 1.0657 Imperial inches
1 pied (foot)	= 12 Paris inches
1 toise (fathom)	= six pied
1 aune	= 120 centimetres

1 livre (pound)	= 500g, each
1 livre	= sixteen once
1 once	= eight gros = approximately 31.25 grams

Russian Measures

(unless otherwise stated, from Clark, Daniel Kinnear, *A Manual of Rules, Tables and Data for Mechanical Engineers*, Blackie & Son, London, 1878 p.172)

liniya (line)	= 0.1 inches (2.54mm)
diuym	= 10 liniya (1 inch, 25.4mm) (had been set precisely equal to an English inch by Peter the Great. See Cardarelli, F. *Encyclopaedia of Scientific Units, Weights and Measures: Their SI Equivalences and Origins*, 2nd ed., Springer, (2004), pp.121–124. ISBN 1-85233-682-X)
Vershok	= 1.75 inches / 44.45mm.
Fuss (Russian foot)	= 13.75 inches, 349.25mm, (but since 1831, the English foot of 12 inches, 305mm, has been used)
Arshine /Arschine	= 16 vershoks = 28 inches, 711.2mm (Gamel, 1826, p.15)
Zolotnik	= 65.833 grains, 0.1505 ounces, 4.25 grams
Pound	= 0.9 pounds avoirdupois, 14.45 ounces, 409 grams.
Pood	= 16.38kg = 36 pounds avoirdupois approximately

Appendix 2

Procédés de la fabrication des armes blanches, publié par l'ordre du Comité de salut public (édition de 1793) with translation

Note

This will appear repetitive to a degree since Rauch commences with a description of the bayonet and then divides his account into three parts – the socket, the locking ring and the blade – and begins each section with a description of the tools required and then goes on to explain the processes involved in producing the three components.

He also does not use 'in-text' illustrations but refers to them; they are parts of large composite engravings. To make things a little easier for the reader, images have been inserted at relevant points in the text here.

It is also noted that so far it has proved impossible to find the answer to questions surrounding two terms Rauch uses – what is "Shuttle oil" and what is meant by "half white-hot"?

Procédés de la fabrication des armes blanches, publié par l'ordre du Comité de salut public (édition de 1793)

Processes for the manufacture of bladed weapons, published by the order of the Committee of Public Safety, 1793

Le Comité de la salut Public a pris, le 12 septembre 1793 (vieux style), un arrêté portant qu'il sera fait un description de tous les procédés de la fabrication des sabres et des bayonnettes dans la manufacture de Klingenthal, et qu'elle sera imprimée et distributée, pour donna aux ouvriers occupés à faire d'autres instrumens tranchans, les lumières dont ils peuvent avoir besoin pour entreprendre de fabrique ces armes si nécessaires à la défense de la République. C'est en conséquence de cet arrêté, que la description suivante éré entreprise.

The Committee of Public Safety on September 12, 1793 (old style), ordered that a description will be made of all the processes for the manufacture of sabres and bayonets in the Klingenthal factory, and that it will be printed and distributed, to give to the workmen occupied in making other cutting instruments, the lights which they may need to undertake the manufacture of these weapons so necessary for the defence of the Republic. It is as a result of this decree that the following description has been undertaken.

DE LA BAYONNETTE

1. La bayonette qu'on va décrire est celle du modèle adopté par ordonnance en 1777. Ce modèle peut changer; mais l'ouvrier qui en connoître bien la fabrication, n'aura probablement pas alors de nouvelle difficulté à vaincre. Cette bayonette est représentée fig. 1, 2, 3.

1. The bayonet we will describe is that of the model adopted by ordinance in 1777. This model can change; but the workman who knows its manufacture well, will probably not have any new difficulty to conquer. This bayonet is represented in Figs. 1, 2, 3.

2. Il faut y considérer trois parties; la doulle a, la virole b, qui sont de fer, et lame c, qui est d'acier.

2. We must consider three parts; socket, a; ring, b, which are iron; and blade, c, which is steel.

3. Il faut les considérer dans deux états; noires, c'est-à-dire, telles qu'elles sortent des maines du forgeur, blanches, c'est-à-dire, telles qu'elles sortent, quant à la douille et à la virole, des mains du limeur, et quant à la lame, de celles de l'aiguisier, après avoir passé par celles du trempeur.

3. They must be considered in two states; black, that is to say, as they come out of the hands of the forger, white, that is to say, as they come out, as to the

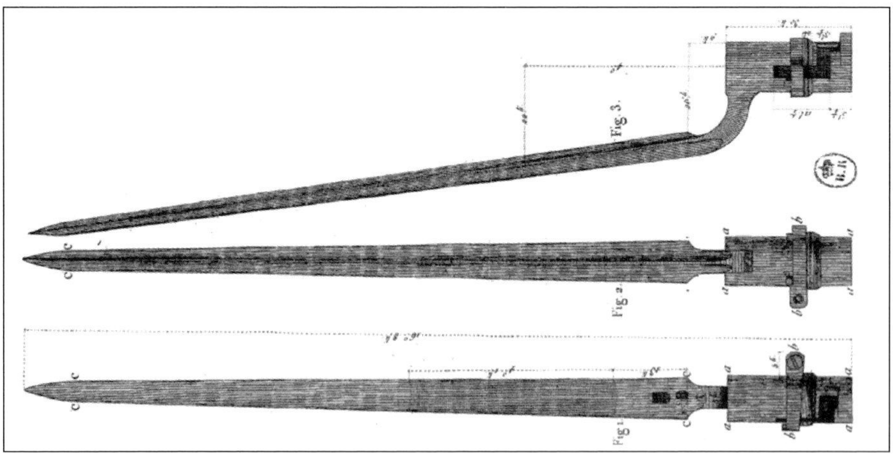

Figs. 1, 2 and 3. The bayonet.

socket and the ring, from the hands of the filer, and as for the blade, of those of the grinder, after having passed through those of the hardener.

Page 2

4. On va d'abord s'occupier de la douille. Elle sert à fixer à volonté la bayonette sur le canon du fusil; elle en embrasse l'extrêmité, et elle y est retenue par le moyen du tenon brasé sur le canon. La virole a une énchancrure intérieur qui, lorsqu'elle se recontre avec l'entaille de la douille, permet au tenon de parcourir cette entaille jusqu'à ce que la virole se trouve au-dessous de lui. Si on tourne alors la virole, le tenon se trouve pris; et pour le dégager, il faut remettre la virole dans la première situation. La suite fera connoître les développmens de ce mécanisme.

4. We will first take care of the socket. It serves to fix at will the bayonet on the barrel of the musket; it embraces its extremity, and it is held there by means of the tenon brazed on the barrel. The ring has an internal notch which, when it meets with the notch of the sleeve, allows the tenon to go through this notch until the ring is below the tenon. If we then turn the ring, the tenon is locked; and to clear it, it is necessary to turn the ring back to the first position. The following will describe the development of this mechanism.

Article Premier. Forger la douille de la bayonette.
Disposition de choses nécessaire au forgeur de douille.

First article. Forging the socket of the bayonet.
Arrangement of things necessary to the socket forger.

5. La disposition de sa forge n'a rien de bien essentiel. Au Klingenthal, l'âtre des toutes les petites forges est un carré long des trois pieds et demi de largeur, sur trois pieds de profondeur. La forge est une cheminée élevée à trent pouces de terre, et murée sur les côtés. La tuyére est à gauche, et une petite auge, qui se remplit par dehors de la cheminée, est encastrée dans le mur, à droite. Le manteau est à vingt-un ou vingt-deux pouces de l'âtre, et il est droit. C'est avec le pied que le compagnon, et quelquefois le maître, fait mouvoir le soufflet.

5. The layout of his forge is not very special. At Klingenthal, the hearth of all the little forges is a square three and a half feet wide, three feet deep. The forge has a chimney raised to thirty inches above the ground, and walled on the sides. The tuyere [nozzle connected to the bellows] is on the left, and a small trough, which is filled by outside the chimney, is embedded in the wall, on the right. The mantle is twenty-one or twenty-two inches from the hearth, and it is straight. It is with the foot that the companion, and sometimes the master, moves the bellows.

6. Le charbon de terre qui convient au forgeur de douilles, doit être médiocrement collant, être lourd et contenir dans sa composition de la terre dans une certaine abondance; mais il ne doit point contenir de pyrite. On le tire au Klingenthal,

de la mine de Villé, près Saint-Marie-aux-Mines, et on en consomme un peu plus de deux quintaux pour forger cent douilles. Le compagnon s'occupe, dans les momens où il n'a rien d'autre à faire, à en casser les morceaux sur l'âtre de la forge, et à les réduire à la grosseur d'une noix au plus.

6. The coal suitable for the forger must not be sticky, heavy and contain in its composition earth in abundance; it must not contain pyrites. It is taken from the Klingenthal mine in Villé, near Saint-Marie-aux-Mines, and consumes a little more than two quintals [a quintal at this time was 100 livres – French pounds] to forge a hundred sockets. The assistant takes care, in the moments when he has nothing else to do, to break the pieces on the hearth of the forge, and to reduce them to the size of a nut at the most.

Page 3

7. Le fer doit être de bonne qualité; il doit n'être cassant ni à chaud ni à froid. Celui dont on se sert dans la même manufacture, est tiré de la forge de Rothau, près Schirmeck, à cinq lieues de route de Klingenthal, et provient de la mine du même endroit.

7. The iron must be of good quality; it must not be brittle when hot nor cold. This, which is used in the same manufactory, is from the forge at Rothau, near Schirmeck, five leagues from Klingenthal, and comes from the mine there.

8. L'enclume du forgeur de douille est telle qu'on la voit fig. 4 et 5; elle est remarquable par les deux énchancrures demi-circulaires qu'on y voit aux deux bouts, et par les deux rainures pratiquées vers la partie qui est à la gauche du maître, et à la droite du compagnon, quand ils forgent ensemble. Elles servent à loger et à fixer solidement les différentes étampes nécessaires, en les y chassant à coups marteau. La partie de l'étampe qui se loge dans rainure, a deux biseau conformes à coux de cette rainure, et, comme elle, elle est de plus taillée un peu en coin. C'est par la tête de ce coin qu'on y chasse l'étampe.

8. The anvil of the socket forger is as shown in Figs. 4 and 5; it is remarkable for the two semicircular incisions which are seen at the two ends, and for the two grooves on the top face to the left of the master, and to the right of the assistant, when they work together. They are used to house and secure the various necessary dies, by driving them in with hammer blows. The part of the die which is lodged in a groove, has two bevels conforming to this groove, and, like it, it is moreover formed with a taper. It is by this taper that the die is fixed.

9. Cette enclume, ainsi que presque toutes celles des petites forges de la manufacture, doit être du poids de 380 à 400 liv.

9. This anvil, as well as almost all those of the small forges of the factory, must weigh 380 to 400 pounds.

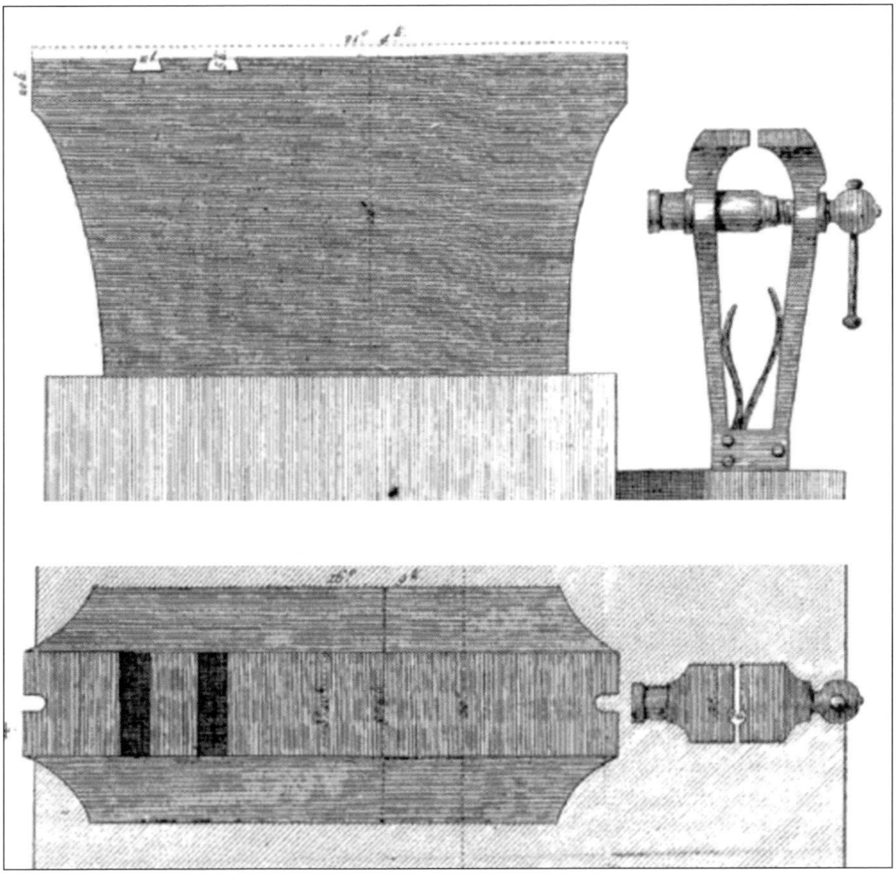

Figs. 4, 5. Side and plan views of the socket forger's anvil.

10. Un étau à chaud, dont on voit la forme, fig. 4 et 5, est fixé sur le bloc de l'enclume, à la droite du maître. Son poids doit être de 40 à 45 livres. Il est remarquable par l'échancrure demi-circulaire qui est pratiquée au milieu de chacune de ses machoires, et par la forme aplatie de lur surface supérieure.

10. A vice, capable of holding hot metal, of which we see the form in Figs. 4 and 5, is fixed on the block of the anvil, on the right of the master. Its weight should be 40 to 45 pounds. It is remarkable for the semicircular notch which is placed in the middle of each of its jaws, and by the flattened form of the upper surface.

Page 4

11. Le maître doit avoir à sa portée un tas, fig. 6, du poids de soixante livres environ, qui est traversé par un mandrin arrondi et un peu conique qui y est

fixé, et qu'on fait entrer dans la douille lorsqu'il est question de la souder.

11. The master must have within reach a stake, Fig. 6, weighing about sixty pounds, which has passing through it a conical round mandrel which is inserted into the socket when welding.

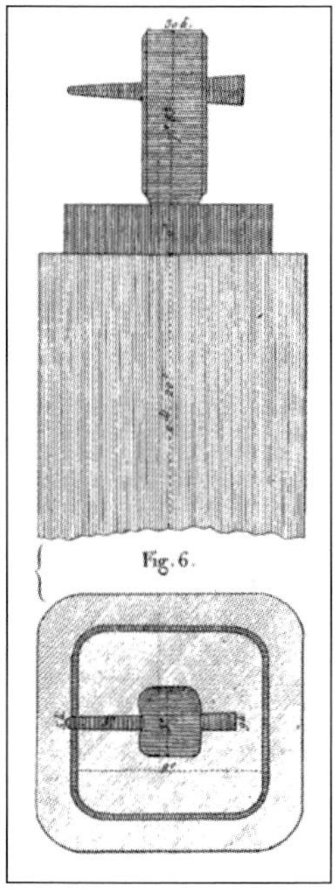

Fig. 6. The stake with mandrel for welding the socket.

12. Le marteau du maître est un marteau ordinaire du poids de 3 à 4 livres.

12. The hammer of the master is an ordinary hammer weighing 3 to 4 pounds.

13. Le compagnon en a deux; l'un à deux têtes, du poids de 16 à 17 livres' l'autre a panne, qui pèse environ 10 livres. Leur manche n'est que d'environ 10 à 11 pouces.

13. The assistant has two; one is double headed, weighing from 16 to 17 pounds, the other has a head and a pein and weighs about 10 pounds. Their handles are only about 10 to 11 inches.

14. Le ratelier doit être garni de tenailles et de pinces ordinaires.

14. The rack must be stocked with ordinary tongs and pincers.

15. Le maître doit avoir sous sa main un calibre, fig. 7, ou l'équivalent, pour vérifier a mesures les dimensions des différentes parties de son ouvrage, et une tranche emmanchée ou tranchoir, qu'il pose dans l'occasion sur les pièces, et sur lequel frappe le compagnon.

15. The master must have to hand a gauge, Fig. 7, or the equivalent, to measure the dimensions of the different parts of his work, and a cutter which he places when required on the pieces to be cut and which the assistant strikes.

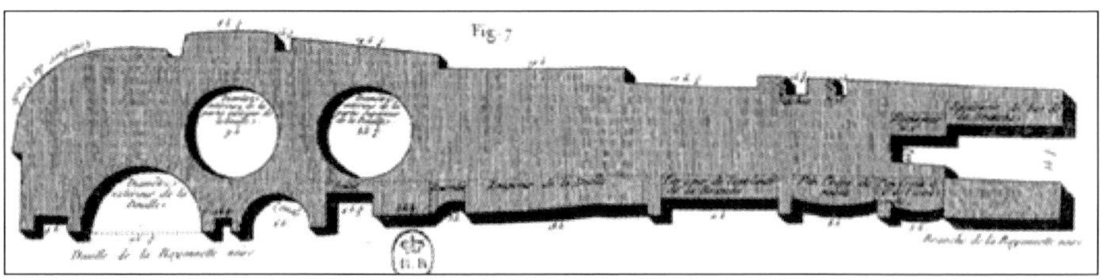

Fig. 7. The gauge.

16. Il doit avoir aussi trois mandrins d'acier, de 10 à 12 poices de long, qu'il puisse tenir à la main par une leurs extrémités, qui est taillée à huit pans, et dont l'autre extrémité, qui est ronde et un peu conique, est trempée, et est destinée a entre dans la douille dans la suite du travail. Ces mandrins ne différent que par les diamétres de la partie arrondie. Ils sont pour le première et le plus mince, de huit lignes à la naissance, et de cinq et demie au bout; pour le second, de neuf lignes et sept lignes et demie; et pour le troisiéme, de neuf lignes et demie et huit lignes.

16. He must also have three mandrels of steel, 10 to 12 inches long, that he can hold by hand at one end, which has eight sides, and the other end, which is round and a little tapered, is hardened, and is destined to enter the socket at various stages of the work. These mandrels differ only in the diameters of the rounded part. They are for the first and the smallest, ranging from eight lines to five and a half lines at the end; for the second, nine lines and seven and a half lines; and for the third, nine lines and a half and eight lines.

17. Il lui faut une petite balance pour peser sa pièce, dans le cas de toute; mais la grande habitude apprend à s'en passer.

17. He needs a small scale to weigh his pieces, but through practice learns to do without it.

18. Il lui faut encore un poincon à sa marque.

18. He needs a punch with his mark.

19. Enfin le compagnon doit avoir à sa portée un étau ordinaire de 40 à 45 livres, montésur en établi, et un carreau de cinq à six livres pour limer les extrémités de la douille, quand elle est forgée.

19. Lastly, the assistant must have within reach an ordinary 40 to 45-pound vise, mounted on a workbench, and a large coarse file of five-to-six-pounds for filing the ends of the socket after it is forged.

Page 5

20. Il doit avoir encore une grande auge remplie d'eau pour rafratîchir les tenailles.

20. He must have a large trough filled with water to cool the tongs.

21. Les étampes de dessous du forgeur de douilles sont au nombre de sept; elles se logent successivement dans les rainures de l'enclume: celles de dessus, que lé maître tient d'une main par le manche de bois qui les traverse, ne sont qu'au nombre de quatre. Le maître donne à la pièce qu'il tient de l'autre main, les mouvement convenables, en la maintenant entre les deux étampes

de dessous er de dessus, tandis que le compagnon frappe sur celle de dessus avec son marteau à deux têtes. Pour le forgeur de douilles, les formes des étampes de dessous et dessus qui se correspondent et sont employées à la fois, sont les mêmes, quant aux faces qui se regardent.

21. There are seven bottom dies used by the socket forger; they are lodged successively in the grooves of the anvil; the top dies, which the master holds with one hand by a wooden handle which passes through them, are only four in number. The master gives to the piece which he holds with the other hand, the proper motions, keeping it between the two dies while the companion strikes the top die with his double-headed hammer. For the socket forger, the forms of the lower and upper dies correspond and are used at the same time.

22. La premiér étampe, fig. 8, sert à arrondir, avant qu'elle soit courbée, la partie qui deviendra le coude de la bayonette. Elle a une étampe de dessus.

22. The first die, Fig. 8, serves to round, before it is bent, the part that will become the elbow of the bayonet. A top die is also used.

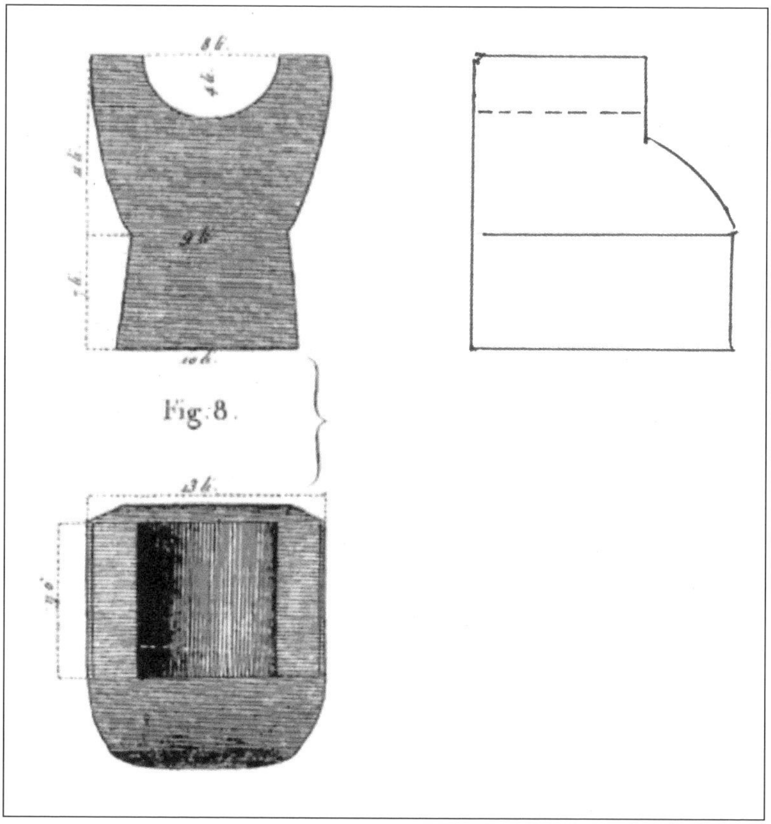

Fig. 8. Die for elbow (with additional sketch to show profile).

23. La seconde, fig. 9, sert à chanfriner les deux bords de la partie qui doit, en se repliant, former la douille, quand ces bords seront soudés. Elle n'a point d'étampe de dessus. Pour former le chanfrin, en appuyant le bord de la pièce sur cette étampe, il suffit qhe le maître frappe sur ce bord, de la tête de son marteau ordinaire.

23. The second, Fig. 9, serves to chamfer the two edges of the part which must overlap when wrapped to form the socket and will be welded. There is no top die. To form the chamfer, by pressing the edge of the piece on this die it suffices that the master strikes on this edge, with the head of his ordinary hammer.

24. La troisième étampe, fig. 10, est crousée en goutière, et sert à rouler le douille; elle n'a point d'étampe de dessus.

24. The third die, Fig. 10, is a half round hollow, and serves to roll the plate to form the socket tube; it has no upper die.

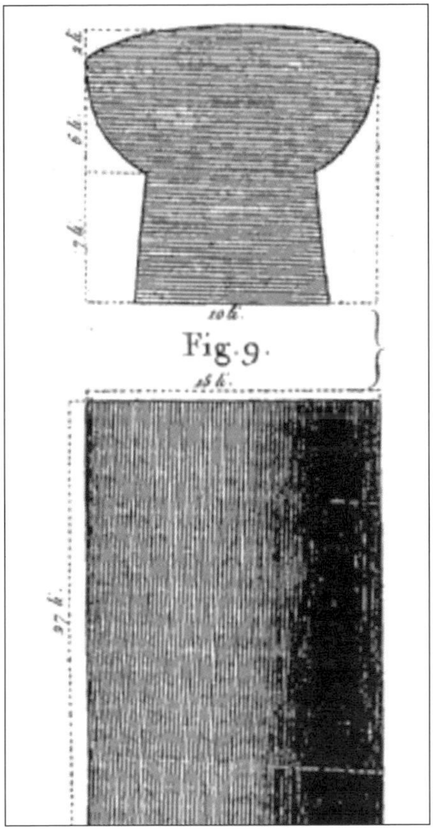

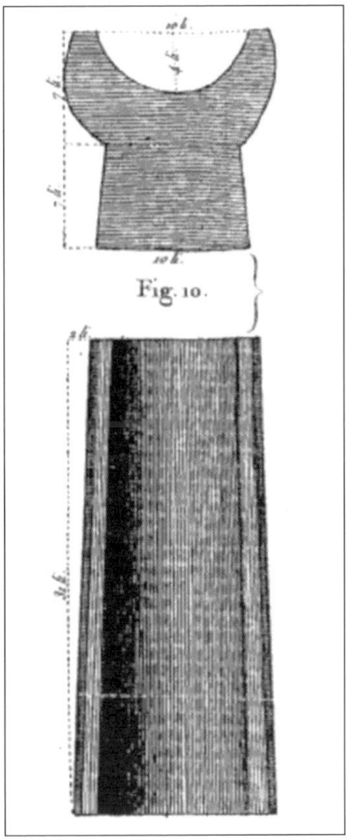

Above left: Fig. 9. Small anvil for chamfering.

Above right: Fig. 10. Die for finish forging the socket.

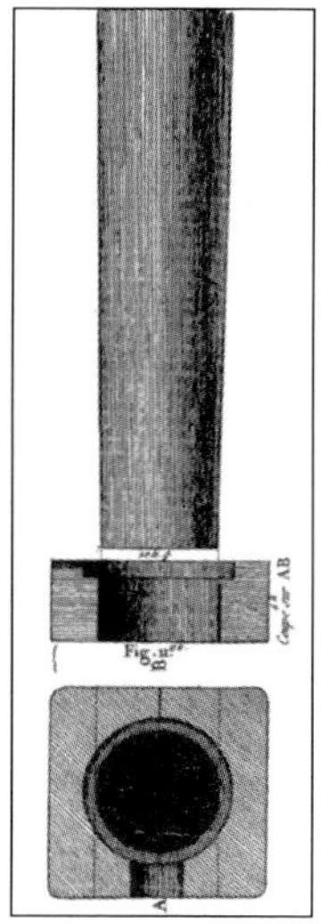

Fig. 11. Die for forming top opening of socket.

25. La quatrième étampe, fig. 11, sert à former l'orifice supérieur de la douille. Pour cela, le maître y a introduit un mandrin, dont il loge le bout dans le trou de l'étampe, en placant le coude de la douille dans la rainure arrondie, marquée A dans la figure; et il forme l'orifice supérieur de la douille, qui se trouve alors renversé, en frappant sur l'extrêmité du mandrin. Il n'y a donc point lieu ici à une étampe de dessus.

25. The fourth die, Fig 11, serves to form the upper orifice of the socket. For this, the master introduces a mandrel, placing the end in the hole of the die and placing the elbow of the socket in the circular groove, marked A in the figure; and he forms the upper orifice of the socket, striking the end of the mandrel which is then withdrawn. There is therefore no place here for a top die.

Page 6

26. Les trois autres étampes, figs. 12,13 et 14, servent à former le bourrelet de la douille, et à en arrondir le corps à l'extérieur, en l'allongeant graduellement, tandis que le mandrin l'arrondit à l'intérieur. Chacune d'elles a son étampe de

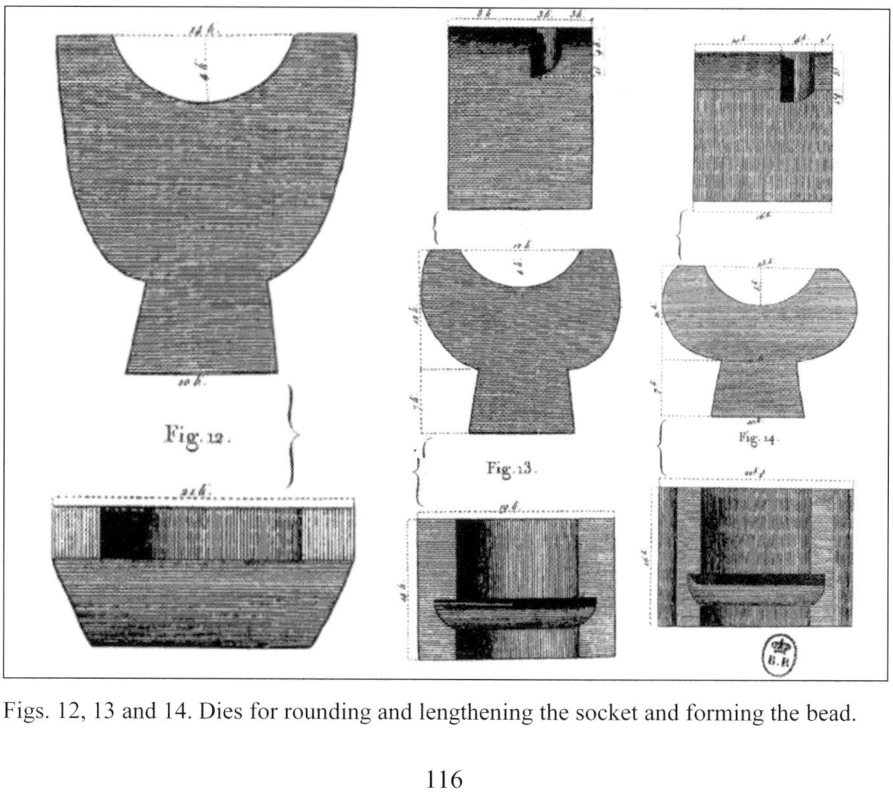

Figs. 12, 13 and 14. Dies for rounding and lengthening the socket and forming the bead.

dessus correspondante et conforme. Les deux dernières ont une gouttière en travers, dans laquelle se loge le bourrelet.

26. The other three dies, Figs 12, 13 and 14, serve to form the bead of the socket, and to round the body outside, gradually lengthening it, while the mandrel rounds it inside. Each of them has its corresponding matching top die. The last two have a gutter formed in which the bead lodges.

27. Tous les forgeurs de la manufacture du Klingenthal, font eux-mêmes leurs outils; ils font leurs étampes; ils taillent leurs limes, etc. Le forgeur de douilles a donc ordinairement tout ce qu'il lui faut pour cela; mais on ne croit pas devoir entrer dans ce détail. On trouve ailleurs les connoissances relatives à la fabrication des outils de serrurier.

27. All the forgers of the Klingenthal factory make their tools themselves; they make their stamps; they cut their files, and so on. The socket forger usually has all he needs for that; but we do not think we ought to enter into this detail. We find elsewhere the knowledge relating to the manufacture of tools of the locksmith.

PROCÉDÉS **du forgeur de douilles**	**PROCEDURES** **of the socket forger**

28. Son opération se partage en quatre époques distinctes, dont on voit les quatre résultats successifs, figures 15, 16, 17 et 18.

28. This operation is divided into four distinct stages, of which we see the four successive results, Figs. 15, 16, 17 and 18.

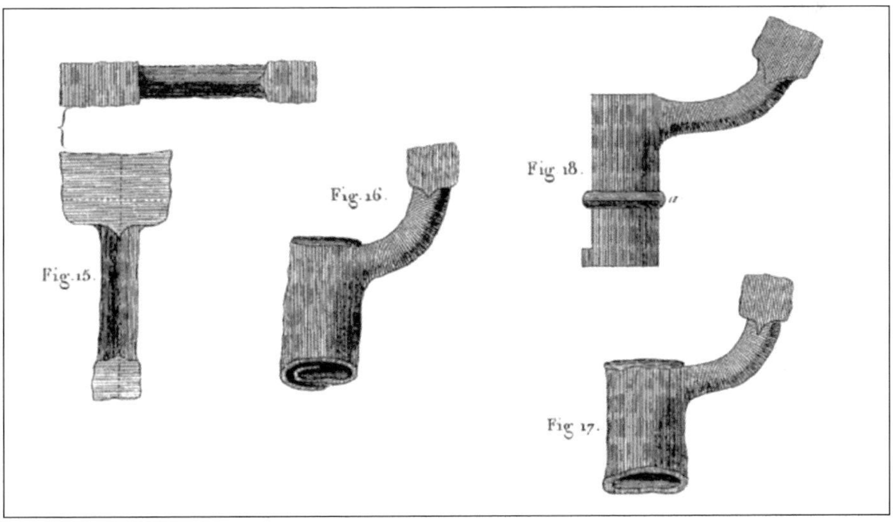

Figs. 15, 16, 17 and 18. Stages in forming the socket and attaching the elbow.

29. La première époque n'exige qu'une chaude; chacune des troits autres en exige plusiers.

29. The first stage requires only one heat; each of the other three require many.

PREMIER ÉPOQUE
Premier chauffement

FIRST STAGE
First heating

30. Un forgeur de douilles, aidé de son compagnon, en forge de trente a trente-six dans sa journée moyenne. Il lui faut pour cela de vingt-deux livres et demie a vingt-sept livres pesant de fer, a raison de douze onces pour chaque douille. Il en prend donc plus que cette quantité, et il en fait trois barres ou d'avantage; il en place trois au feu par l'extremité; celle qui est près du vent de la tuyère sera la première employée: quand on tire celle-ci du feu, on porte sa voisine près du vent, a sa place.

30. A socket forger, with the help of his assistant, forges from thirty to thirty-six in his average day. For this he requires twenty-two and a half to twenty-seven pounds of iron, twelve ounces for each socket. He takes more than this quantity and makes three bars or more; he places three at the fire by the extremity; that which is near the blast from the nozzle will be the first used: when he pulls it off the fire, he replaces it with its neighbour close to the air blast from the nozzle.

Page 7

31. L'échantillon de ces barres est de dix-huit lignes sur sept à huit d'épaisseur.

31. The specification for these bars is eighteen lines by seven to eight thick.

32. Le maître prend d'abord une de ces barres chauffée à blanc par son extrêmitée, il la porte sur l'enclume, où il la forge avec son compagnon sur environ un pouce, pour porter cette longeur au double à peu près, en l'écarrisant et la réduissant a sept lignes environ sur chaque face. Le compagnon se sert d'abord de la tête et ensuite de la panne de son marteau à panner; de la tête, lorsque le maître forge sur le milieu de l'enclume; et de la panne, quand il forge sur le bord poure faire les épaulemens.

32. The master first takes one of these bars, heated at its extremity, and places it on the anvil, where he forges it with his assistant for about an inch, to bring this length to about twice as much and reducing it to seven lines on each side. The assistant first uses the head of his hammer when the master forges on the middle of the anvil and then the pein, when it is forged on the edge to make the shoulders.

33. Le maître porte ensuite le bout, qu'il a écarri, sur l'étampe, fig. 8, et prend d'une main l'étampe de dessus correspondante, sur laquelle frappe son compagnon avec son marteau à deux têtes, tandis qu'il tourne et afit avancer le pièce pour

l'arrondir sur une longeur de deux pouces, en réservant une extrêmité du huit lignes, qui doit demeourer simplement écarrie. La partie arrondie formera le coude de la bayonette; et l'extrêmité écarrie, qu'on nomme la masselote, est l'amorce sur laquelle on soudera l'acier qui doit former la lame.

33. The master then places the end which he has reduced on the die, Fig. 8, and takes with one hand the corresponding die on which his companion strikes with his double-headed hammer, turns and move the piece round to a length of two inches, reserving one end of eight lines which must be left square. The rounded part will form the elbow of the bayonette; and the extremity, which is called the masselote (thick/heavy part), is the piece on which the steel forming the blade is welded.

34. Pour détacher la portion de la barre qui n'a pas été forgée encore dans cette opération, et qui doit former le corps de la douille, le maître remet la barre sur l'enclume, prend son tranchoir par le manche, le pose à l'endroit convenable, et le compagnon frappe jusqu'à ce que la pièce soit presqu'entièrement détachée. L'habitude apprend à saisir parfaitement l'endroit où il faut couper. Si le maître avoit do doute, il vérifieroit le poids de la pièce; si elle pesoit trop peu, il la mettroit au rebut; si elle pesoit trop il en retrancheroit un peu par la suite, on il en laisseroit consumer un peu par le feu dans les chaudes suantes.

34. To detach the portion of the bar that has not been forged yet in this operation, and which must form the body of the socket, the master puts the bar on the anvil, takes his chisel by the handle, positions the bar, and the assistant strikes until the piece is almost entirely detached. Through habit he learns to position it perfectly where it needs to cut. If the master had any doubt, he would check the weight of the piece; if it weighed too little, he would throw it away; if it weighed too much a little more would be cut off, or it would be allowed to burn a little in the blast in the fire.

Page 8

35. Quand la pièce esta peu près dètachèe, le maître retourne la barre, frappe de la pièce sur l'enclume, la met à angle droit de la barre, la porte entre les mâchoires de l'étau à chaud, où sa partie arrondie se loge dans le trou que forment les deux mâchoires en se serrant.

35. When the piece is almost detached, the master turns the bar over, strikes the piece on the anvil, puts it at a right angle to the bar, places it between the jaws of the hot vice, where its rounded part lodges in the hole formed by the two jaws closing.

36. Il détachée alors la pièce de la barre par des mouvemens rèpètès de haut et bas, que le compagnon seconde de quelques coups.

36. He then detaches the piece of the bar by repeated movements up and down, the mate helping with a few strokes.

37. Celui-ci frappe ensuite sur le sommet de la plaque détachée de la barre, pour la refouler et pour en former les épaulemens par le contre-coup, sur les mâchoires de l'étau. Ceci seroit inutile si la barre étoit parfaitement d'échantillon, et si les ouvriers, en forgeant les épaulemens sur le bord de l'enclume, avoient frappe assez juste pour les former tous deux quarrément et bien niveau.

37. The latter then strikes on the top of the detached plate of the bar, to depress it and to form the shoulders on the jaws of the vise. This would not be necessary if the bar conformed to the sample, and if the workers, by forging the shoulders on the edge of the anvil, had forged them both square and level.

38. Enfin, le compagnon saisit la pièce avec une tenaille, et desserre l'étau; si la pièce n'est par droite, il la porte sur l'enclume pour achever, en la forgeant avec le marteau du maître, de lui donner la forme qu'on lui voit fig. 15.

38. Finally, the assistant seizes the piece with tongs, and loosens the vise; if the piece is not quite right, he places it on the anvil to correct by forging it with the hammer of the master, to give it the shape seen in Fig. 15.

39. Alors il la jette par terre pour refroidir; et pareille opération se continue pour toutes les autres pièces qui doivent être terminées dans la journée.

39. Then he throws it on the ground to cool; and such an operation is continued for all the other pieces which are to be made during the day.

SECONDE ÉPOQUE ***Deuxième chauffement***	**SECOND STAGE** ***Second heating***

40. On reprend les pièces l'une après l'autre en les serrant dans une tenaille par la masselote, et on les porte au feu.

40. We take the pieces one after the other by grasping them in tongs by the portion to which the blade will be welded and place them in the hearth.

Page 8/9

41. On laissee chauffer la pièce a blanc, et le maître la porte sur l'enclume en se placant devant. Il y aplatit la masse qui formera la douille, vers le bord opposé à la masselote. Il se place ensuite en face d'un des côtés de l'enclume, sur lequel il pose la tenaille. En frappant alors sur la plaque qui doit former la douille, il commence à en plier le coude à cause du porte-à-faux; et la plaque elle-même prend un peu de courbure dans le même sens.

Il reporte aussi-tôt la pièce dans l'étau en placant le coude dans le trou que forment les machoires rapprochées. Alors le compagnon frappe de la tête de son marteau a panne sur le dos de la courbure de la plaque. Il frappe d'abord de biais de manière à chasser la plaque un peu au-delà du pied du coude, parce que ce coude ne doit maître qu'un peu au-dessous de l'orifice supérieur de la douille. Il frappe ensuite d'aplomb pour aplatir la plaque. Il prend enfin la tenaille, desserre l'étau, et reporte la pièce au feu.

41. When the piece is heated, the master places it on the anvil and flattens the portion which will form the socket. He then places himself in front of one of the sides of the anvil, on which he places the tongs holding the shank of the elbow and, striking then on the plate which will form the socket, begins to bend it over.

He then fits the piece into the vise as soon as possible by placing the elbow in the hole formed by closing the jaws. Then the assistant strikes with the pein of his hammer on the back of the bend of the plate. He first strikes at a slant so as to drive the plate a little beyond the foot of the elbow, because this elbow should only be a little below the upper orifice of the socket. He then strikes to flatten the plate. He finally takes the tongs, loosens the vise, and takes the piece back to the fire.

SECONDE ÉPOQUE
Troisième chauffement

SECOND STAGE
Third heating

42. Il se donne au demi-blanc. On porte la pièce dans l'échancrure circulaire de l'enclume pour achever de forger carrément la plaque qui doit former la douille, en y réservant de la matière en travers du mileau pour servir à faire le bourrelet a fig. 18, qui sera l'embase de la virole. On réserve aussi de la matière aux deux angles qui se trouveront à la partie inférieure de la douille, parce que ces deux angles rapprochés, quand on roulera la plaque, et soudés, formeront l'éminence b, fig. 18, dans laquelle on doit prendre le pontet a, fig. 19; ce pontet sert de passage au tenon du canon de fusil.

42. He heats it to half-white hot [?]. The piece is brought into the circular indentation of the anvil to complete the forging of the plate which is to form the socket, by reserving material therein to form the bead, a, Fig. 18, against which the ring will rest. He also reserves material at the two angles which will be at the lower part of the sleeve, because these two angles, when we roll the plate, and weld it, will form the eminence b, Fig 18, in which we must make the bridge, b, Fig. 18; this bridge serves as a passage for the tenon on the musket barrel.

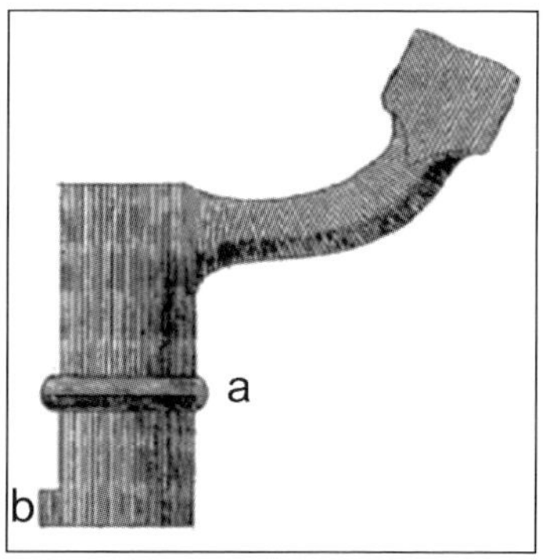

Fig. 18. Noting the bead, a, and the bridge, b.

43. C'est avec la panne de leur marteau que le compagnon et le maître retirent la matière vers les angles.

43. It is with the peins of their hammers that the master and the assistant draw the metal towards the corners.

Page 10

SECONDE ÉPOQUE **SECOND STAGE**
Quatrième chauffement ***Fourth heating***

44. On ne chauffe qu'au rouge de cerise. Il s'agit de chanfriner les deux bords de la plaque, de droite et de gauche. C'est ce qu'opère le maître seul, en posant ces bords sur l'étampe, fig. 9, et en frappant de la tête de son marteau. Quelques ouvriers se passent de cette étampe, et chanfrinent sur l'enclume en posant la pièce sur le bord. Il vaut mieux se servir de l'étampe.

44. We only heat to cherry red. It is a matter of chamfering the two edges of the plate, right and left. This is done by the master alone, by placing these edges on the small anvil, Fig. 9, and striking with the head of his hammer. Some workers do without this small anvil, and use the main anvil by placing the plate on the edge. It is better to use the small anvil.

SECONDE ÉPOQUE **SECOND STAGE**
Cinquième chauffement ***Fifth heating***

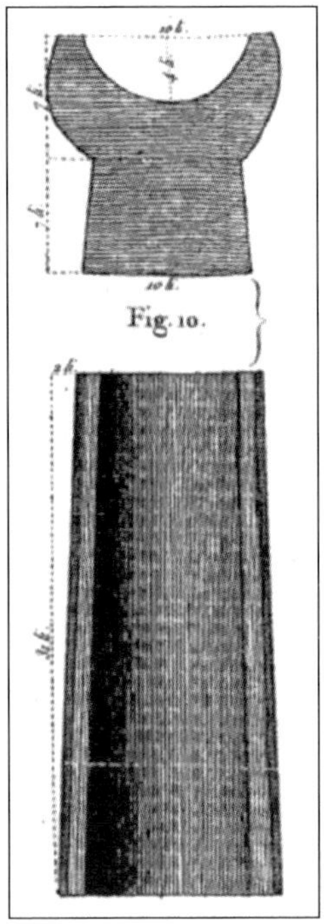

Fig. 10. Die for finish forging the socket.

45. On chauffe encore au rouge de cerise. Il s'agit de rouler la plaque pour commencer à lui donner la forme d'une douille. Pour cela le maître porte la pièce entre les machoires demi-ouvertes de l'étau à chaud; il donne deux au trois coups de la panne de son marteau en travers de la plaque, et la plie. Il porte la pièce sur l'enclume, et il continue d'arrondir en frappant de côté avec la tête du marteau; il y passe le plus mince de ses mandrins à main, et continue de rouler en croissant les deux bords chanfrinés, d'environ huit lignes l'un sur l'autre; il pose la pièce sur l'étampe, fig. 10, qui est en goutière; et il achève d'arrondir la douille.

45. We still heat to cherry red. It is about rolling the plate to begin to give it the shape of a socket. For this, the master places the piece between the half-open jaws of

the hot vise; he gives two or three strokes of the pein of his hammer across the plate and folds it. He places the piece on the anvil, and he continues to wrap it by striking with the hammer's head; he passes the thinnest of his hand mandrels, and continues to roll up the two chamfered edges, about eight lines one on the other; he places the piece on the die, Fig. 10, which is hollow, and he finishes rounding the socket.

46. Il dégage la pièce du mandrin; la jette à terre pour refroidir, et continue pareille opération pour toutes les autres pièces.

46. He removes the piece from the mandrel, throws it on the ground to cool, and continues the same operation for all the other pieces.

47. Quelques maîtres emploient ici une des étampes a goutière en travers, pour employer une étampe de moins; mais ils usent d'autant celle-ci qui est plus difficile à faire.

47. Some masters here use one of the cross hollow dies, to use one less die, but that makes for more difficulty.

Page 11

TROISIÈME ÉPOQUE
Sixtième, septième et huitième chauffemens

THIRD STAGE
Sixth, seventh and eighth heatings

48. Ce sont trois chaudes suantes, qui ont pour objet de souder la douille. La première est pour souder l'extrêmité supérieur; la seconde pour l'inférieur; et la troisième pour terminer la soudure. C'est le maître seul qui faite cette opération, en passant chaque fois la douille dans le mandrin du tas, fig. 6, et en rappant vîte et a petits coups sur les bords qu'il s'agit de réunir. À la fin, il fait passer la douille sur son mandrin à main de moyenne grosseur; et en posant la pièce horisontalement sur le tas, et la faisant tourner, il forge pour faconner sur ce mandrin l'intérieur de la douille.

48. These are three heats which aim to weld the socket. The first is to weld the upper extremity; the second for the lower; and the third to complete the weld. It is the master alone who does this operation, passing each time the socket onto the mandrel of the block, Fig. 6,

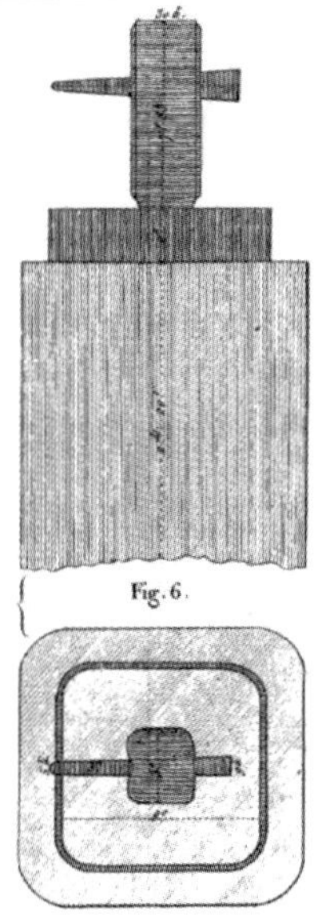

Fig. 6. The stake with mandrel for welding the socket.

and rapping quickly and gently on the edges to be joined. At the end, he passes the sleeve on his medium-sized hand mandrel, and by placing the piece horizontally on the block, and turning it, it forges to shape on this mandrel the inside of the socket.

49. A la fin de ce travail il jette la douille à terre; et soude de la même manière toutes les autres pièces qui doivent l'être. Le compagnon n'est occupé pendant cette époque qu'à tenir les pièces prêtes pour le travail du maître.

49. At the end of this work he throws the socket on the ground; and welds in the same way all the other pieces that must be done. The assistant is busy during this time keeping the pieces ready for the master's work.

QUATRIÈME ÉPOQUE — **FOURTH STAGE**

Neuvième chauffemens — *Ninth heating*

50. Cette époque a pour objet;
1, de porter le corps de la douille a la longueur qui lui est prescrite, en y faconnant le bourrelet; 2 d'en bien dégager le coude; et 3, de former l'éminence qui deviendra le pontet.

50. This stage has for its objects;
1, to form the body of the socket to the length which is prescribed and forming the bead; 2, to clear the elbow; and 3, to form the eminence that will become the bridge.

51. On chauffe la douille a demi-blanc. Le maître y fait entrer son mandrin de médiocre grosseur, et la pose sur l'étampe étroite, fig. 12, il y applique de l'autre main l'étampe de dessus corespondante, et le compagnon frappe avec son marteau à deux têtes. Le maître fait tourner la pièce pendant ce temps-là. Il lui donne cessivement deux positions sur l'ètampe; l'une au-dessus et l'autre au-dessus de la place où doit se former le bourrelet.

51. The socket is heated to red heat. The master inserts his mandrel of mediocre thickness, and places it on the narrow die, Fig. 12, he applies the corresponding

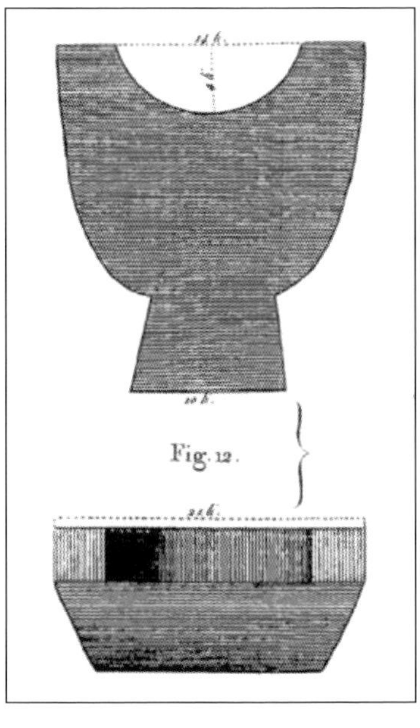

Fig. 12. Die for forging the socket either side of the bead.

die with the other hand, and the companion strikes with his double-headed hammer. The master rotates the workpiece during this time. He ceaselessly gives him two positions on the die, one above the other where the bead is to be formed.

Page 12

QUATRIÈME ÉPOQUE	**FOURTH STAGE**
Dixième chauffement	***Tenth heating***

52. On chauffe encore la douille à demi-blanc; le maître y fait encore entrer son mandrin de médiocre grosseur. Il la place sur l'étampe étroite a goutière en travers, fig. 13, et continue d'allonger la douille et de former le bourrelet en tournant la douille, et faissant frapper le compagnon sur l'étampe de dessus correspondante, qu'il tient de l'autre main. Le bourrelet se moule sur la goutière en travers.

52. The socket is still half white; the master still has his mandrel of mediocre size inserted in it. He places it on the narrow die at the cross-piece, Fig. 13, and continues to lengthen the socket and form the bead by turning the sleeve, and the companion striking the corresponding top die, which he holds with the other hand. The bead is moulded in the transverse channel.

QUATRIÈME ÉPOQUE	**FOURTH STAGE**
Onzième chauffement	***Eleventh heating***

53. On ne chauffe de nouveau à *demi-blanc*, que pour continuer de la même manière, et perfectionner l'ouvrage de la chaude précédente.

53. It is heated again half white, only to continue in the same way, and perfect the work of the previous heating.

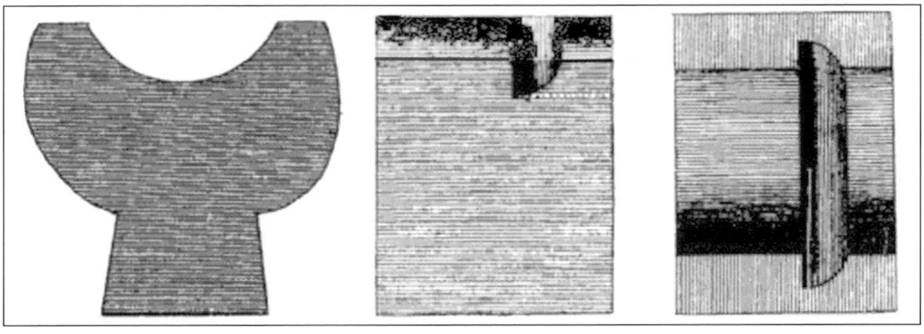

Fig. 13. The two dies used for forging the bead.

QUATRIÈME ÉPOQUE
Douzième chauffement

FOURTH STAGE
Twelfth heating

54. Cette chaude est un peu moins forte que la précédente; le maître y employe le plus gros de ses trois mandrins à main et la plus large des deux étampes a goutière en travers, fig. 14; pour le surplus, tout se passe comme dans les deux chauffemens précédens. Mais comme les étampes ne suffisent pas pour bien dégager le coude de la douille a sa naissance, le maître finit par le faire avec la panne de son marteau; il s'occupe aussi de perfectionner la forme extérieure du pontet.

54. This heat is a little weaker than the previous one; the master employs the largest of his three hand mandrels, and the larger of the two transverse gusseted dies, Fig. 14; for the rest, everything happens as in the two previous heatings. But as the dies are not sufficient to clear the elbow of the socket at its root, the master ends up doing so with the pein of his hammer; he is also busy perfecting the external shape of the bridge.

55. La pièce est alors terminée telle qu'on la voit, fig. 18.

55. The piece is then finished as it is shown in Fig. 18.

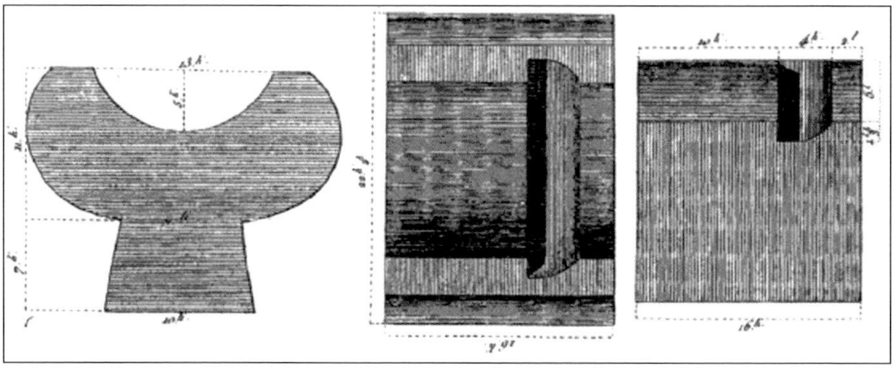

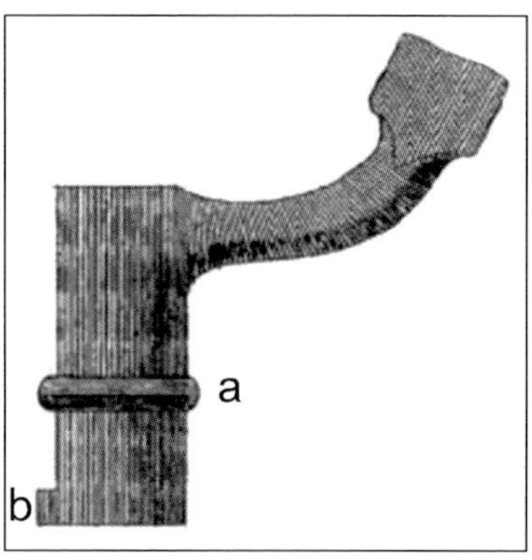

Above: Fig. 14. Dies for finishing the forging of the bead.

Left: Fig. 18. Noting the bead, a, and the bridge, b.

Page 13

Trezième et dernier chauffement. ***Thirteenth and last heating.***

56. Il n'a pour objet que de recuire la pièce, qui seroit trop dure pour le foret ou l'alezoir, parce que le maître a été obligé, dans le chauffement précédent, de la forger à froid.

56. The only task remaining is to anneal the piece, which would be too hard for the drill or the reamer, because the master was obliged, in the preceding heat, to forge it cold.

57. Le compagnon lime ensuite, avec son carreau, les deux orifices de la douille, qu'il ne s'agit plus que de porter un magasin, après l'avoir frappée, a la naissance du coude, de la marque du maître.

57. The assistant then files, using his square file, the two openings of the socket, and it is then taken to the store, after having stamped the mark of the master at the root of the elbow.

ARTICLE SECOND
Premier contrôle de la douille au magasin.

SECOND ARTICLE
First inspection of the socket at the store.

58. Les douilles de baionettes sortent des mains du forgeur pour passer, une à une, au magasin, dans celles du contrôleur d'armes noires.

58. The bayonet sockets leave the hands of the forger to go, one by one, to the store, into the care of the inspector of black weapons.

59. Il mire l'intérieur pour s'assurer si la pièce est bien saine dans cette partie, ou si les défants qui y restent peuvent être emportés par l'alezoir, à la forerie.

59. He looks to make sure the socket is good in the bore, or if any defects can be removed by the reaming/boring.

60. Il examine ensuite toutes les parties pour s'assurer si elles ont les dimensions prescrites. Si, malgré son habitude, il lui reste du doute, il y porte le calibre, fig. 7.

60. He then examines all parts to make sure they have the required dimensions. If, in spite of his inspection, he remains in doubt, he uses the gauge, Fig. 7.

61. S'il soupconne quelque paille ou crevasse déguisée, pour la decouvrir il frappe sur la pièce avec un petit marteau qui est toujours sons à main.

61. If he suspects some small flaw or disguised crevice, to check he strikes the piece with a small hammer that is always to hand.

62. Si le défaut, lorsqu'il s'en trouve, est irréparable, il met la pièce au rebut. Lorsque le défaut pente se réparer, il fait sur l'endroit, à la craie on avec son marteau, une marque convenue qui indique son espèce. Les pièces de rebut sont cassées. Celles qui peuvent se réparer sont rapportées chez le maître, qui les soumet à un nouvel examen du contrôleur, quand il les a raccomodées.

62. If the defect, when it is found, is irreparable, he will discard it. When the defect can be repaired, he marks the defect, with chalk or with his hammer, an agreed mark which indicates its position. The pieces of waste are broken. Those which can be repaired are reported to the master, who submits them to a new examination of the controller, when he has corrected them.

Page 14

63. Les douilles recues sont marquées à froid, sur la masselote, du poincon du contrôleur.

63. The sockets received are marked cold, on the portion to be welded to the blade with the punch of the controller.

64. Le forgeur est présent à l'examen, on bien il envoie une personne a sa place; c'est ordinairement lui ou son substitut qui frappe le poincon, en posant la piêce sur la coussinet, fig. 19, qui est toujours près de la table du contrôleur. Ce coussinet est de fer avec une mise d'acier.

64. The forger is present at the examination, or he sends a representative; it is usually he or his substitute who strikes the mark, placing the socket on the support, Fig. 19, which is near the controller's table. This cushion is of iron with a setting of steel. *[elsewhere this is described as a brass cushion – see bottom page 41]*

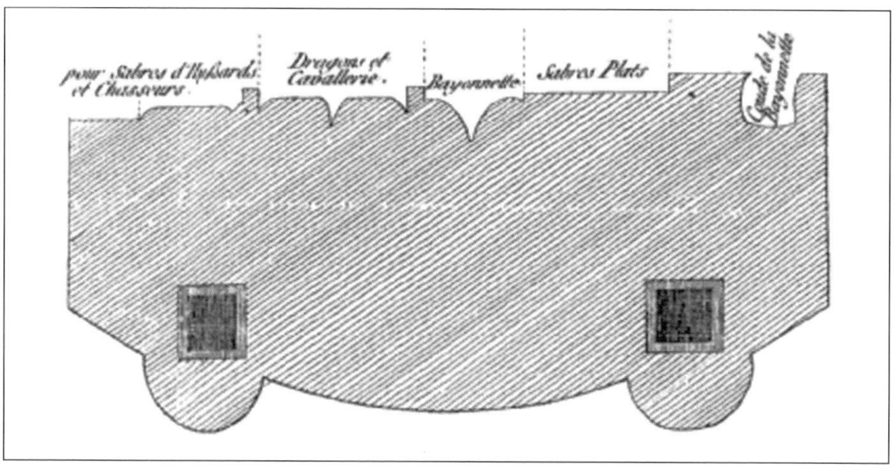

Fig. 19. The 'cushion' used to support edged weapons when being stamped with various marks.

65. Les douilles sont alors prêtes à être envoyées à la forerie.

65. The sockets are then ready to be sent for drilling.

ARTICLE TROISIEME
Alezer la douille de la bayonnette

THIRD ARTICLE
Reaming the socket of the bayonet

66. Le forerie est une usine où une roue a eau fait tourner l'alezoir a, fig. 20, qu'on fait entrer dans la douille, et qui doit la traverser, en la rendant parfaitement cylindrique à l'intérieur, et exactement du calibre de dix lignes.

66. The boring workshop is a factory where a water wheel turns the reamer, a, Fig. 20, which is entered into the socket, and which must pass through, making it perfectly cylindrical inside, and exactly the calibre of ten lines.

67. L'alesoir fait cinq révolutions et demi pour une de la roue a eau, qui en fait de vingt à vingt-cinq par minute.

67. The reamer makes five and a half revolutions for one of the water wheels', which makes twenty to twenty-five per minute.

68. Il passe dans chaque douille six alesoirs différens, depuis le diamètre de neuf lignes jusqu'à celui de dix, dans leur partie la plus large; la plus étroite a toujours environ une ligne de moins. Chaque alesoir passe de suite dans toutes les douilles qui compléteront le travail de la journée. Il faut en avoir toujours au moins trois fois plus de la première espèce que de toutes les autres, parce que cette espèce, devant mordre sur une surface qui a en le contact immèdiat du feu, et devant, par cette raison, être trempée plus dur, tandis qu'elle est exposée à des saccades à cause des inégalités de cette surface, s'use aussi beaucoup d'avantage.

68. In each case he passes six different reamers, from the diameter of nine lines to that of ten, in their widest part; the narrowest still has about one line less. Each

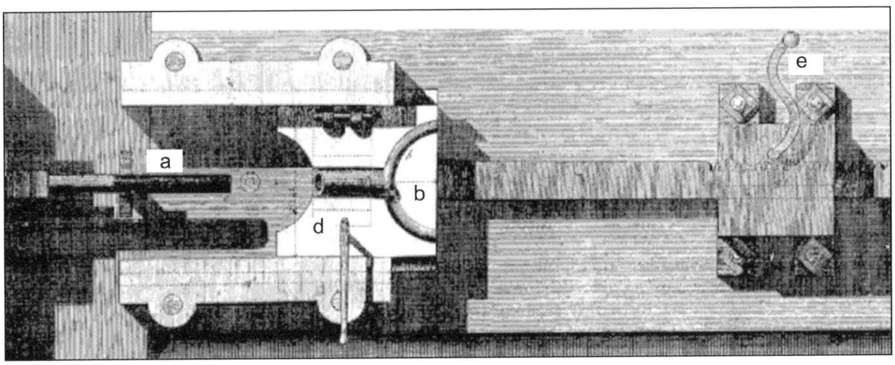

Fig. 20. The socket boring machine with a reamer, a.

reamer goes right through all the sockets, which will complete the work of the day. We must always have at least three times more of the first kind than of all the others, because this reamer, having to bite on a surface which has been in immediate contact with the fire, and for this reason is harder, is exposed to jerking cuts because of the inequalities of this surface and is worn more rapidly.

Page 15

69. Deux enfans de dix à douze ans suffisent au travail journalier de cette forerie. Un homme prend soin de l'usine et des outils, et surveille les opérations; et il a le tems de s'occuper à autre chose.

69. Two children from ten to twelve years old are sufficient for the daily work of this drilling operation. A man takes care of the plant and tools, and monitors operations; and he has the time to take care of other things also.

70. L'un des enfans a soin d'huiller l'intérieur des douilles avec une barbe de-plume, et de les tenir continuellement sous la main de celui qui les place dans le chariot b, fig. 20, et qui le fait avancer en tournant la manivelle du cric e, fig. 20. Les enfans se relayant; car l'effort sur la manivelle est trop grand pour être supporté par un enfant pendant toute la journée.

70. One of the children is careful to oil the inside of the sleeves with a feather and to keep them continually under the hand of the one who places them in the carriage b, Fig 20, and makes it move forward by turning the handle of the rack, e, Fig. 20. The children take turns because the effort on the crank is too much to be carried out by one child all day long.

71. Pour fixer solidement la douille dans le chariot, il faut appliquer dessus, la fermeture a charnière d, fig. 20, et la contenir par l'arrétoir e. Il faut faire le contraire pour retirer la douille de sa place.

71. To securely fix the socket in the carriage, apply the hinged closure d, Fig. 20, and secure it by locking the handle, e. The reverse is done to remove the socket from its fixture.

72. L'enfant qui opère, commence donc par le placer la douille dans le chariot, il abaisse la fermeture et tourne l'arretoir; tou cela d'une main. Il tourne de l'autre, la manivelle du cric pour faire avancer la douille, jusqu'à ce que la partie de alesoir, dont le diamétre est le plus grand, l'ait entiérement traversée; il en est averti, parce que la résistance cesse. Il tourne aussi-tôt la manivelle du cric dans l'autre sens, pour ramener la douille; et de l'autre main, il détourne l'arrétoir, lève la fermeture et enlève la douille. Voilà toute l'opération.

72. The child who operates begins by placing the socket in the carriage, lowers the clamp and turns the lever; all this with one hand. With the other hand, he turns the crank of the rack to advance the socket until the portion of the

reamer whose diameter is the largest, has entirely traversed it, indicated by the resistance ceasing. He turns the rack crank in the other direction as soon as possible, to bring back the socket; and with the other hand he releases the clamp, raises the closure and removes the socket. That is the whole operation.

73. On en peut alezer à l'aise deux cents dans la journée moyenne.

73. Two hundred can be processed in the average day.

74. L'eau qui coule continuellement vers l'extrêmité de l'alesoir par un petit canal, rafraîchit les parties qui s'échauffent dans ce travail.

74. The water flowing continuously towards the end of the reamer through a small channel, cools the parts that warm up in this work.

Page 16

ARTICLE QUATRIEME	**FOURTH ARTICLE**
Second contrôle de la douille au magasin.	***Second inspection of the socket at the store.***

75. Le forage peut avoir découvert des vices dans l'intérieur de la matière de la douille, il peut aussi avoir été imparfait; l'examen par le contrôleur d'armes noires est destiné à découvrir ces défauts, afin de ne pas continuer le travail sur une pièce qu'ils forceroient à rebuter après cet examen, celles qui sont recues sont frappées sur le coude, du poincon du contrôleur d'armes noires.

75. The drilling may have uncovered defects in the inside of the socket material, it may also have been imperfect; the examination by the controller of black weapons is intended to discover these defects, so as not to continue the work on a piece they would be forced to discard later; those that are accepted are struck on the elbow with the mark of the inspector of black weapons.

ARTICLE CINQUIEME	**FIFTH ARTICLE**
Forger la lame de la bayonette	***Forging the bayonet blade***

Disposition do choses nécessaire au forgeur de lames de bayonettes.
Arrangement of things necessary to the bayonet blade forger.

76. La forge est de la même construction que pour la douille. Le charbon de terre est le même, est sa consommation moyenne est d'un peu plus d'un quintal et demi pour cent lames de bayonettes. L'acier doit être de bonne qualité, mais il est inutile qu'il ait tout le liant qu'exigent les longues lames de sabres. Au Klingenthal, il est tiré brut de Nassau-Sigen, et s'affine dans

la manufacture. On n'y emploie pour la bayonette qu'un acier de seconde qualité, dit à deux marques. L'affineur le prépare pour cet emploi, en barres de huit lignes sur six.

76. The forge is of the same construction as for the socket. The charcoal is the same, its average consumption is a little over a quintal and a half per hundred bayonet blades. The steel must be of good quality, but it is unnecessary for it to have all the refinement/quality required by long sword blades. At Klingenthal, it is crude from Nassau-Sigen, and is refined in the blade manufacture. For the bayonet only steel of second quality is needed, having two marks. The refiner prepares it for this job in bars of eight lines by six. [20mm x 13.5mm]

77. Il en faut plus de quinze ou seize livres au forgeur pour sa journée; car il peut souder et forger de trente-six a quarante lames de bayonette qui, chacune, exigent six onces et demi d'acier.

77. It requires fifteen or sixteen pounds for the forger for his day; he can weld and forge from thirty-six to forty bayonet blades which each require six and a half ounces of steel.

Page 17

78. L'enclume ne différe que parce qu'il n'y a point d'échancrure au bord des deux extrémités, mais qu'elle a sur la gauche du maître un trou carré qui peut loger un tranchoir, si le maître le préfère au tranchoir à main, comme cela seroit peut-être à propos pour-ménager les forces du compagnon, voyez fig. 21.

78. The anvil differs only because there is no indentation at the edge of both ends, but it has on the left of the master a square hole which can accommodate a cutter if the master prefers it to the hand-held cutter, as perhaps it would be advisable to spare the assistant's strength, Fig. 21.

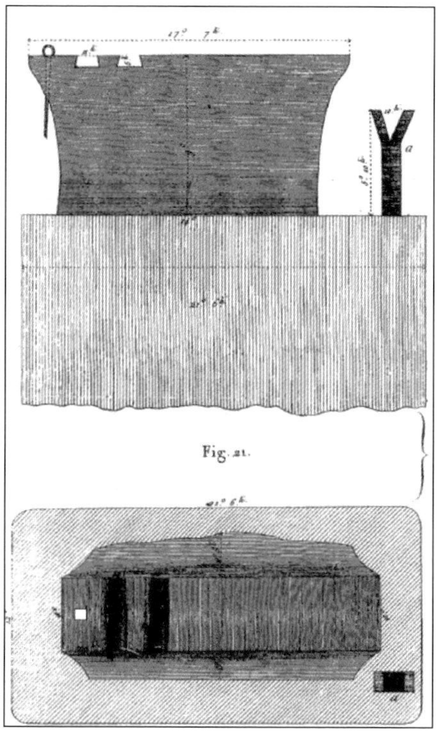

Fig. 21. The blade forger's anvil.

79. On y a placé dans le trou carré une broche applatie de fer, qui est très-nécessaire au compagnon pour nettoyer de temps en temps le fond de la cavité de l'étampe, fig. 22, où des petites lamelles d'acier brulé dans les chaudes à la surface des pièces, et qu'on nomme écailles de fer, sont sujettes à se loger. Il met en effet la broche dans cette place, quand elle est libre, pour l'avoir tout-à-fait sous la main. Il faut graisser de temps en temps le fond de la cavité; on se sert pour cela d'huille de navette, ou même de saindoux.

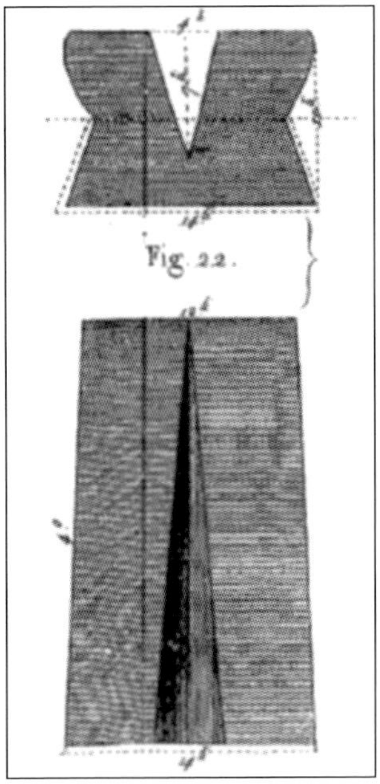

Fig. 22. Blade forging die/stamp

79. There is placed in the square hole an iron pin, which is very necessary for the companion to use to clean from time to time the bottom of the cavity of the die, Fig. 22, where small flakes of steel burned on the surface of the pieces [scale], are prone to lodge. He puts the pin in this place, when it is free, to have it all at hand. The bottom of the cavity must be greased from time to time; for this shuttle oil, or even lard, is used.

80. Cette enclume doit, pour le mieux, peser autant que celle du forgeur de douille. Elle peut cependant ne peser que trois cent trente livres a trois cent cinquante.

80. This anvil must, for the better, weigh as much as that of the socket forger. It may, however, weigh only three hundred and thirty pounds to three hundred and fifty.

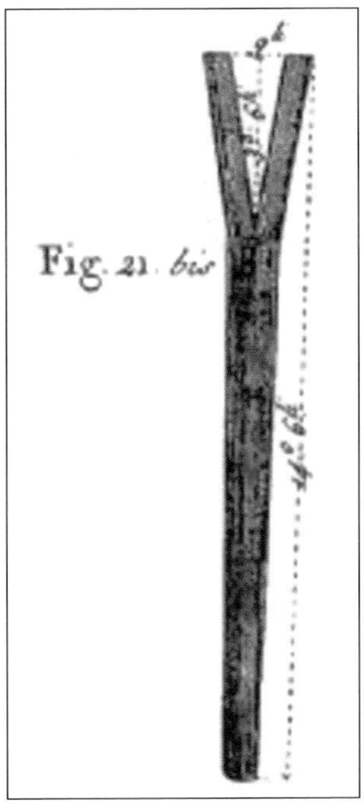

Fig. 21 *bis*. The hand dresser.

81. Au lieu d'étau à chaud, c'est un dressoir, a, qui est implanté dans le billot de l'enclume. Un pareil dressoir à main est toujours à la portée du maître. Il arrête la lame de bayonette dans le dressoir fixe, et la tord avec le dressoir a main pour le dressoir lorsqu'elle se fausse dans le travail, voyez fig. 23.[should be Fig. 21 bis]

81. Instead of a vise for hot metal, there is a dresser [fork used for correcting or creating any twists or bends], a, which is implanted in the block of the anvil. Such a dresser is always within the reach of the master. He puts the bayonet's

blade in the fixed dresser and twists it with the hand-dresser to straighten it when bent, Fig. 21 bis.

82. Le seul étau necessaire au forgeur de lames est un étau ordinaire de trente-six a quarante livres, monté sur un établi. Le compagnon y lime la pièce, quand elle en a besoin, avec un carreau d'environ trois livres pesant.

82. The only vice required for the blade forger is an ordinary thirty-six to forty-pound vise mounted on a workbench. The assistant files the piece when needed, with a square file about three pounds.

83. Le marteau du maître doit peser quatre livres ou quatre livres et demi. Le compagnon a les deux mêmes marteaux que chez le forgeur de douilles.

83. The hammer of the master must weigh four pounds or four and a half pounds. The assistant has the same two hammers as in the forging of sockets.

84. Ils ont aussi besoin d'un ratelier garni de tenailles et de pinces ordinaires, et d'une auge pour les rafraìchir; ils ont besoin d'un calibre, d'une petite lance, et d'un poincon à la marque du maître.

84. They also need a rack filled with tongs and ordinary pincers, and a trough to cool them down; they need a caliber [gauge], a small spear (?), and a punch with the mark of the master.

Page 18

85. Il faut deux étampes de dessous; la première, fig. 23, n'a pas d'étampe de dessus correspondante; elle sert pour former l'épaulement de la lame à sa base; l'autre fig. 22 sert seule pour y mouler l'arrête du dos de la lame, tandis qu'il en faut quatre correspondantes de dessus pour la concavité de la face opposée, voyez fig. 24, 25, 26 et 27.

85. Two bottom dies are needed; the first, Fig. 23, has no corresponding top die; it serves to form the shoulder of the blade at its base; [the other, Fig. 22 above] alone serves to mould the end of the back of the blade, while it requires four top matching dies for the concavity ['fuller' or 'hollow'] of the opposite side, Figs. 24, 25, 26 and 27.

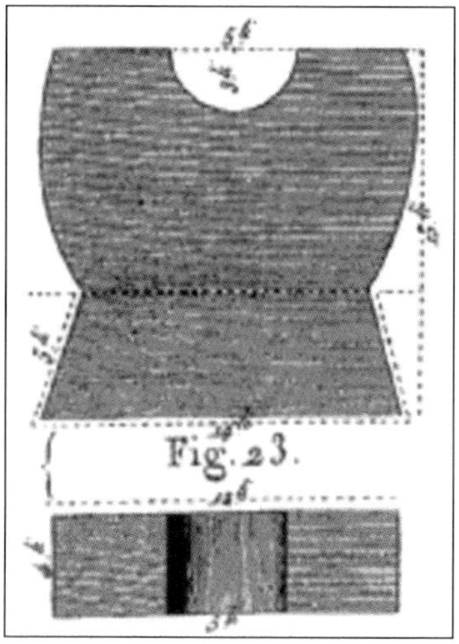

Fig. 23. Die for forming the shoulder of the blade.

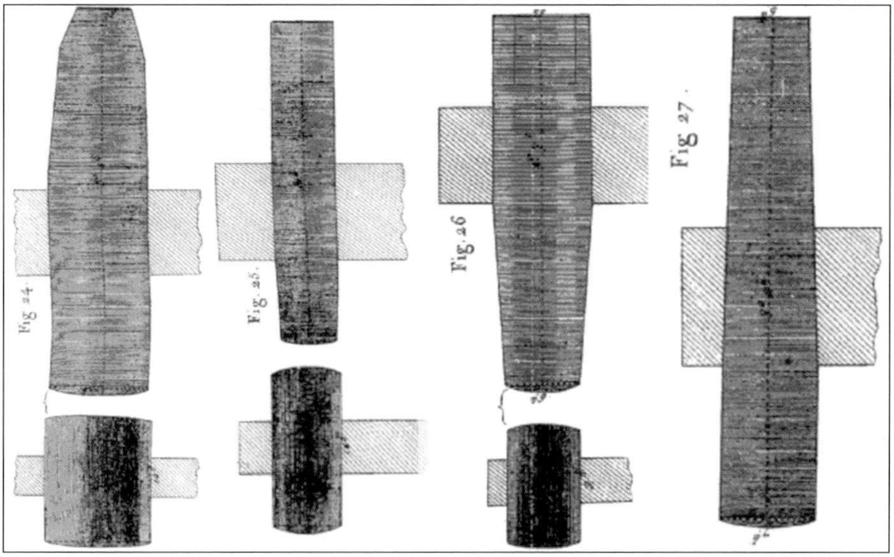

Figs. 24, 25, 26 and 27. Tools for forging the hollow faces of the blade.

PROCÉDÉS	**PROCEDURES**
du forgeur de lames de bayonnettes	***of the bayonet blade forger***

86. Il y a ici autant d'époques que chauffemens, c'est-à-dire la pièce qu'on tire chaque fois du feu pour le travail, est différente de celle sur laquelle on vient d'opérer. Les chauffemens sont au nombre de neuf.

86. There are as many stages here as there are heatings, that is to say, every time the piece is drawn from the fire, is for a different operation from that on which we have just performed. The heatings are nine in number.

Premier chauffement	***First heating***

87. Il pour objet d'étirer le bout du barreau d'acier en écarissant et amincissant, pour obtenir la maquette qu'on en sépare et qui doit former la lame.

87. Its aims are to draw out the steel bar by tapering, to obtain the model [*mood* in Sheffield cutler's terminology] that is then separated and which will form the blade.

88. Le maître retire d'auprès du vent de la forge l'un des barreaux d'acier chauffé à demi blanc; il le porte sur l'enclume, où il le forge avec son compagnon. Il en coupe ensuite le bout a la longeur d'environ sept pouces, et de manière que la partie séparée pèse environ six onces et demi. C'est ce bout destiné à faire une lame, qui se nomme maquette. Le maître peut se servir pour couper, on du

tranchoir dont la queue se loge dans le trou carré de l'enclume, et alors il pose le barreau sur le tranchant, et frappe lui-même, on du tranchoir emmanché qu'il pose sur le barreau, et alors c'est le compagnon qui frappe avec son marteau à deux têtes. Les maîtres en général préfèrent la seconde méthode.

88. The master removes from the blast of the forge one of the bars of steel heated half white [?]; he places it on the anvil and he forges it with his companion. He then cuts the end about seven inches long, so that the separated part weighs about six and a half ounces. This, which is called model [*mood* in English terminology], is then used to make the blade. In cutting off the mood, the master uses one of the cutters which is housed in the square hole of the anvil; he puts the bar on the cutter and strikes it himself, or he places one of the chisels on the bar, and then it is the assistant who strikes with his double-headed hammer. Masters in general prefer the second method.

Page 19

89. Le compagnon s'occupe à passer ces maquettes à mesure que le maître les détache, et il en fait trois tas; l'un, de celles qui pesent six onces et demie juste; un autre, de celles qui pesent un peu plus; et le troisième, de celles qui pesent un peu moins.

89. The assistant takes these models [moods] as the master detaches them, and he makes three heaps of them; one contains models which weigh just six and a half ounces; another, of those a little more; and the third, of those which weigh a little less.

90. Il fait aussi trois tas des douilles, a raison de la grosseur de leurs masselotes. Il insère les maquettes légères dans les douilles dont les masselotes sont les plus grosses, et les lourdes, dans celles dont les masselotes sont foibles; et c'est conformément à cette convenance, qu'on les soudera l'une sur l'autre.

90. He also makes three heaps of sockets, based on their weights. He inserts the light moods into the heavy sockets, and the heavy ones into the light sockets, to match them for welding to one another.

91. Si par une erreur qu'on ne commet guères, il se trou voit des maquettes beaucoup trop lourdes ou trop légères, on rebuteroit celles-ci, et on retrancheroit quelque chose de celles-là.

91. If, by chance there were moods too heavy or too light, they would be rejected and a part cut off to prevent them being used in error.

Deuxième chauffement ***Second heating***

92. On chauffe à la fois une douille par la masselote, en la tenant avec une pince dont une des branches entre dans la douille, et une maquette par le gros

bout, en prenant le petit bout dans une tenaille. Aussi tôt que ces parties sont parvenus au rouge de cerise, le maître porte la douille sur l'enclume et chanfrine la masselote, en tournant le biais vers la douille; et, pendant ce tems-là, le compagnon chanfrine aussi maquette, de manière qui les deux chanfrins s'appliquent l'un sur l'autre pour former la soudure. On reporte aussi tôt les deux pièces ay feu, et quand elles sont parvenues au blanc suant et étincellant, le maître les prend toutes deux, chacune d'une main, et les applique l'une sur l'autre sur l'enclume. Le compagnon frappe aussi-tôt vîte et a petits coups de la tête de sonne marteau a panne, jusqu'à ce que le maître juge la soudure fait. Celui-ci desserre alors la tenaille et la retire; et il se met à forgeur carrément avec le compagnon, jusqu'au tiers environ de la longeur que devra avoir de lame, à partir de sa naissance.

92. At the same time, the end of the neck of a socket is heated, holding the socket with one branch of the tongs in the socket, and a mood at the wide end, taking the small end into a pincer. As soon as these parts have reached the cherry red, the master carries the socket to the anvil and chamfers the end of the neck, turning the bias *[slope]* towards the socket; and during this time, the assistant chamfers a blade, so that the two chamfers match one another to form the weld. The two pieces are immediately returned to the hearth and when they have reached the sparkling white heat, the master takes them both, each with one hand, and applies them to one another on the anvil. The assistant strikes as early and quickly as he can with the hammer head, until the master deems the weld to be done. He then loosens the pincer and removes it; and he begins to forge with the companion, up to about a third of the length of the blade from its root.

Page 20

93. Il pose ensuite le coude et la douille dans le dressoir fixe, et avec le dressoir à main qu'il applique tout près il tord la maquette a sa naissance, de manière à placer une des carres au droit de la douille. Celle-ci sera aplatie dans la suite du travail; mais la carre opposée formera l'arrête du dos de la lame. Il pose ensuite la naissance de la lame horisontalement et la douille en bas sur-l'étampe, fig. 23, qui est fixée sur le bord de l'enclume; et pour former l'embase de la lame, il frappe successivement de la tête de son marteau sur les deux faces plates de la maquette dans la partie opposée à l'étampe, en faisant faire à la pièce un huitième de tour de chaque côté sur cette étampe; l'étampe laisse son empreinte sur la partie qui y a tête appliquée et la séparation se marque dans cette partie entre le coude et la lame. Le maître frappe ensuite quelques coups de la panne de son marteau, mais de biais en recommençant le même mouvement, pour retirer de la matière vers le haut, à la naissance du dos de la lame.

93. He then places the elbow and the socket in the fixed dresser, and with the hand-dresser applied close he twists the model *[mood]* at its root,

so as to place one of the edges to the right of the socket. This one will be flattened in the continuation of the work; but the opposite square will form the ridge of the back of the blade. He then lays the root of the blade horizontally and the socket down on the die, Fig. 23, which is fixed on the face of the anvil, and to form the base of the blade, he strikes successively with the head of his hammer on the two flat faces of the model [mood] in the part opposite to the stamp, by making the piece rotate an eighth of a turn of each side on this stamp; the stamp leaves its imprint on the part which has been hammered there and the separation between the elbow and the blade is made. The master then strikes a few strokes with the pein of his hammer, but on the sides, starting again the same movement, to move the material upwards to begin forming of the back of the blade.

Troisième chauffement ***Third heating***

94. Il n'a pour objet que de continuer de forger carrément et en amincissant depuis le tiers on le milieu où on est resté, jusqu'au bout. La chaude se donne à demi-blanc. Le maître et le compagnon forgent d'abord ensemble; mais sur la fin, le maître forge seul, et il s'assure si la partie écarrie a la longeur précise de onze pouces qu'il doit lui donner.

94. It only remains to continue forging squarely and slimming down from the centre towards the point. The heat is half-white. The master and the companion first forge together; but at the point the master forges alone, and he makes sure that the forged blade has the precise length of eleven inches.

95. Le compagnon emploie le temps qui lui reste libre, à examiner si, parmi les pièces qui ont subi cette opération, il n'en est pas qui aient quelques crevasses de brùlure, et il enlève ces crevasses à la lime.

95. The assistant uses the time which remains free to him, to examine whether, among the pieces which have undergone this operation, there are some which have some cracks/ faults from burning, and he removes these with a file.

Page 21
Quatrième chauffement ***Fourth heating***

96. Ce chauffement et le suivant ont pour objet de commencer à former sur l'étampe, fig. 22, l'arrête du dos de la lame. Om n'emploie ni dans l'un ni dans l'autre aucune étampe de dessus.

96. This heating and the following are intended to begin to form with the die, Fig. 22, the back of the blade. No top dies are used.

97. Il y toujours deux ou trois pièces au feu, et celle qui sort d'auprès du vent de la tuyère, y est remplacée aussi-tôt par une autre, jusqu'à ce qu'il n'en reste plus.

97. There are always two or three pieces in the fire, and the one coming out from close to the blast from the bellows, is replaced by another until all have been worked.

98. On graisse l'étampe avec de l'huile de navette ou du sain-doux en commençant, et toutes les fois qu'on le juge nécessaire. Il faut nétoyer le fond de l'étampe chaque fois, et le mieux est de la graisser aussi chaque fois. Quelques forgeurs recommandent au compagnon de la rafraîchir souvent avec de l'eau qu'il y jette en la prenant dans l'auge avec le creux de la main; d'autres forgeurs blâment cette méthode; ceux qui l'adoptent, craignent que l'étampe ne se détrempe, et ceux qui la rejettent assurent que cela n'arrive pas, si on ne chauffe qu'au dégré convenable.

98. The die is greased with shuttle oil or lard at the outset, and whenever it is deemed necessary. It is necessary to clean the bottom of the die every time, and it is best to grease it also each time. Some forgers recommend the assistant cools it often with water, which he throws into the channel with the hollow of his hand; other forgers reject this practice; those who adopt it fear that the stamp may be softened, [by heat from the hot forging] and those who reject it assure that this does not happen if the forging is only heated to the proper degree.

99. Ce dégré est le rouge vif.

99. This degree is bright red.

100. Le maître porte la pièce sur l'étampe, en dirigeant constaminent sa carre extérieure vers le fond de l'angle aigu; il ne donne à la pièce que des mouvemens d'avant en arrière, et aucun mouvement de côté. Le compagnon et lui frappent de la tête de leur marteau sur la carre opposée, afin de l'effacer entièrement et d'applatir complettement la face intérieure.

100. The master places the piece on the die, directing its outer edge towards the bottom of the acute angle; he only moves the piece backwards and forwards with no movement sideways. The assistant and he strike with their hammers on the opposite square, in order to erase it completely and completely flatten it.

101. Cette quatrième chaude ne suffit que pour dégrossir ainsi la lame depuis le coude jusqu'aux deux tiers de sa longueur.

101. This fourth heat is only enough to roughly shape the blade from the elbow to two-thirds of its length.

Cinquième chauffement ***Fifth heating***

102. Dans celui-ci qui est de la même nature, on achève l'opération sur le dernier tiers jusqu'à la point.

102. In this one, which is of the same nature, the operation on the last third to the point is completed.

Page 22

103. S'il arrive que la pièce se fausse dans le travail, le maître emploie le marteau et quelquefois le dressoir.

103. If it happens that the piece is not quite right, the master uses the hammer and sometimes the dresser to correct it.

Sixième chauffement ***Sixth heating***

104. On se propose ici de perfectionner et de terminer l'ouvrage, en employant les quatre étampes de dessus, qui déterminent la forme de la face intérieure de la lame. Cette face est d'abord applatie jusqu'à un pouce de la base, et elle prend ensuite une concavité sensible jusque près de la pointe.

104. It is proposed here to perfect and finish the work, using the four stamps above, which determine the shape of the inner face of the blade. This face is first flattened an inch from the base, and then takes a sensible concavity towards the point.

105. On chauffe quatre fois au rouge de cerise.

105. It is heated four times to a cherry red.

106. Cette fois en chauffe près le coude, et après avoir posé l'arrête du dos de la lame dans l'étampe de dessous, fig. 22, qui sert constamment jusqu'à la fin, le maître pose sur la face opposée l'étampe de dessus, fig. 24, dont la forme applatie, ou qui du moins à très-peu de courbure, se moule sur cette face à la naissance de la lame, par l'effet des coups du marteau à deux têtes du compagnon.

106. This time heating near the elbow, and having placed the ridge of the back of the blade in the bottom die, Fig. 22, which serves constantly until the process is finished, the master places on the opposite side the stamp used from above, Fig. 24, with a face that is flat, or at least has very little curvature, is used to form the face at the start of the blade, by the effect of the blows of the double headed hammer of the assistant.

107. Le maître achève ensuite, en forgeant seul sur l'enclume, de donner à cette partie de la lame la forme qu'elle doit avoir, et particulièrement aux arrêtes, qui doivent être mousses, comme on le voit fig. 2 et 3.

107. The master then finishes, by forging alone on the anvil, to give this part of the blade the shape which it must have, and particularly to the edges, which must be formed as shown in Figs. 2 and 3 [above].

108. Le compagnon frappe ensuite deux poincons sur la face applatie; celui du maître forgeur et celui de l'affineur qui lui a fourni l'acier.

108. The assistant then strikes two marks on the flattened face; that of the forging master and that of the refiner who supplied him with the steel.

Septième chauffement ***Seventh heating***

109. Ici on opère sur les deux tiers environ de la lame, à partir de la face applatie qu'on a formée dans le chauffement précédent. Le maître emploie les deux étampes de dessus, fig. 26 et 27. Il commence par la plus étroite, qui étend mieux le maître, et qui la fait mieux pénétrer dans l'angle de l'étampe de dessous, et il emploie ensuite la plus large, dont la forme s'adapte mieux à la concavité que doit prendre la face intérieure de la lame, surtout vers la base.

109. Here one operates on about two thirds of the blade, from the flattened face which was formed in the previous heating. The master uses the two top stamps, Figs. 26 and 27. It starts at the narrowest point, which the master extends better, and makes it better penetrate into the angle of the die below, and then employs the widest, the form of which is better adapted to the concavity that the inner side of the blade must have, especially towards the base.

Page 23

110. Si la pièce se fausse, il emploie le marteau pour la redresser, et quelque fois le dressoir, et le finit, comme dans le chauffement précédent, par la forger seul sur l'enclume, et particulièrement par donner aux arrêtes la forme requise, voyez fig. 3.

110. If the piece is not quite correct he uses the hammer to straighten it, and sometimes the dresser, and finishes it, as in the preceding heating, by forging it alone on the anvil, and especially by giving the edges the required form see Fig. 3.

111. Il est bon d'avertir que si, dans ce moment ou dans tout autre, le maître y découvroit une paille, ou une autre défectuosité remédiable, il la feroit enlever à la lime par le compagnon; et que, s'il le falloit, il chaufferoit exprés la pièce pour réparer le défaut.

111. It is good to note that if at this moment or at any other, the master discovers a small flaw or another remediable defect, he would get it removed by the assistant with a file; or, if it were necessary, he would heat up the piece to repair the defect.

Huitième chauffement ***Eighth heating***

112. Il ne sert qu'à terminer l'opération précédent jusqu'à la pointe, avec les deux mêmes étampes arrondies, et à porter la lame a la longeur prescrite.

112. It only remains to complete the preceding operation up to the point, with the same two rounded stamps, and to bring the blade to the prescribed length.

Neuvième et dernier chauffement ***Ninth and last heating***

113. Il se donne sur le dernier tiers de la lame, et il a pour objet d'en perfectionner entièrement la forme. On y emploie l'étampe, fig. 25, qui est la plus étroite des quatre. Le maître achève au marteau sur l'enclume.

113. He works on the last third of the blade, and his object is to perfect the whole form. The die used, Fig. 25, is the narrowest of the four. The master finishes with a hammer on the anvil.

ARTICLE SIXIEME **SIXTH ARTICLE**
Contrôle de la lame au magasin. *Inspecting the blade at the store.*

114. Toutes les pièces terminées ainsi par le forgeur de lames sont portées au magasin pour y être examinées une à une par le contrôleur d'armes noires, qui vérifie les dimensions des différentes parties de lame, et s'il ne lui reste pas quelque défectuosité qui ne puisse pas être emportée à l'aiguisage. Tout se passe comme dans les examens précédens, et on marque du poincon du contrôleur d'armes noires, sur le coude, les pièces recues.

114. All the parts thus completed by the blade forger are brought to the store for examination by the black weapons inspector, who checks the dimensions of the different parts of the blade, and if there is any defect which cannot be removed during grinding. Everything proceeds as in the previous examinations, and the mark of the controller of black weapons is stamped on the elbow of the pieces received.

Page 24

ARTICLE SEPTIEME **SEVENTH ARTICLE**
Tremper la lame de la bayonnette. *Heat treatment of the blade of the bayonet.*

115. L'acier a la propriété d'acquérir de la dureté lorsqu'ayant été rouge à feu, on le réfroidit subitement. Le dégré de dureté qu'il acquiert dépend:

    1. De la quantité relative de charbon qui est entrée dans la combinaison avec le fer qui en est la base; c'est-adire-dire qu'il devient d'autant plus dur dans cette opération, qu'il est plus acier.

2. Cette dureté croit aussi avec la différence entre la température chaude qu'il avoit éprouvée et la température froide à laquelle on l'a exposé, et avec la rapidité du passage de l'une à l'autre.

115. Steel has the property of acquiring hardness when, at red heat, it is suddenly cooled. The degree of hardness that it acquires depends on:

1. The relative amount of carbon that has entered into combination with the iron is a defining property; that is to say, it becomes all the harder in this operation when the carbon level is higher.
2. This hardness also depends on the difference in temperature between the hot steel and the cold water, and with the rapidity of the cooling.

116. En acquiérant de la dureté par la trempe, l'acier prend un peu plus de volume qu'il n'en avoit; il garde des dimensions approchantes de celles que la chaleur lui avoit données, et que le refroidissement subit l'a empêché de perdre.

116. In hardening, the steel takes a little more volume than it had; it retains dimensions approaching those which the expansion from heat had created during forging, and which the sudden cooling prevented it from losing.

117. Il suit de la, comme le fait le démontre, qu'une pièce d'acier doit tendre à se tourmenter, à se déformer, même à se briser à la trempe, dans les circonstances suivantes:

1. Lorsque ses parties ne sont pas précisément du même acier, ou du moins des mêmes aciers semblablement distribués; ce qui arrive lorsque l'affinage n'en a pas été bien fait;
2. Lorsqu'elles n'ont pas éprouvé toutes également le même dégré de chaleur au feu, et le même refroidissement dans l'eau; au du moins, lorsque ces dégrés n'ont pas été les mêmes pour les parties semblables et semblablement posées; car des efforts inégaux de chaque partie pour changer de volume, tendent à changer la position respective des parties.

117. It follows from the fact, as it is demonstrated, that a piece of steel must be put under stress to deform itself, or even break with hardening and tempering, under the following circumstances:

1. When its parts are not exactly of the same steel, or at least the same steels similarly distributed, which is what happens when the refining has not been well done.
2. When they have not all been equally heated and quenched in water; at least, when these temperatures have not been the same for similar and similarly placed parts; the unequal efforts of each part to change its volume, tend to change the respective positions of the parts.

Page 25

118. Du bon acier découvre à la trempe, quand elle est bonne: voici en quoi consiste cette seconde propriété. Quand on fait rougir de l'acier entre les charbons, il s'y couvre toujours d'une pellicule d'acier brûlé, qui en rendroit la surface noirâtre, si on le laissoit refroidir lentement. L'acier se débarrasse de lui-même de cette pellicule, quand on le trempe; et il l'éclat métallique a sa surface, quand on le retire de l'eau.

118. Good steel is tempered well and this is what this second property consists of. When steel is made red hot in a bed of charcoal, it is always covered with a burnt steel film, which renders the surface blackish if it is allowed to cool slowly. This film is lost when it is quenched and it has a metallic lustre on its surface when it is removed from the water.

119. Une troisième propriété de l'acier, cest de prendre de la couleur au recuit. On recuit l'acier après la trempe, c'est-à-dire, qu'on lui donne un dégré de chaleur incapable de la rougir, afin de détruire l'état de contraction où la trempe l'a mis, et qui l'exposeroit à rompre au premier effort. Il prend successivement, en s'échauffant, des couleurs a sa surface, parmi lesquelles on distingue trois nuances très-sensibles: ce sont pour l'acier de forge qui n'a été blanchi ni à la meule, ni à la lime,

1. le jaunâtre, couleur de paille
2. le bleuâtre
3. le grisâtre cendré

On arrête le recuit au dégré ou on le veut, en retirant la pièce du feu, et on la plonge dans l'eau. Elle conserve d'autant plus dureté, qu'on la retirée moins chaude.

C'est d'après ces propriétés que le trempeur se dirige.

119. A third property of steel is to show colours when annealing. The steel is annealed after hardening, that is to say, it is given a degree of heat less than red in order to destroy the brittleness caused by quenching and which would allow it to break under stress. It takes successively, while warming up, colours on its surface, among which are distinguished three very sensitive shades: it is used for steel from the forge which has not had its surface cleaned either with the millstone, nor with the file,

1. yellowish, straw colour
2. bluish
3. grey or greyish

We stop the annealing at the required temperature, removing the piece from the fire, and we plunge it into water. It retains greater hardness if heated to a lower degree.

It is by these properties that the hardener is guided.

[At this point there are 2 pages devoted to describing the workshop and equipment of the temperer at Klingenthal which have been omitted for brevity.]

Page 28

Procédé du trempeur pour la bayonette ***Process of hardening the bayonet***

131. Il commence par dresser a froid les bords de la lame, s'ils en ont besoin.

131. He begins by cold-setting (straightening) the edges of the blade if they need it.

132. Si l'acier est tel qu'il convient, la chaleur à donner à la lame est toujours le rouge de cerise ordinaire; c'est toujours celle que donne le trempeur a la pièce par laquelle il commence. Il la présente au feu, la douille en haut; c'est la douille qu'il prend dans la pince; il donne à la pièce des mouvemens d'avant et d'arrière, pour que la chaleur se répande également sur tout la lame. Quand elle est à son point de chaleur, il la retire; il passe deux fois l'arrête du dos de la lame, d'un bout à l'autre, dans le residu mouillé d'écailles de fer qui est amoncelé sur une petite planche posée sur le bord de l'auge, et il la plonge dans l'eau dans cette même position, c'est-à-dire, l'arrête du dos en bas, en commencant par la pointe et tirant a lui en inclinant, à mesure qu'il enfonce.

132. If steel is suitable, the heat to be given to the blade is always ordinary cherry red; it is always that which the forger gives to the piece to commence working. He presents it to the fire, the socket above and held in the tongs and he moves the blade around so that it heats equally all over. When the blade is at the correct temperature, it is withdrawn and passed twice through moistened iron scales which are heaped up on a small board placed on the edge of the trough, and he plunges it into the water in this same position, that is to say, starting with the point and keeping it inclined while it is submerged.

133. En la retirent, il examine si l'acier découvre bien; si cela est, il recuire cette lame jusqu'à la couleur bleuâtre.

133. In withdrawing it, he examines whether the steel appears good; if it is, the blade will be annealed to a blue colour.

134. Si cela n'étoit pas, il ne la recuiroit que jusqu'au jaunâtre couleur de paille; mais comme cela indiqueroit un acier foible, il chaufferoit la pièce suivante un peu davantage, et ainsi de suite jusqu'à ce qu'il eût attaint le degré qui mettra la pièce dans le cas de bien découvrir à la trempe, et c'est à ce degré qu'il se fixera pour toutes les autres pièces, qu'il faudra recuire alors jusqu'au bleuâtre.

134. If it were not so, he would only retrieve it when it was a yellowish straw colour; but as this would indicate a weak steel, he would heat the next blade

a little more, and so on until he had attained the degree which will make the blade harden well, and it is to this degree that all the other blades will be heated and which will have to then be annealed until blue.

Page 29

135. Il ne faudroit recuire jusqu'au grisâtre que dans le cas où la lame trempée, après n'avoir été chauffée qu'au rouge sombre, découvriroit. Cela indiqueroit dans l'acier une dureté que n'a pas celui qu'on employe au Klingenthal pour les bayonnettes.

135. It would only be found necessary to anneal until greyish in the case where the blade was hardened after having been heated only to dark red. This would indicate in the steel a hardness different from that used at Klingenthal for bayonets.

136. Lorsqu'en retirent la lame du feu, elle lui paroît plus chaude qu'il ne le desire, il passe l'arrête du dos dans le residu mouillé d'écailles de fer; trois fois au lieu dedeux.

136. When the blade is removed from the fire, if it seems hotter to him than he wishes, he passes the ridge on the back in the moistened residue of iron scales three times instead of two.

137. Si elle lui paroît, au contraire, moins chaude, il ne la passe qu'une.

137. If it appears to him, on the contrary, less hot, he passes it only once.

138. La bayonnette est trempée; il s'agit de la recuire.

138. The bayonet is hardened; it is now ready for annealing [tempering].

139. Le bonne méthode pour cela est de ne passer la lame sur le charbon allumé et non pas au travers.

139. The best way to do this is to pass the blade over the hot charcoal and not through it.

140. Le trempeur la retire lorsque la couleur qu'elle a prise lui paroît celle qui convient; mais pour s'en assurer, pendant qu'il la retire d'une main, il tient de l'autre un linge sec avec lequel il frotte la lame au jour pour l'examiner mieux. S'il se trou voit que la chaleur du recuit eût été trop forte, il faudroit chauffer au rouge et tremper de nouveau. Le trempeur ne s'expose guères à cette perte de tems. Si la chaleur, au contraire, a été trop foible, ce qui arrive quelquefois, il repasse la lame sur les charbons. Si la couleur indique la chaleur convenable, ce qui arrive presque toujours, il n'est plus question que de redresser la lame, si elle en a besoin.

140. The annealer removes it when the colour which it has taken appears to him to be the right one; but to make sure of it, while he takes it out with one hand, he holds in the other a dry cloth with which he rubs the blade to examine it better in the daylight. If it be found that the heat of the tempering would have been too high, it would be necessary to heat to red and to quench again. The hardener is hardly exposed to this loss of time. If the heat, on the contrary, has been too weak, which happens sometimes, he passes the blade over the coals again. If the colour indicates the proper heat, which is almost always the case, it is only a question of straightening the blade, if it needs it.

141. C'est ce qu'il fait en portant le pièce aussitôt sur son enclume, en la placant dans la canelure qui lui convient en frappant des coups gradués avec la tête on avec la panne de son marteau, sur toutes les élévations qui se présentent, lorsqu'il donne à la lame des mouvemens d'avant et d'arrière, ou enfin en se servant s'il est nécessaire, du dressoir fixe et du dressoir a main.

141. He does this by immediately placing it in the suitable groove on his anvil and, while moving the blade, striking graduated blows with the pein of his hammer on all the imperfections, or finally, if it is necessary, using the fixed dresser and the hand dresser.

142. Aussitôt que la lame est droite, il la plonge dans l'eau. L'acier trempé ne se prêteroit pas a froid aux coups de marteau; mais une foible chaleur lui suffit pour les supporter.

142. As soon as the blade is straight, he plunges it into the water. Hardened steel would not lend itself to cold hammering; but a low heat suffices.

Page 30

Aiguiser la lame de la bayonnette ***Grinding the bayonet blade***

143. Une aiguiserie est usine ou une roue a eau, dont les révolutions sont supposées au Klingenthal de vingt a vingt-cinq par minute, fait mouvoir.

    1. Une meule de grès nommée la grande meule, dont l'epaisseur est d'environ sept a huit pouces, et dont le diamètre varie depuis celui d'environ sept pieds, qu'elle a lorsqu'on commence à en faire usage, jusqu'à celui d'environ quatre pieds. Quand elle est usée à ce point, on la casse pour en faire de petites meules, et on la remplace. La grande meule fait huit révolutions pour une de la roue a eau.

143. A grindery is a factory with a water wheel, whose revolutions are supposed to be, at the Klingenthal factory, from twenty to twenty-five per minute.

    1. A sandstone called the great millstone, whose thickness is about seven to eight inches, and whose diameter varies from that of about seven feet,

which it has when one begins to make use of it, down to that of about four feet. At this point, it is used to make small millstones, and it is replaced. The big wheel makes eight revolutions for one of the water-wheel.

144. Dans celle des cinq aiguiseries du Klingenthal, qui passe pour la mieux entendue, le rez-de-chaussée ost dispose pour recevoir de plus.

2. Quatre meules moyennes auxquelles le mouvement est communiqué par des courroies, et qui, si la courroie ne glisse pas, font vingt révolutions pour une de la roue a eau. Les meules qui occupent le plus ordinairement cette place, sont des meules d'un granit tendre et rougeâtre, dont la partie des Vosges ou se trouve le Klingenthal est presqu'entièrement compose. On y pratique, en les usant avec des crochets de fer, des canelures dont les differentes formes sont adaptées a celles des parties qu'on y veut aiguiser. Ces meules s'employent a sec, tandis que celles de grès doivent toujours ètre arrosées d'eau. Le diamétre des meules de granit qui occupent le plus communément cette place, varie de deuz pieds et demi a quinze pouces.
3. Quatre polissoires en bois ou d'autres très-petites meules en grès ou en granit; auxquelles le mouvement est communiqué aussi par des courroies, et qui font quarante huit révolutions pour une de la roue a eau.

144. In the five Klingenthal workshops, which are considered the best, the ground floor can accomodate more.

2. Four medium wheels, to which the movement is communicated by belts, and if the belt does not slip, make twenty revolutions for one of the water-wheel. The grindstones which ordinarily occupy this place are of soft, reddish granite, of which the part of the Vosges where Klingenthal is situated is almost entirely composed. Using iron tools, grooves of different shapes are formed which are adapted to those parts that need to be ground. These millstones are used dry, while those of sandstone must always be used with water. The diameter of the granite millstones which most commonly occupy this place varies from two and a half feet to fifteen inches.

3. Four wooden polishing wheels or other very small grinding stones in sandstone or granite, to which the movement is communicated by belts, make forty-eight revolutions for one of the water wheel.

Page 31

145. Le mouvement est transmis de plus au premier étage par un second renvoi de courroies,

4. A quatre polissoires en bois qui font cinquante révolutions pour une de la roue a eau.

145. The movement is transmitted moreover to the first stage by a second set of belts,

4. Has four wooden polishing wheels that make fifty revolutions for one of the water wheel.

146. Cet état des mouvemens pour tout ce qui tourne par le moyen des courroies, varie dans les aiguiseries selon la fantaisie ou la convenance particulière des maîtres aiguiseurs; car rien ne les empêche de changer les rapports de grandeur des differentes poulies.

146. The speed of rotation of everything driven by belts varies according to the whim or the peculiar convenience of the master grinders, because nothing prevents them from changing the size ratios of the different pulleys.

147. Les changements de cette espece ne peuvent cependant pas se faire au Klingenthal d'un moment à l'autre, et cela mème a un grand inconvénient.

147. The changing of the pulleys, however, cannot be made at Klingenthal from one moment to the next, and this has a great disadvantage.

148. Par example, pour faconner les canelures, en les tournant avec le crochet de fer, il faut que le meule tourne beaucoup moins vite que son train ordinaire, afin que l'ouvrier voye mieux ce qu'il fait; la dépendance des roue entr'elles oblige, pour ce besoin momentané, à suspendre le travail de toutes les autres meules. Ces suspensions momentanées, ajoutées a celles qui ont lieu toutes les fois que la grande meule s'arrête pour quelque autre cause, retardent beaucoup le travail; il paroît cependant facile de les éviter.

148. For example, to shape the grooves by turning them with iron tools, it is necessary that the wheel turns much slower than its ordinary speed so that the workman sees better to perform this task; for this momentary need, it is necessary to suspend the work of all the other wheels. These momentary suspensions, added to those which take place whenever the great wheel stops for some other cause, delay much work; however, it seems easy to avoid them.

149. Toutes les meules, excepte la grande, peuvent s'enlever et se changer avec la plus grande facilite, ainsi que les polissoires. Elles tournent sur deux pointes, et le tasseau mobile qui recoit l'une de ces pointes, se serre et se fixe à volonté au moyen d'un plusiers coins et d'une pièce buttant. On les arrête quand on le veut, en retirant courroie de dessus leur poulie. Les grandes poulies qui menent n'ont point de rebord. Quant a la grande meule, on ne peut l'arrêter, indépendamment de la roue a eau qu'en désenrayant la lanterne qui sert à lui communiquer le mouvement.

149. All grinding wheels, except the big one, can be removed and changed with the greatest ease, as well as polishers. They turn on two points, and the movable

block which receives one of these points, is tightened and fixed at will by means of several wedges against its housing. We stop them when needed by removing the belt from their pulley. The large pulleys that lead have no rim. As for the great millstone, it cannot be stopped independently of the water wheel except by disengaging the lantern gear which serves to communicate the movement to it.

Page 32

150. Il faut avoir la plus grande attention a ce que les meules de granit, et sur-tout celles de grès, n'aient ni fentes Niger sûres; car s'il vient à s'en détacher des morceaux, ils sont sujets à blesser les ouvriers, sur-tout ceux des meules de grès, qui se détachent avec éclat.

150. The greatest attention must be given to the fact that the granite wheels, and especially those of sandstone, have no black cracks; for if it breaks into pieces they are liable to injure the workmen, especially those of the sandstones which fragment easily.

151. Les polissoires sont des meules étroites des bois de chêne. Elles polissent au moyen de l'émeri délaye dans l'huile de navette, dont on enduit les pièces qu'on leur charbon d'aulne ou de hêtre avec lequel on a frotte pour cela leur circonférence. Le charbon s'y attache, et on le fixe dans le fil du bois avec une agathe qui polit cette circonférence, ou avec un morceau de sanguine dure. Les cailloux demi-transparens qu'on désigne ici sous le nom agathe, se trouvent dans le lit de la petite rivière de Neim, qui coule au Klingenthal.

151. The polishers are narrow wheels of oak. They polish by means of a paste of emery and shuttle oil [it has not been possible so far to identify what 'shuttle oil' is] which one coats on the pieces, and charcoal of alder or beech which is rubbed on their circumference. The charcoal is fixed in the grain of the wood with an agate which polishes this circumference, or with a piece of hard red haemetite. The semi-transparent pebbles, which are here called agate, are found in the bed of the little river Neim, which flows at Klingenthal.

152. Il y a des polissoires de vingt-quatre ou trent pouces de diamètre; il y en a de deux pouces au plus. Leurs diamètres et la forme de leurs circonférences doivent s'adapter aux parties sur lesquelles elles doivent agir. Quand leur grandeur le permet, elles sont faites d'assemblage; car c'est toujours le fil du bois qu'elles doivent présenter à la pièce lorsque faire se peut. On doit choisir du chêne âgé et a fil piqueté fin, et de préférence celui qui, place vers le haut des montagnes, en face du midi, avoit son tronc expose aux rayons du soleil: on conseille de le laisser un an ou dix-huit mois dans l'eau avant de

l'employer, pour qu'il ne se travaille pas, et ce seroit le mieux; mais-le-plus souvent on n'a pas cette prévoyance. On ne peut admettre aucun nœud du bois dans les polissoires.

152. There are polishers of twenty-four or thirty inches in diameter; they are two inches wide at most. Their diameters and the shape of their circumferences are adapted to the parts on which they must act. When their size permits, they are composite because it is always the thread [grain] of the wood that they must present on the edge when possible [this would be the same as devices known as 'glazing wheels' used in the Sheffield cutlery trades made from segments]. We should choose old oak with a fine grain, and preferably one which grows towards the top of the mountains on the southern side and had its trunk exposed to the rays of the sun: we advise to leave it a year or eighteen months in water before using it, so that it does not warp, but often one does not have this foresight. There must be no knots in the polishing wheels.

153. Il faut de tems en tems rafraìchir le grain des polissoires et des meules, et leur en donner un nouveau.

153. It takes time to refresh the rims of polishers and grinders and to expose a new surface.

Page 33

154. Pour les polissoires, on se sert d'un ciseau de menuisier qu'on appuye sur une pièce de bois qui se place exprès.

154. For polishers, we use a carpenter's chisel for that purpose.

155. Pour les meules de granit tendre, on se sert d'un crochet de fer, qu'on chanfrine, et qu'on faconne a froid au bout de la barre avec un marteau ordinaire, sur un tas de vingt a trente livres que l'aiguiseur doit avoir pour cet usage.

155. For soft granite wheels, we use a chamfered iron hook, that is cold-formed at the end of the bar with a hammer of twenty to thirty pounds which the grinder must have for this purpose.

156. Pour les meules de grès, on se sert du grand marteau courbe deux pannes tranchantes, qu'on nomme hachoir, parce qu'il sert à faire des hachures sur la meule.

156. For the sandstones, the large, curved hammer is used with two sharp edges, which is called a chopper [in the Sheffield trades this is referred to as a 'hack hammer'], because it is used to make hatches [cross-hatched cuts] on the rim of the grindstone.

157. Si la meule a perdu sa rondeur, ce qui arrive assez fréquemment, parce qu'elles sont plus tendres dans certaines parties que dans d'autres, il faut, après s'en ètre assure, en la faisant tourner et l'approchant avec un crochet, de fer bien fixe, l'user avec ce mème crochet toujours bien fixe, qu'on fait avancer jusqu'à ce qu'il touche toute la circonférence.

157. If the wheel has lost its roundness, which happens quite frequently, because they are softer in some parts than in others, it must, after being checked, be turned by using an iron hook, always fixed well, so that one advances the hook until it touches all the circumference when it rotates.

158. L'aiguiseur taille des morceaux de bois pour y appliquer les pièces par une de leurs faces, afin qu'elles ne se courbent point lorsqu'il appuie la face opposée sur la meule. Il a besoin pour cela d'une hachette.

158. The grinder cuts pieces of wood to apply to one of the faces of the pieces, so that they do not bend when he presses the opposite face on the grinding wheel [in the Sheffield trades these are referred to as 'flat sticks']. He needs a hatchet for that.

159. Le morceau de bois qu'il employe de cette manière pour la bayonnette, est creuse pour recevoir le dos de la lame. On le nommera support.

159. The piece of wood that he uses in this way for the bayonet is hollow to receive the back of the blade. We will call it a support.

160. Il doit toujours avoir à côté de lui, quand il aiguise sur les meules, une auge pleine d'eau pour y plonger les pièces, quand il craint qu'elles ne se détrempent en s'échauffant. Cette auge est ordinairement taillée dans une pièce de bois de trois à quatre pieds de long.

160. He must always have beside him, when he sharpens on the millstones, a trough full of water to plunge the pieces into it, when he fears that they will become softened by being heated up. This trough is usually carved in a piece of wood three to four feet long.

161. Il faut escabelles à toutes les places, pour que l'ouvrier puisse s'y asseoir; elles s'inclinent vers la meule.

161. There must be stools in all places, so that the workman can sit there because they lean over the grindstone.

162. La disposition du jour n'est bonne que quand l'ouvrier l'a en face ou sa gauche: la meule tournant en dedans on de haut en bas, par rapport a lui.

162. Their disposition of the day depends whether the workman has the grindstone in front of him or his left: the grindstone rotating anti-clockwise or towards him.

Page 34

163. Pour travailler à la grande meule, l'ouvrier a besoin non-seulement d'un tablier, mais de genouillères en cuir, car il se sert souvent du genou pour appuyer la pièce contre la meule.

163. To work at the large grindstone, the worker needs not only an apron, but leather knee pads, because he often uses the knees to press the piece against the grinding wheel.

164. Il tient auprès de lui un creux de la forme extérieure et de l'epaisseur de la piêce; on le nomme fourreau. La pièce doit y entrer juste après l'aiguisage. Ce fourreau est de fer forge, et monte sur une pièce de bois.

164. He holds near him a sheath for the blade. The blade should just enter after grinding. This scabbard is of wrought iron and is fitted upon a piece of wood.

165. L'ouvrier a aussi un calibre qui lui sert à vérifier les autres dimensions.

165. The worker also has a template [gauge] to check the other dimensions.

166. Il lui faut un marteau a deux têtes, de quinze ou seize livres, pour frapper les coins et les pièces buttantes, et pour piler, sur une plaque de fer coule à rebord de trois cotes, l'émeri qui reste sur le tamis.

166. He needs a hammer with two heads, fifteen or sixteen pounds, to strike the wedges and the bearing blocks, and to crush, on a plate of iron with a rim on three sides, the emery which remains on the sieve.

167. Il lui faite de l'huile pour délayer l'émeri. On se contente d'huile de navette pour les lames de bayonnettes; mais pour celles des sabres, il est bon de n'employer que de l'huile d'olive, qui se nétoye mieux; car au brunissage, les parties on l'huile n'a pas été parfaitement enlevée, font tache.

167. He uses oil to mix with the emery. We are satisfied with shuttle oil for bayonet blades; but for swords, it is good to use only olive oil, which is better cleaned; because in burnishing, the parts where the oil has not been perfectly removed become stained.

168. Il lui faut enfin un poincon pour frapper sa marque.

168. Finally, he needs a punch to strike his mark.

169. Les meules et polissoires nécessaires pour la bayonnette sont: la grande meule, une autre meule de grès d'environs six pouces de diamètre pour la face plate de l'intérieure de la lame, et pour commencer la partie en gouttière; une autre de grès de deux a trois pouces seulement, pour achever cette partie; une meule de granit tendre a canelure de vingt-quatre a trente pouces environ

de diamètre pour les bords de la lame. Il faut enfin trois polissoires, l'une de vingt-quatre pouces de diamètre; une autre de six pouces, et la dernière de ceux a trois pouces.

169. The grinding wheels and polishers necessary for the bayonet are: the large grinding wheel, another sandstone grinding wheel of about six inches in diameter for the flat face of the blade's interior, and to begin the part in the gutter; another sandstone of only two to three inches to complete this part; a millstone of soft granite with ribs of about twenty-four to thirty inches in diameter for the edges of the blade. Finally, there are three polishers; one of twenty-four inches in diameter, another six inches, and the last three inches.

Page 35

Procedés de l'aiguisage de la bayonnette. Procedures for grinding the bayonet.

170. Cette opération se partage naturellement en trois tems, celui de l'aiguisage proprement dit, celui du polissage a l'émeri et celui du brunissage au charbon mais il faut distinguer aussi le travail à faire sur le dos de la lame, de celui qui se fait sur sa face intérieure. L'aiguiseur opère ordinairement sur cinquante on soixante bayonnettes, qui doivent être l'ouvrage de deux journées de lui et de son aide. Chaque opération se fait sur toutes successivement, et on ne reprend la première que pour une opération nouvelle.

170. This operation is naturally divided into three parts; that of grinding itself, that of polishing with emery and that of burnishing with charcoal but it is necessary to distinguish also the work to be done on the back of the blade from that on its inside face. The grinder usually operates on fifty or sixty bayonets, which is two days' work for him and his assistant. Each operation is done on all successively, and we only take one as an example.

Aiguisage ***Grinding***

171. 1. Il faut mettre la lame a sa longeur précise, en usant la pointe si elle en a besoin. Cela se fait en la présentant directement à l'une des faces plates de la meule canelée. L'aiguiser se place donc de côté, debout ou assis, de manière que la meule tourne à gauche par rapport à lui; il tient la bayonnette d'une main en appuyant la lame sur le tasseau qui porte le pivot de l'axe de la meule, et, de l'autre, il tient le fourreau pour vérifier la longeur.
2. Il se porte à la grande meule, et il s'asseoit devant, de manière qu'elle tourne de haut en bas par rapport a lui. Il y aiguise en travers, et carrément, les deux bords de la lame; il blanchit l'arrête du dos, et il forme la point en usant les trois faces: il vérifie les largeurs en présentant au fourreau.

171. 1. It is necessary to make the blade the precise length, if it needs it. This is done by presenting the tip directly to one of the flat sides of the grooved

grinding wheel. Sharpening is therefore placed aside. Standing or sitting, so that the grinding wheel turns anticlockwise with respect to him; he holds the bayonet with one hand while pressing the blade on the bearing block which carries the pivot of the axis of the wheel, and he uses the scabbard to check the length.

2. He transfers to the large grindstone, and he sits before it, so that it rotates in line with him. He grinds square across the face of the blade and the two edges of the blade; he grinds the edge of the rib at the back, and forms the point using the three faces and checks the widths using the opening in the scabbard.

Page. 36

172. Cette opération faite sur toutes les bayonnette, il quitte la grande meule pour n'y plus revenir.

3. Il retourne à la meule canelée, et se place encore de côté, pour aiguiser en long, sur les canelures, les pans creux du dos de la lame. Cela se fait en trois tems, a cause de la chaleur que prennent les pièces qu'il faut plonger dans l'auge a chaque tems pour qu'elles ne se détrempent pas; il aiguise d'abord un des pans creux depuis la base jusqu'aux deux tiers environ de la lame. Il l'appuye sur la canelure, en pressent de la main sur l'autre tiers. Il en fait autant pour toutes.
4. Il aiguise de même l'autre pan creux do dos, sur le même longeur.
5. Enfin, il aiguise successivement les deux pans creux sur l'autre tiers, jusqu'à la pointe. Ceci exige une canelure plus étroite. Toutes les fois qu'il a des doutes, il vérifie avec son calibre la courbure des pans creux.

172. This operation done on the bayonet, the use of the large grindstone is finished.

3. He returns to the grooved millstone, and still stands to one side, to grind along each side of the rib on the back of the blade. This is done in three stages, because of the heating of the blades which must be plunged into the trough of water each time so that they do not become softened; he first grinds one of the hollows from the base to about two-thirds of the blade. He presses it in the groove, his other hand pressing his hand on the part not being ground. He does the same for all.
4. He then grinds the other hollow on the back to the same length.
5. Finally, he grinds successively the two hollows on the remaining third of the blade, to the tip. This requires a narrower groove. Whenever he has doubts, he checks with his gauge the curvature of the hollows.

Face Intérieure de la lame. *The inner face of the blade*

173. La concavité de cette face se distingue en trois parties; l'une a la base, sur environ un pouce de longueur, qui a très-peu de courbure; une seconde, qui en a beaucoup d'avantage, depuis cette première jusqu'à la moitié de la

longueur de la lame; et une troisième, depuis celle-ci jusqu'à a la pointe, dont la courbure est ordinairement plus grande, et devroit cependant être la même. Cette dernière s'aiguise en long: on la polit et on la brunit; les deux autres s'aiguisent en travers: on les polit, mais on ne les brunit pas.

1. Pour aiguiser le première, l'ouvrier passe à une petite meule d'environ six pouces de diamètre, soit de grès, soit de granit tendre. Ces meules sont sujettes à varier beaucoup dans leurs qualités: celle qui mord le mieux est la préférable pour cette opération. L'ouvrier y aiguise non-seulement la base de la lame, mais il y blanchit ce que le meule peut atteindre de la seconde partie de la concavité.

Page 37

2. Il passe à une meule pareille, dont le diamètre est de trois pouces au plus, et il aiguise la seconde partie.
3. Pendant l'opération précédente faite sur toutes les lames, la petite meule s'est usée considérablement, et son diamètre est presque réduit à un pouce et demi. Elle devient propre à perfectionner le travail de cette opération: c'est à quoi l'ouvrier l'emploie alors pour toutes les lames qui lui paroissent en avoir besoin. Il vérifie la courbure avec son calibre toutes les fois qu'il a du doute.

173. The concavity of this face is divided into three parts; one at the base, about an inch in length, which has very little curvature; a second, which has much more, from this first to half the length of the blade; and a third, the half to the point, whose curvature is ordinarily greater, and yet should be the same. The latter is ground lengthwise: it is polished and burnished; the two others are ground across: they are polished, but they are not burnished.

1. To grind the first, the workman uses a small millstone about six inches in diameter, either of sandstone or of soft granite. These grinding wheels are liable to vary greatly in their qualities: the one that bites the best is the best for this operation. The worker grinds not only the base [forte] of the blade, but cleans what the grinding wheel can reach of the second part of the concavity.
2. He passes to a similar wheel, the diameter of which is not more than three inches, and grinds the second part.
3. During the preceding operation made on all the blades, the small wheel has worn out considerably, and its diameter is almost reduced to an inch and a half. It becomes suitable for perfecting the work of this operation; so the workman then employs it for all the blades which appear to him to need it. He checks the curvature with his gauge whenever he has doubts.

174. Il est remarquer que les meules dont nous venons de parler sont presque toujours coniques, ou de la forme d'un troncon de pain sucre, quand l'ouvrier

les emploie. Il est donc naturel à l'observateur de croire qu'elles doivent avoir cette forme. Il n'en est rien. Si les meules ne s'usoient pas, et si les pans creux de la bayonnette étoient aiguises en travers d'un bout l'autre, ils devroient l'être par une même meule cylindrique qui pénétreroit davantage dans la lame vers sa base que vers la pointe, sans jamais changer de direction par rapport a l'axe de la lame. La meule auroit donc plus à travailler par le bord du côté de la base de la lame, que par l'autre bord. En se pénétrant de cette réflexion, on expliquera pourquoi les meules deviennent coniques, quoiqu'elles ne doivent pas l'être: et pourquoi la courbure des pans creux varie ordinairement de la base a la pointe, quoiqu'elle doive être la même.

4. Le reste de la concavité jusqu'à la pointe s'aiguise en long sur la meule canelée. Le plat de cette meule sert aussi pour dresser parfaitement les bords de la lame et faconner la pointe. On vérifie en présentant au fourreau: et cette fois, la lame doit y entrer juste.

Page 38

5. L'ouvrier arrondit les bords de la lame en les présentant en long entre deux cannelures.

   C'est alors qu'il frappe sa marque a la base de la lame, sur la partie qui est presque platte.

174. It is noticed that the millstones of which we have just spoken are almost always conical, or of the form of a slice of sugar loaf, when the workman employs them. It is therefore natural for the observer to believe that they must have this form. It is not so. If the grinding wheels do not wear out, and the hollow sides of the bayonet are sharp across the other end, they must be made by the same cylindrical grinding wheel which penetrates more into the blade towards its base than towards the tip, without ever changing direction with respect to the axis of the blade. The grinding wheel would therefore have to work more by the edge on the side of the base of the blade than by the other edge. On consideration, it can be seen why the grindstones become conical, though they must not be so: and why the curvature of the hollow varies ordinarily from the base to the point, although it should be the same.

4. The rest of the concavity up to the point is ground lengthwise on the grooved grindstone. The flat of this wheel is also used to perfectly dress the edges of the blade and shape the tip. It is checked by trying in the scabbard, and this time, the blade must just enter.

Page 38

5. The worker rounds the edges of the blade by grinding them lengthwise between two grooves.

   It is then that he strikes his mark at the base [forte] of the blade, on the part that is almost flat.

Dos de la lame	**Back of the blade**
Polissage	***Polishing***

175. 1. L'ouvrier passe à la grande polissoire de vingt-quatre a trente pouces de diamètre. Il frotte, d'émeri délayé dans l'huile, les pans creux du dos de la lame, et il les polit tous deux en long.
2. Il remet l'émeri vers la pointe pour achever d'y polir les deux pans creux: car la chaleur de la pièce ne lui auroit pas permis, dans l'opération précédente, d'appuyer sur le milieu de la lame pour polir l'extrêmité.
3. Il saupoudre la pièce de sable fin ou de cendre, pour enlever l'huile avec un vieux linge; et il polit à sec les deux pans creux du dos sur toute leur longeur.
Il les saupoudre encore, et les essuie avec un linge sec.

175. 1. The workman passes to the large polishing wheel, twenty-four to thirty inches in diameter. He rubs a paste of emery and oil in the hollow sections of the back of the blade, and he polishes them both lengthwise.
2. He puts the emery paste towards the point to complete the polishing of the two hollows because the heat of the blade would not have allowed him, in the previous operation, to press on the middle of the blade to polish to the point.
3. He sprinkles the piece with fine sand or ash, removes the oil with a linen rag, and he polishes the two hollow sides of the back along all the length. He repeats the process and wipes them with a dry cloth.

Face intérieure de la lame	**Inner face of the blade**
Polissage sue une moitié de sa longeur	*Polishing on one half of its length*

176. La circonférence de la grande polissoire doit présenter un arrondissement plus étendu et moins convexe pour cette opération que pour la précédente: l'aiguiseur la faconne en la tournant avec le ciseau de menuisier, ou un bout de lame de sabre qui lui en teint lieu.

Page 39

1. Il doit polir en long la face intérieure de la lame, depuis la pointe jusqu'à moitié de la longeur. Pour cela, il frotte cette partie de la lame, d'émeri délayé dans l'huile: mais il est obligé de la présenter un peu de biais a la grande polissoire, par la crainte qu'il a de toucher cette polissoire avec la douille.
2. La difficulté d'appuyer la main sur le bout de la lame, l'a forcé à laisser le poli imparfait vers la pointe; il y remet de l'émeri délayé dans huile, et il achève de la polir.
3. Il saupoudre de sable ou de cendre, il essuie, et polit à sec la moitié entière sur laquelle il avoit déjà opéré en deux fois.
Il saupoudre de nouveau et essuie avec un linge sec.

176. The circumference of the large polishing wheel must present a wider and less convex edge for this operation than for the preceding one: the grinder shapes it by turning it with the joiner's chisel, or a piece of sabre-blade as a substitute.

1. He must polish the inner side of the blade lengthwise, from the tip to half the length. For this, he rubs this part of the blade with a paste of emery and oil: but he is obliged to present it at a small angle to the large polishing wheel so that the socket does not come into contact with it.
2. The difficulty of pressing the hand on the tip of the blade forced him to leave it imperfectly polished towards the point; he puts more emery and oil paste, and he finishes polishing it.
3. He sprinkles with sand or ashes, he wipes, and polishes the whole half on which he had already operated twice.

He sprinkles again and wipes with a dry cloth.

177. Si quelques lames s'étoient déjetées dans toutes ces opérations, ce qui arrive très-rarement aux bayonnettes, on les mettroit a part, et on les renverroit au trempeur pour les dresser.

177. If a few blades were damaged in all these operations, which happens very seldom to bayonets, they should be put aside, and returned to the temperer to correct them.

Dos de la lame	**Back of the blade**
Brunissage	***Burnishing***

178. L'aiguiseur tourne de nouveau sa grande polissoire au cisseau, pour rendre la circonférence propre à brunir en long les deux pans creux du dos de la lame.

178. The grinder turns his large polisher with a chisel again, to make the circumference fit to burnish along the two hollow sides of the ridge on the back of the blade.

179. Il frotte cette circonférence en mouvement avec un charbon d'aulne ou de hêtre, et la polit avec l'agathe ou la sanguine dure.

1. Il l'emploie pour brunir l'un pans creux sur toute sa longeur, jusque près du bout.
2. Il brunit de même l'autre pan creux.
3. Il brunit enfin successivement et en une fois les deux pans creux vers le bout.

179. He rubs the rim of his rotating polishing wheel with charcoal of alder or beech and polishes it with agate or hard red haemetite.

1. He uses it to burnish the hollow section all the way to the end.
2. He also burnishes the other hollow.
3. Finally, he burnishes successively and at once both hollows towards the end.

Page 40

180. Quand la polissoire encor a besoin d'être rechargée de charbon, l'ouvrier interrompt son travail pour l'en frotter de nouveau, et y repasser l'agathe.

180. When the polisher needs to be recharged with charcoal, the worker interrupts his work to rub it again, and to dress with agate.

Face intérieure de la lame.
Brunisage

Inner face of the blade.
Burnishing

181. L'aiguiseur tourne encore la circonférence de cette polissoire, pour la rendre propre à brunir en long cette face, depuis le milieu jusqu'à la pointe; et il le recharge de charbon. Dela fait, il brunit ensuite cette concavité, en commencant par la pointe, et en continuant jusqu'au dela de la moitié de la longeur.

181. The grinder still turns the circumference of this polisher, to make it fit to burnish along this face, from the middle to the point; and he reloads it with charcoal. When that is done, he burnishes this concave face, beginning at the point, and continuing to halfway down the length.

Base et première moîtié de la face intérieure de la lame
Polissage

Base and first half of the inner side of the blade
Polishing

182. Cette opération a été remise à cette époque, pour que le bruni de la moîtié supérieure de cette face se détache nettement du simple poli de la seconde moitié; car on polit ici en travers jusqu'à la moîtié juste, et l'émeri fait disparoître le bruni.

1. L'ouvrier se porte à la seconde polissoire de six pouces de diamêtre. Il enduit légèrement aussi d'émeri délayé dans l'huile, las base de la face intérieure de la lame, et en polit cette base travers.
2. Il met la plus petite polissoire en place; il enduit légèrement aussi d'émeri la concavité jusqu'au milieu a-peu-près de la lame, et il polit en travers la seconde partie de la face intérieure, jusqu'au milieu bien juste.

182. This operation was postponed until this time, so that the burnished upper half of this face is clearly separate from the simple polish of the second half; for here we polish right up to the half-way, the emery removing the lower part of the burnishing to make a clean separation of the two finishes.

1. The workman goes to the second polisher, six inches in diameter. The base of the inner face of the blade is lightly coated with emery and oil paste, and polishes this base across.
2. He puts the smallest polisher in place; he also smeared the concavity slightly as far as the middle of the blade, and he polishes across the second part of the inner side, right down to the middle.

183. Il saupoudre enfin de sable fin ou de cendre; il nétoye avec un linge bien sec, et ses opérations sont terminées.

183. He finally sprinkles with fine sand or ashes, wipes with a dry cloth, and his operations are finished.

Page 41

184. Les fonctions des compagnons dans les aiguiseries n'out rien de remarquable. La plupart d'entr'eux font tout ce que fait le maître, qui ne se réserve que le choix et l'inspection; car leur apprentissage n'est ni long ni difficile. Le long exercice ne donne que la facilite de faire plus vite et mieux.

184. The functions of the assistants in the grinding processes are nothing remarkable. Most of them do all that the master does, who reserves only the choice and the inspection, because learning the trade is neither long nor difficult. Long experience only allows the work to be done faster and better.

ARTICLE NEUVIÈME
Quatrième contrôle au magasin

ARTICLE NINE
Fourth inspection at the store.

185. Après l'aiguisage, le bayonnette est reportée au magasin pour ètre examinée par les contrôleurs d'armes blanches, dont l'attention principale dans cet examen, ne porte que sur la lame.

185. After grinding and polishing, the bayonet is returned to the store to be examined by the inspector of edged weapons whose main attention in this examination relates only to the blade.

186. Il en vérifie d'abord la longeur ainsi que l'inclinaison des cotes et leur epaisseur, en la placant dans la pièce nommée fourreau dont il a été parlé ci-dessus. S'il a du doute sur la forme des autres parties, il y porte sou calibre.

186. He checks first the length as well as the width and inclination by placing it in the scabbard spoken of above. If he has any doubt about the shape of the other parts, he refers to his gauge.

187. Il place ensuite la lame, en appuyant le pointe dans l'angle du fond, sur le milieu de la piêce, fig. 29, qu'on nomme mentonnet; il la plie une fois de chaque côté jusqu'à ce que la base de lame touche. Elle pourroit se fausser ou se casser dans cette épreuve; mais cela n'arrive presque jamais.

187. He then places the blade on the middle of the piece, [B, Plate 6] fig. 29, which is called a mantlet, and the point in the angle of the end piece A; he bends it once on each side until the blade base [forte] touches. It could be permanently bent or broken in this ordeal; but that hardly ever happens. *[An interpretation of this process is shown below]*

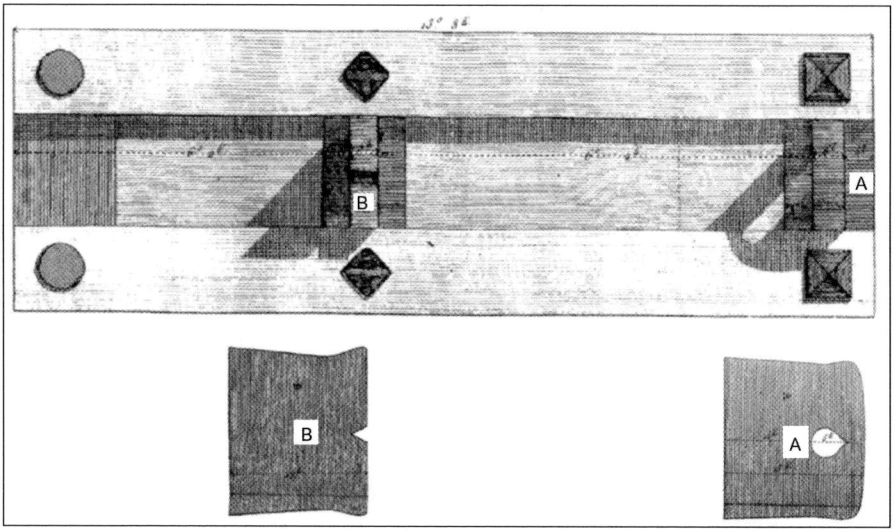

Fig. 29. The 'mantlet' – bending test fixture.

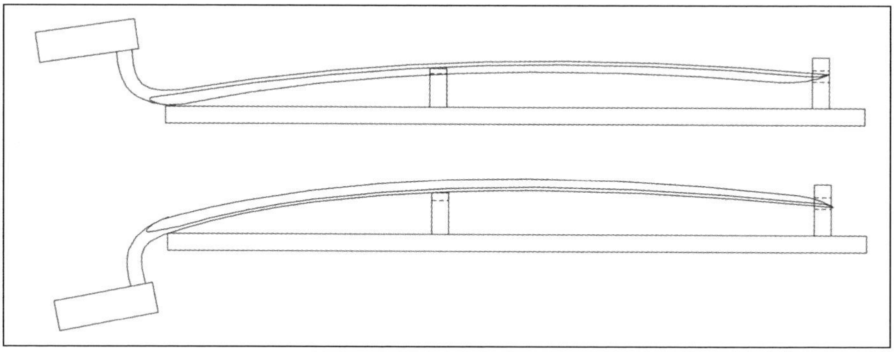

Fig. 29A. Interpretation of how the bending test jig was used.

188. Il finit par examiner si le poli de la moitie de la face intérieure et le bruni de tout le reste sont tels qu'ils doivent ètre, s'il n'y a des doublures ou des fentes longitudinales nulle part, et s'il n'y a pas des travers ou des fentes en travers, sur les bords ou sur l'arrête du dos.

188. He finally examines whether the polish of the half of the inner face and the burnishing of everything else are as they should be, and if there are longitudinal or scratches across on the edges or on the rib of the back.

189. S'il y a quelque défaut irrémédiable, il rebute la piêce; si le défaut peut se répare, il le marque d'un petit coup de son marteau, d'une manière convenue; et s'il regarde la piêce comme sans défaut, il la fait marquer de son poincon la

base dans la face aplatie, sur le coussinet laiton, dont la forme est semblable a celui dont il a été question plus haut, fig. 19.

189. If there is some irreparable fault, he rejects the item; if the defect can be repaired, he marks it with a little stroke of his hammer, in an agreed manner; and if he views the item as without flaw, he has it stamped with his mark at the base in the flattened face of the blade, placing the blade on the brass cushion, whose shape is similar to that mentioned above, Fig. 19.

Page 42

ARTICLE DIXIEME
Forger la virole et la vis

ARTICLE TEN
Forging the ring and the screw

190. Quoiqu'il y ait dans le manufacture des ouvriers qui ne se livrent qu'a cette partie, plusiers limeurs de douilles s'en chargent eux-mêmes. Alors il leur faut une forge, qui sans cela leur seroit inutile. Les opérations de forger la virole et la vis, et de les limer, ainsi que la douille, ne sortent guère du cercle des opérations ordinaires de le serrurerie, et elles ne se traitent pas, à proprement parler, en manœuvreriez. Les dispositions nécessaires pour ce travail n'ont que très-peu de particularités, qu'on se contrera d'indiquer dans le cours de la description des procédés.

190. Although there are workmen in the factory who only engage in this task, many socket filers make them themselves. Then they need a forge, or would otherwise be useless. The operations of forging the ferrule and the screw, and of filing them, as well as the socket, hardly depart from the circle of the ordinary operations of locksmithing, and they are not, strictly speaking, handled. The arrangements necessary for this work have but very few peculiarities, that we will refrain from indicating in the course of the description of the processes.

FORGER LA VIROLE
premier chauffement

FORGING THE RING
first heating

191. L'ouvrier prend une verge de fer mâchée au martinet, du poids d'environ demi-livre le pied; il en chauffe le bout a blanc sur environ deux pouces, et il le forge carrément sur l'enclume jusqu'à ce qu'il l'ait porté a environ trois pouces et demi de long, quatre lignes de large et deux lignes d'épais.

191. The workman takes a rod of iron forged under a tilt-hammer, weighing about half a pound; he heats the end to white heat for about two inches, and he forges it squarely on the anvil until it is about three and a half inches long, four lines wide, and two lines thick.

192. Il le pose sur l'étampe, fig. 30, de manière a faire d'abord, au moyen de la carre intérieure de l'étampe, le talon, a, fig. 31 et 32, de l'extrémité, sur la largeur de la pièce; il lui fait faire un demi-tour, et fait, sur le carre-extérieure de l'étampe, le premier épaulement, c, fig. 32, du petit pontet, a, fig. 33, puis l'autre épaulement sur la carre intérieure; et enfin il fait faire de nouveau le demi-tour a sa barre, et il forge l'autre talon, b, fig. 31 et 32, sur la carre extérieure de l'étampe.

192. He places it on the die, Fig. 30, so as to make first, by means of the inner edge of the die, the heel, a, Fig. 31 and 32, from the end, across the width of the piece; he rotates it a half-turn, and makes, on the outer edge of the die, the first shoulder, c, Fig. 32, the small bridge, a, Fig. 33, then the other shoulder on the inner edge; and finally he rotates the bar again, and he forges the other heel, b, Fig. 31 and 32, on the outer edge of the die.

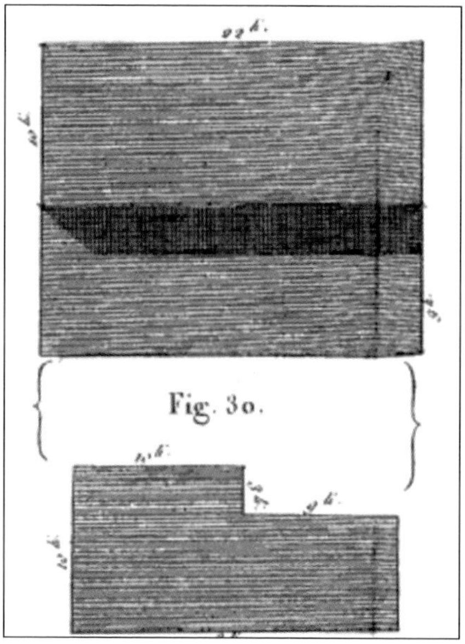

Left: Fig. 30. The die for forging the ring.

Below: Figs. 31 [top] and 32 [bottom].

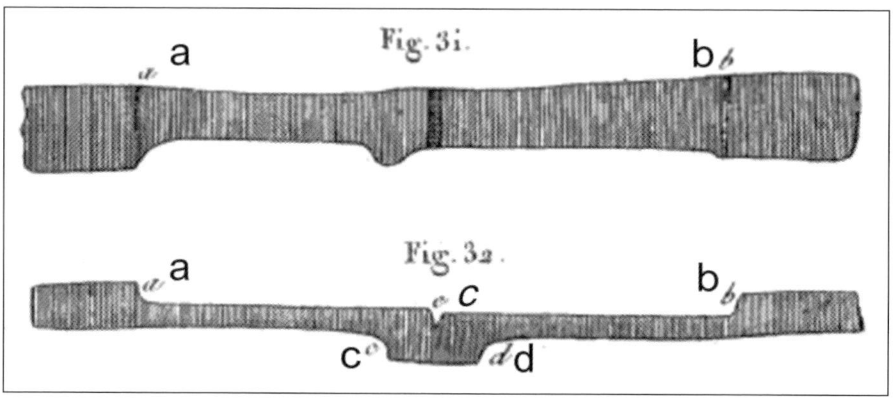

Page 43

193. Il faite ensuite, dans l'epaisseur de la piêce et sur la carre extérieure de l'étampe, l'épaulement, a, fig. 31, au talon; et sur la carre intérieure, celui, b, fig. 34, de l'arrêtoir, b, fig. 33. La place de celui-ci est déterminée par une convenance a laquelle tous les ouvriers ne s'assujettissent pas. On desire que, lorsque l'arretoir, b, bute contre le pivot, c, fig. 2, de la douille, alors les deux pontets, celui de la douille et celui virole, soient juste en opposition l'un de l'autre, ou, ce qui est la mème chose, qu'alors les deux oreilles de la virole, qu'on nomme la tête, quand elles sont rénies par la vis, tombent au droit du pontet de la douille. Pour satisfaire à cette condition, il faut que les deux épaulemens dont il vient d'ètre question, soient à la distance juste d'un pouce l'un de l'autre sur la virole développée. Si l'ouvrier n'est pas sûr de son coup-d'œil, il faut donc qu'il a'assurer de cette distance avec son pied de roi ou autrement. L'autre épaulement, c, fig. 34, qui décide la forme ébauchée de l'arretoir se fait aussitôt sur la carre extérieure de l'étampe. Comme il faut que la partie de l'epaisseur, adjacente a de dernier épaulement, montes-en talud depuis le fond de l'épaulement jusqu'au talon du mème cote, l'ouvrier a soin, en forgeant cette partie, de soulever la barre a laquelle la pièce tient encore, et de ménager graduellement ses coups.

193. He then makes, in the thickness of the piece and on the outer edge of the die, the shoulder, a, Fig. 31, in the heel; and on the inner edge, that, b, Fig. 34, of the stop, b, Fig. 33. The place of this one is determined by a convenience to which all the workers do not subjugate themselves. It is desired that when the stop, b, abuts against the pin, c, Fig. 2, of the socket, then the two bridges, that of the socket and the ring, are just in line with each other, or, what is the same thing, that then the two ears of the ring, which one calls the head, when they are fitted with the screw, fall to the right of the bridge of the socket. To satisfy this condition, it is necessary that the two shoulders of which it has just been mentioned, be at a distance of just one inch from each other

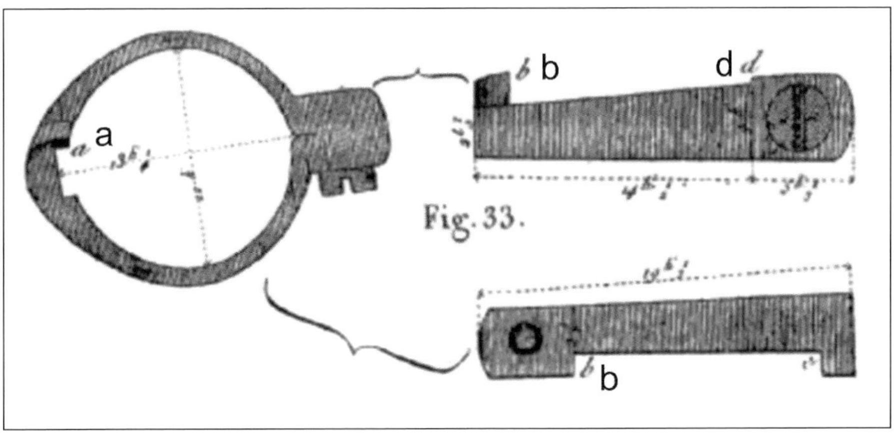

Fig. 33. Features of the finished ring.

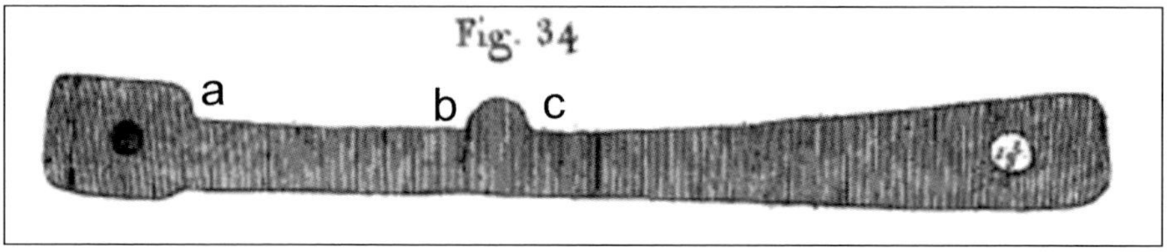

Fig. 34. Features of the ring forging.

on the developed ring. If the worker is not sure of his work, he must check this distance with his imperial measure or otherwise. The other shoulder, c, fig. 34, which decides the rough form of the stop is made immediately on the outer edge of the die. As it is necessary for the part of the thickness adjacent to the last shoulder to rise up from the bottom of the shoulder to the heel of the same side, the workman takes care, by forging this part, to lift the bar to which the piece is still attached, and to gradually reduce his blows.

194. Cela fait, et en supposant que son coup l'œil lui ait suffi pour mettre trente-deux lignes juste de distance entre les deux talons, il mesure à la vue la moitie de cette distance, pour y poser la pièce sur le tranchoir implante dans le trou de son enclume, et il frappe un coup pour faire l'encoche, c, fig. 32, qui détermine le milieu du pontet de la virole; enfin il pose la pièce sur le tranchoir, a la place ou il doit frapper, pour la détacher la barre, et il sépare; elle doit peser dans cet état trois quarts d'once.

194. This done, and supposing that his eye was good enough for him to put thirty-two lines just between the two heels, he measures at sight half of this distance, to put the piece on the cutter implanted in the hole of his anvil, and he strikes a blow to make the notch, c, Fig. 32, which determines the middle of the bridge of the ring; finally he places the piece on the cutter at the place he must strike to detach the bar, and he separates the forged part; it must weigh in this state three quarters of an ounce.

Page 44

195. Si l'ouvrier craint d'avoir été trompé dans son coup-d'œil, il vérifie avant de porter sur le tranchoir, et il continue de forger pour parvenir aux véritables dimensions, s'il s'en est écarté.

195. If the workman suspects he has been deceived by his eye, he checks before using the cutter and he continues to forge to reach the true dimensions, if he has departed from them.

196. Tout cela doit se faire dans une chaude; mais on est force quelquefois à le faire en deux.

196. All this must be done in one heating, but he is sometimes forced to do it in two.

Second chauffement ***Second heating***

197. L'ouvrier prend la pièce dans une pince plate, par le talon, a, fig. 31, qui étoit au bout de la barre; il chauffe l'autre talon au rouge, et il y perce avec un poincon le trou qui doit donner passage à la vis. Ce trou doit avoir une ligne et demi au moins. Il fait cela en frappant deux coups d'un côté, et deux coups de l'autre. Il en fait autant à toutes les pièces.

197. The worker takes the piece in flat tongs by the heel, a, Fig. 31, which was at the end of the bar; he heats the other heel red, and he pierces with a punch the hole for the passage of the screw. This hole must be a line and a half diameter at least. He does this by striking twice on one side, and twice on the other. He does the same to all the pieces.

Troisième chauffement ***Third heating***

198. Il prend la pièce par le talon déjà perce, il chauffe l'autre au rouge, et il y perce avec un autre poincon le trou qui doit ètre taraude, et qui doit n'avoir qu'une ligne au plus.

198. He takes the piece by the heel already pierced, he heats the other end to red heat and he pierces with another punch the hole which must be tapped, and which must be only one line diameter at most.

Quatrième chauffement ***Fourth heating***

199. Il se donne au demi-blanc. L'ouvrier met l'éminence du milieu de la pièce dans le trou de son enclume destine au tranchoir; il frappe sur la partie opposée ou est l'encoche, avec la panne de son marteau, pour commencer à donner à la virole sa courbure: il la saisit alors avec sa pince par cette partie du milieu, et il appuie la pince sur l'enclume; alors il frappe avec la tête du marteau, des coups de biais de chaque côté, pour continuer à courber la virole.

199. It is heated to half-white. The workman puts the eminence at the middle of the ring in the hole of his anvil for fitting the cutter and he strikes on the opposite side where the notch is, with the pein of his hammer to begin to give the ring its curvature: he then grasps it with his pincers in the middle of this part, and he rests the pincer on the anvil; he then strikes with the head of the hammer, skewing it on each side, to continue to bend the ring.

Page 45

Cinquième chauffement ***Fifth heating***

200. Il la jette au feu: quand elle y a pris le rouge demi-blanc, il la pose sur l'enclume avec le crochet qui sert à attiser le charbon. Il y passe un mandrin a main de la grosseur de l'extérieur de la douille; il la fait remonter sur le mandrin on

la poussant et relevant avec le carre du marteau, et il le pos sur l'étampe, fig. 35, pour achever d'arrondir et pour former les deux replis qui sont nécessaires pour mettre les talons des extrémités en contact, comme ils doivent l'être, pour loger la vis qui doit les traverser.

200. He puts it in the hearth, and when it is half-white to red, he puts it on the anvil with the hook which serves to stoke the coal. He inserts a hand mandrel the size of the outside of the socket; he makes the ring go up on the mandrel by pushing it and raising with the edge of the hammer; he then puts it on the die, Fig. 35, to complete rounding and to form the two folds that are necessary to put the heels at the ends in contact, as they must be, to accommodate the screw that must pass through them.

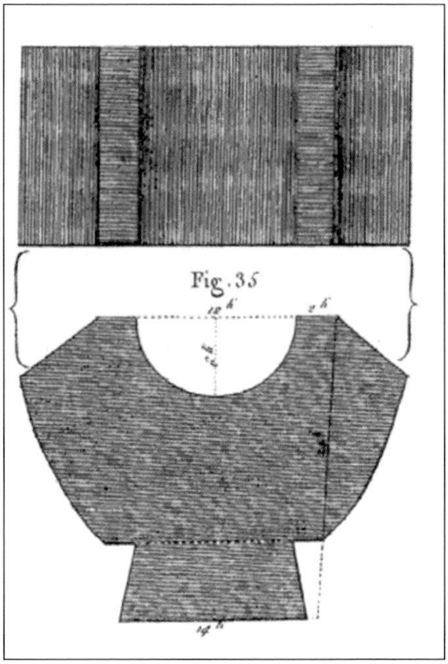

Fig. 35. Die for forming the 'ears' or 'heels' which when together form the 'head' of the ring.

201. Pour remplir ce dernier objet, il applique alternativement a plusiers fois, la face extérieure de chacun de ces replis sur les deux rebords aplatis de l'étampe, et frappe d'abord de la panne du marteau, et ensuite de la tête, sur la face opposée de l'autre repli. Il a soin, en accolant ainsi les deux replis, qu'on nommera oreilles par la suite, de diriger bien les deux trous en face l'un de l'autre. Cela fait, il recuit la virole.

201. To achieve this last object, he places alternately several times, the outer face of each of these folds on the two flattened flanges of the stamp, and strikes first with the pein of the hammer, and then of the head, on the opposite side of the other fold. He takes care in joining the two folds, which will be called ears thereafter, to align the two holes. That done, he anneals the ring.

Forger la vis ***Forging the screw***

202. Il ne faut chauffer qu'une fois pour en forger quatre; et les ouvriers habiles ne chauffent deux fois, que quand il leur arrive quelqu'accident.

202. It is only necessary to heat once to forge four; and the skilful workmen do not heat twice, unless a mishap occurs.

203. On chauffe au demi-blanc. C'est toujours le forgeur de viroles qui forge les vis. S'il fait que cela, il en peut forger environ huit cents dans sa journée moyenne.

203. We heat to half-white. It is always the forger of the rings who forges the screws, and he can forge about eight hundred in his average day.

204. On emploie pour les vis, le fer du même échantillon que pour les viroles.

204. For the screws, the same iron is used as for the rings.

205. Le maître forge d'abord au bout de la barre, sur une longeur d'environ deux pouces, deux portions arrondies en forme d'olives, qui se tiennent par le bout, fig. 36. Le plus grand diamètre des olives est quatre lignes; et la pièce a deux lignes dans ses moindres grosseurs.

205. The master forges first at the end of the bar, on a length of about two inches, two rounded portions in the shape of olives, Fig. 36. The largest diameter of the 'olives' is four lines, and two lines at the smallest diameter.

Page 46

206. Comme il faut éviter de frapper du marteau sur l'enclume dans cette opération, qui exige qu'on frappe de biais, tantôt d'arrière en-avant, et tantôt d'avant en arrière, le maître a soin de porter le bout de la barre, ou devant lui, près de la carre intérieure de l'enclume, on sur la partie opposée, près de la carre extérieure.

206. As one must avoid hammering the anvil in this operation, which requires striking at an angle, sometimes from behind and sometimes from the front, the master is careful to place the end of the bar on the inner and outer edges of the anvil as required.

207. Il tourne continuellement la barre pour arrondit la pièce pendant cette opération.

207. He continuously turns the bar to round the piece during this operation

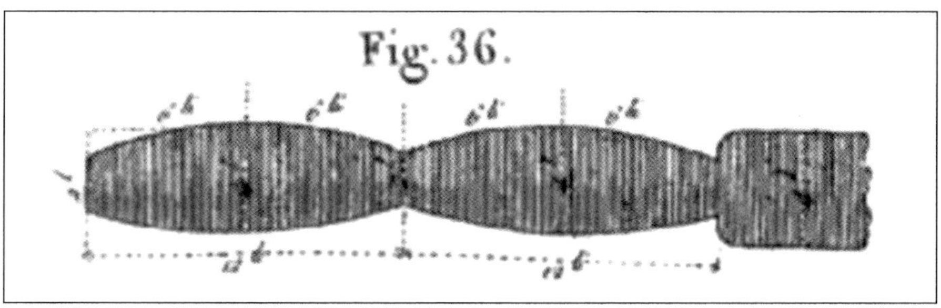

Fig. 36. The screws commencing as two 'olive-shaped' forgings on the bar.

208. Les olives faites, il les met par paires, l'une après l'autre, sur l'étampe de dessous, fig. 37, et il y applique une étampe de dessus de pareille forme; et il continue de tourner, pendant les intervalles des coups que frappe le compagnon. Celui-ci n'y emploie qu'un marteau du poids de dix livres au plus.

208. The olives made, he puts them in pairs, one after the other, on the bottom die, Fig. 37, and there applies the top die of similar form, and he continues to turn the piece in the intervals between blows struck by the companion. He only uses a hammer weighing ten pounds or less.

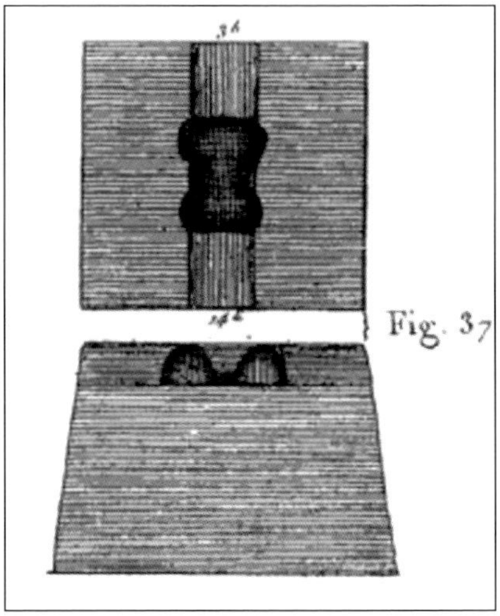

Fig. 37. The die used in making the screw.

209. Les olives s'étendent sous l'étampe et s'y moulent. L'operation finie sur la seconde paire, le maître les sépare l'une de l'autre; et celle-ci du bout de la barre en les posant aux endroits convenables sur son tranchoir, et frappant de son marteau.

209. The olives extend under the dies. The operation finished on the second pair, the master separates them one from the other, and the one from the end of the bar, by placing them at the proper places on his cutter and striking with his hammer.

210. L'étampe doit être graissée d'huile de navette avec une barbe de plume, au commencement de chaque opération pareille.

210. The stamp must be greased with shuttle oil with a feather at the beginning of each such operation.

ARTICLE ONZIÈME
Limer la douille, la virole et la vis

ELEVENTH ARTICLE
Filing the socket, ring and screw

211. L'ordre à mettre dans ce travail est presque la seule chose à remarquer. Tous les limeurs en petits ouvrage de fer en sont capables; et la description en peut leur servis qu'a leur éviter quelques pertes de tems dans les commencemens, et à leur indiquer deux ou trois outils particuliers qui y procurent de la célérité et de la perfection. On se contentera de renvoyer aux figures, en parlant de leur emploi.

211. The order of this work is almost the only thing to notice. All filers in small iron work are capable, and the description can be used to save some loss of time at the outset, and to point out to them two or three particular tools which

procure speed and perfection. We will content ourselves with referring to the figures in describing their employment.

212. Le compagnon fait ici les mêmes choses que le maître, qui ne se réserve que l'inspection et le choix, et qui peut en diriger plusiers.

212. The assistant here does the same things as the master, who reserves only inspection and choice, and who can direct.

213. Trois ou quatre douilles suffisent pour la journée moyenne d'un limeur.

213. Three or four sockets are enough for the average day of a filer.

214. Des circonstances particulières font que l'ordre est quelquefois interverti dans les details. On peut cependant classer les opérations comme il suit.

214. Special circumstances sometimes cause the order to be reversed. However, we can classify the operations as follows.

1. DEGRAISER LA DOUILLE 1. DEGREASING THE SOCKET

215. On commence par rougir les douilles pour enlever l'huile qui a dû s'y attacher pendant le polissage de la lame, et pour adoucir la matière. On en met trois ou quatre à la fois au feu. Une forge n'est point nécessaire au limer pour cela; il les met au feu do forgeur le plus voisin.

215. We start by heating the sockets to a low red heat to remove the oil that has been used during the polishing of the blade, and to soften the material. Three or four at a time are put in the fire. A forge is not necessary to the filer; he puts them in the nearest neighbour's fire.

2. BIEN METTRE LA DOUILLE DE LONGEUR 2. MAKING THE SOCKET TO CORRECT LENGTH

216. On le met droite dans l'étau, la lame en haut. On met son orifice supérieur bien de niveau, en le limant avec une lime plate, aprés s'être servi du carreau, s'il y avoit trop de matière à emporter. On en fait autant a l'autre orifice, aprés avoir place la douille dans l'étau, la lame bas. Il n'est guères possible d'obtenir de la précision dans la distance des orifices entre eux, combinée avec leurs distances au bourrelet, sans vérifier avec le calibre.

216. It is fixed square in the vise, the blade up. Its upper orifice is well squared by filing it with a flat file. The same is done at the other orifice, after placing the socket in the vise, the blade down. It is not possible to obtain precision in the distance between the orifices, combined with their distances to the bead, without checking with the gauge.

3. Y FAIRE LES ENTAILLES. 3. MAKING THE SLOTS.

217. Il faut commencer par entamer dans le pontet, l'échan, crure qui doit donner passage au tenon. Pour cela on a un burin d'établi de la largeur exacte de l'canal, c'est-à-dire de deux lignes et demie. On le frappe d'abord sur les côtes, et ensuite sur le fond de l'ouverture à faire, en tournant le biseau du burin de dehors en dedans.

217. It is necessary to begin by starting in the bridge with the notch through which tenon passes. For this a bench chisel the exact width of the channel, that is, two lines and a half, is used. It is struck first on the sides and then on the bottom of the opening to be made, turning the bevel of the chisel from outside to inside.

Page 48

218. Ce premier travail n'a pour objet que favoriser l'introduction du mandrin, fig. 38, qui porte un long tenon d'acier trempe, qui a lui-même la forme d'un burin, dont le biseau est très-peu incliné. Ce mandrin est destiné à emporter la matiere de l'entaille verticale, et dans le pontet auquel elle aboutit, et dans le corps même de la douille.

218. This first work is intended to promote the introduction of the mandrel, Fig. 38, which carries a long tenon of hardened steel, which itself has the form of a chisel, whose bevel is very little inclined. This mandrel is intended to remove the material of the vertical channel in the bridge and in the body itself of the socket.

219. On frappe de la tête du marteau sur celle du mandrin, pour l'enfoncer dans la douille, jusqu'à une marque qui doit arraser l'orifice quand l'entaille est faite. Alors on le retire; la matiere entraînée et coupes par le burin encastre dans mandrin, s'est roulée pour lui laisser passage; il suffit, pour l'enlever tout-la-fait, de frapper pour la rompre; mais il vaut mieux encore l'emporter avec la scie a main.

219. The hammer's head is struck against the mandrel head, to push it into the socket, until a mark is reached to indicate the end of the slot to be cut. So we remove it; the material entrained and cut by the chisel embedded in the

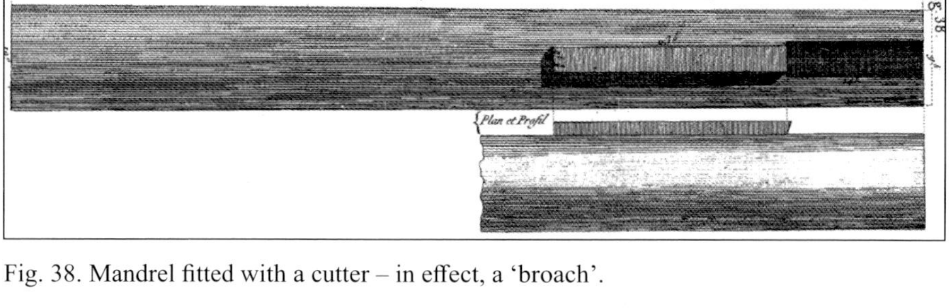

Fig. 38. Mandrel fitted with a cutter – in effect, a 'broach'.

mandrel, curled in its passage and it can be removed by breaking it off, but it is better still to remove it with the hacksaw.

220. Après cette entaille, on fait celle qui est en travers. On commence, après avoir fixe la douille horisontalement dans l'étau, par entamer les bords de cette entaille avec les carres d'une lime plate taillée en carreau.

220. After this cut, we do the one that is across. We begin, after fixing the sleeve horizontally in the vice, to cut the edges of this slot with the edges of a coarse flat file.

221. Ensuite on en emporte en entier la matiere avec une autre lime de deux lignes et demie d'épaisseur sur dix a douze de largeur, taillée en grosse lime d'Allemagne. C'est par l'arrondissemont qui règne sur ses côtés, qu'on attaque la douille pour faire l'entaille.

221. Then the whole material is removed with another large German file two and a half lines thick by ten to twelve in width. It is through the rounding which reigns on its sides that we attack the socket to make the notch.

222. Après celle-ci, il faut faire l'entaille verticale qui coupe le bourrelet. Pour cela, on emporte d'abord avec la lime dout on vient de parler, la matiere du bourrelet à l'endroit convenable; ensuite on entame avec le burin d'établi les bords de l'entaille à faire.

222. After this one must make the vertical cut that cuts through the bead. To do this, first remove with the file just mentioned the material of the bead at the proper place; then start with the chisel to make the edges of the slot.

Page 49

223. On retire alors la douille de l'étau; on y passe un mandrin de neuf lignes de gros, qui porte un tenon d'acier trempe, en faisant parcourir à ce tenon la première entaille longitudinale et l'entaille en traverse; et ça appuyant l'orifice supérieur de la douille sur les machoires de l'étau, et frappant sur le mandrin avec le marteau, on fait sortir dehors, en se roulant, la matiere à emporter pour former la troisième entaille.

223. The socket is removed from the vise; a mandrel of nine lines, which carries a hardened steel tool, is passed through the first longitudinal slot and the lateral slot; and pressing the upper orifice of the socket on the jaws of the vice, and striking on the mandrel with the hammer, it removes the material to form the third part of the slot.

224. Après avoir retiré le mandrin, on détache cette matiere avec la panne d'un petit marteau.

224. After removing the mandrel, we detach this material with the pein of a small hammer.

225. Alors on place la douille horizontalement dans l'étau, en la serrant par le coude, et on enlevé toutes les bavures superficielles avec un lime plate, et celles de l'interieur avec une lime demi-ronde.

225. Then put the sleeve horizontally in the vise, holding it by the elbow, and remove all superficial burrs with a flat file, and those inside with a half-round file.

226. Ensuite on retire la pièce de l'étau; on la prend aux mains, la lame en haut; on y introduit par le bas un troisième mandrin qui est d'acier trempe, et n'a point de tenon; ce mandrin a un peu d'entrée, et il a dix lignes foibles de gros. On le chasse dans l'intérieure en frappant sur l'étau; puis on frappe sur la circonférence de la douille dans tous les sens, avec la tête du marteau, pour en bien appliquer au mandrin toute la surface intérieure.

226. Then remove the piece from the vise; it is taken in the hand, the blade up; a third mandrel is introduced from below, which is of tempered steel, and has no tenon; this only enters about ten lines at most. It is lodged in the interior by striking on the vice; then strike on the circumference of the socket in all directions, with the head of the hammer, to properly shape its inner surface to the mandrel.

4. BLANCHIR LE COUDE **4. CLEANING THE ELBOW**

227. Le limeur serre douille dans l'étau, en y laissant le mandrin dont on vient de parler; et il l'y place successivement dans toutes les positions nécessaires.

227. The filer clamps the socket in the vice, leaving the mandrel of which we have just spoken in place, and he places the socket successively in all the necessary positions.

228. Il lime d'abord le coude de la douille, comme s'il vouloit l'écarri, avec un grosse lime Allemagne, dont les bords sont demi-rondes. C'est en mesurant le coude dans l'état ou le met cette première opération, qu'il s'assure de la grosseur qu'il doit lui donner.

228. He first files the elbow of the socket, as if he wanted to scrape it, with a large German file, whose edges are half-round. It is by measuring the elbow in the state when he commences this first operation that he determines the size that he must make it.

Page 50

229. Il le lime ensuite avec la même lime, comme pour le mettre à huit pans, et il l'y porte rèellement. Ce n'est qu'ensuite qu'il arrondit entièrement le coude.

229. He then files it with the same file, as if to put on it eight sides. Only then does he round the elbow completely.

5. BLANCHIR LE CORPS DE LA DOUILLE

5. CLEANING THE BODY OF THE SOCKET

230. Le limeur le dégrossit au-dessus du bourrelet avec un carreau. Quand il y a peu de matière à enlever, il n'emploie pour cela qu'une lime Allemagne. Au-dessous du bourrelet, c'est toujours de cette dernière seule qu'il fait usage; et il en prend une plus étroite pour dégrossir et arrondir le bourrelet.

230. The filer cleans the bead with a coarse file. When there is little material to be removed, he only uses a German file. Below the bead, it is always the latter that he makes use of; and he takes a narrower one to rough and round the bead.

231. Pendant cette opération, il s'assure continuellement, avec le calibre, des dimensions de toutes les parties.

231. During this operation, he continuously ensures, with the gauge, the dimensions of all parts.

232. Pour perfectionner la forme du bourrelet et sa rondeur, ainsi que celle de la douille, dans une étendue adjacente de six lignes par le haut, et dix lignes par le bas, il prend la douille dans l'étau, la lame en bas, vers l'orifice près du coude, en laissant le mandrin dedans. Il embrasse le bourrelet avec l'outil a charnière, fig. 39. [the text from here is partly illegible] ... surface circulaire intérieure est taillée en lime; ... tournant cet outil des deux mains avec vivacité, il ... cette partie de son ouvrage.

232. To perfect the shape of the bead and its roundness, as well as that of the socket, in an adjacent extension of six lines by the top, and ten lines by the bottom, it takes the mandrel with the socket on it in the vise, the blade down. He embraces the bead with the hinge tool, Fig. 39, [incomplete text] whose inner circular surface is cut to form a file; and vigorously turning this tool with both hands, he completes this part of his work.

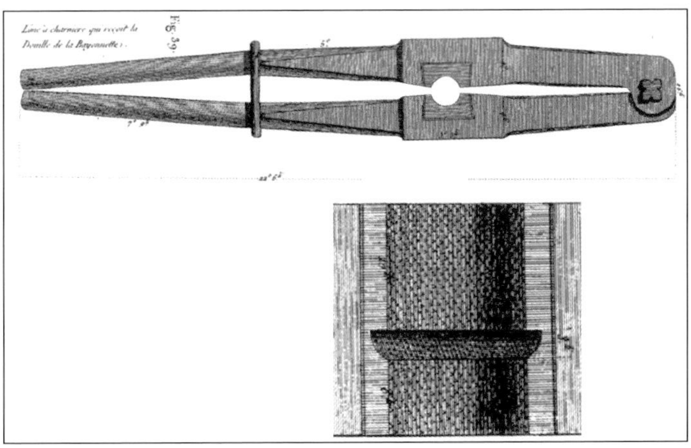

Fig. 39. Device for filing the outside of the socket and the bead.

6. POLIR ET BRUNIR LE COUDE

6. POLISHING AND BURNISHING THE ELBOW

233. On remet alors la douille dans une situation horizontale, en la fixant dans l'étau par le mandrin seul. On commence à polir le coude avec une lime demi-douce, arrondie sur ces deux faces; et on achève avec une lime de même forme, entièrement douce.

On prend ensuite un brunissoir d'acier trempe, a deux manches, et on brunit le coude dans toutes ses parties.

233. The socket is then placed in a horizontal position, fixing it in the vise by means of the mandrel alone. One begins to polish the elbow with a second-cut file, rounded on both sides; and finish with a fine-cut file of the same form.

We then take a hardened steel burnisher, with two handles, and burnish the elbow in all its parts.

7. COMMENCER LE TRAVAIL DE LA VIROLE.

7. STARTING WORK ON THE RING.

234. Le limeur prend une virole telle qu'elle sort de la forge; il la serre dans l'étau par les bords de celui des deux replis, qui doit être taraudé; et pour être libre de la faire, il détourne l'autre; il perfectionne le trou du premier avec un écarissoir à main proportionne, qui a un manche comme une vrille, et il taraudé ce trou.

234. The filer takes the ring as it leaves the forge; he clasps it in the vise by the edges of the one of the two 'ears' which must be tapped; and to be free to do it, he turns away the other; he perfects the hole of the first with a hand-held square broach, which has a handle like a gimlet, and then he taps this hole.

Page 51

235. Il retire ce repli, ou cette oreille de l'étau, et il y met l'autre, pour y passer le même écarissoir, qui etant conique, peut aussi perfectionner le trou, quoique d'une demi-ligne plus grand.

235. He withdraws this ear from the vice, and puts the other in it, to pass the same broach, which being conical, can also perfect the hole, though of a half-line greater.

236. Pour limer le plat de l'oreille qui est dans l'étau, il soulève l'autre; et pour en faire autant à celle-ci, il la place ensuite dans l'étau. Il vaut mieux, dans ces deux opérations, emporter trop peu que trop de matiere, au risque d'y revenir, si on trouve par la suite que la virole soit lâche sur la douille; car il est essentiel qu'il n'y ait point d'interstice entre les deux oreilles, quand la virole est en place.

236. To file the flat of the ear that is in the vise, he lifts the other ear; and to do the same with it, he then places it in the vise. It is better, in these two operations, to remove too little material, at the risk of returning to it if it is found later that the ring is loose on the socket; for it is essential that there be no gap between the two ears when the ring is in place.

237. Le limeur met ensuite les deux oreilles en contact, en faisant bien coïncider les deux trous; il prend une vis étalon, qui ordinairement est d'acier, et s'assure, en lui faisant traverser l'un des trous, et la vissant dans l'autre, que les opérations précédentes ont été bien faites.

237. The filer then puts the two ears in contact, making the two holes coincide well; he takes a standard screw, which is usually steel, and makes sure by passing it through one of the holes, and screwing it into the other, that the preceding operations have been well done.

238. Alors, il place la virole dans l'étau, en saisissant dans les machoires le tête et l'extrémité de la vis étalon, de manière à présenter vers le haut et horizontalement, le plate du dessous de la virole qui doit porter sur l'embase du bourrelet. Il blanchit et il polit ensuite avec des limes plates, tout ce qui s'offre à lui de surface horizontale, y compris celle des deux oreilles réunies. Il chanfrine enfin avec une lime demi-ronde, du dehors au dedans, l'intérieure de la circonférence de la virole, pour que rien n'empêche cette partie de s'appliquer toujours exactement sur l'embase du bourrelet.

238. Then he places the ring in the vise, grasping the head and the end of the standard screw in the jaws, so as to present upwards and horizontally, the flat of the underside of the ferrule which must bear on the base of the bead. He cleans and then polishes with flat files all of the exposed horizontal surface, including that of the two ears together. Finally, he chamfers with a half-round file, from outside to inside, the inside of the circumference of the ring so that nothing prevents this part from always seating exactly on the base of the bead.

239. Cela fait, il retourne la pièce, en la saisissant toujours par la tête, a l'extrémité de la vis étalon. On voit fig. 33 la forme que doit avoir la virole dans sa partie supérieure, qui se présente alors eu haut. Il faut done limer avec des limes plates, et la partie horizontale de la circonférence, depuis l'oreille jusqu'à l'arretoir, b; et cet arrêtoir lui-même, et la partie en talus, depuis l'arretoir jusqu'à l'autre oreille, d, et enfin la face plate que présentent les deux oreilles réunies.

239. That done, he turns the ring over, still grasping it by the head and the end of the standard screw. We see in fig. 33 the shape that the ring must have in its top edge which is then uppermost. It is therefore necessary to file with flat files the horizontal part of the circumference, from the ear to the stop, b; and this stop itself, and the sloping portion, from the stop to the other ear, d, and finally the flat face of the two ears together.

Page 52

8. FAIRE LE PETIT PONTET DE LA VIROLE
8. FINISHING THE SMALL BRIDGE OF THE RING

240. On serre pour cela la virole dans l'étau, par l'extrémité du plat de l'éminence, dans laquelle l'entaille doit être faite.

240. For this purpose, the ring is grasped in the vise by the end of the flat of the eminence in which the notch must be made.

241. On prend une petite lime plate de deux lignes et demie d'epaisseur et de quatre lignes de large, dont on s'est déjà servi pour ébarber les entailles de la douille; et on enfonce par le bord de la lime jusqu'à ce que l'entaille ait la profondeur requise pour le passage du tenon cette profondeur est d'une ligne.

241. Take a small flat file two and a half lines thick and four lines wide, which has already been used to trim the notches in the socket, and use the edge of the file until the notch has the depth required for the passage of the tenon, which depth is one line.

9. EN POLIR ET BRUNIR LE TETE, EN PARTIE
9. POLISHING AND BURNISHING THE HEAD, IN PART

242. On ûte la vis étalon; on prend la virole dans l'étau par le réunion des deux oreilles, de manière à présenter l'un de leurs trous en haut, et à permettre de limer la face extérieure de l'oreille que traverse ce trou, en faisant que cette face affleure ou déborde peu les machoires. C'est l'éminence que forment les deux oreilles, réunies que les ouvriers nomment tête de la virole.

242. We use the standard screw; we take the ferrule in the vise by the union of the two ears, so as to present one of their holes at the top to allow filing the outer face of the ear in which that hole is situated, making that face flush or slightly over the jaws. The eminence which the two ears form when united that the workers call the 'head' of the ring.

243. On commence par blanchir à la lime la face plate dont il vient d'être parle, et la partie adjacente de la circonférence de la virole, jusqu'au quart a peu près de cette circonférence.

243. We begin by cleaning with the file the flat face of which we have just spoken, and the adjacent part of the circumference of the shell, up to a quarter of its circumference.

244. On retourne la pièce, et on en fait autant du côté oppose.

244. We turn the ring, and we do the same on the opposite side.

Page 53

245. On polit ensuite avec des limes douces ces mêmes parties, et de même, en deux tems.

245. These same parts are then polished with a fine/smooth file twice.

246. On les essuie enfin pour enlever l'huile que les limes douces peuvent y avoir laissée, et on les brunit, toujours en deux tems, avec un brunissoir d'acier trempé a un seul manche.

246. Finally, they are wiped over to remove the oil that the fine files may have left, and they are burnished, always twice, with a hardened steel burnisher with a single handle.

247. Le sommet de la tête de la virole demeure encore tel qu'il est sorti de la forge, parce qu'on peut avoir à frapper dessus par la suite, si la virole se trouvoit trop serrée sur la douille; et qu'on ne veut point s'exposer à en gâter l'ouvrage.

247. The top of the head of the ring still remains as it came out of the forge, because one may have to hit it later, if the shell was too tight on the socket; and one does not wish to spoil the work done.

10. PERCER DANS LA DOUILLE LE TROU DU PIVOT
10. DRILLING HOLE IN THE SOCKET FOR THE PIVOT [stop-pin]

248. Il faut pour cela placer la virole sur la douille, et y mettre la vis d'épreuve. Les ouvriers nomment pivot le petit étau, c, fig. 2, qui est implante sur la douille, et qui borne le mouvement de la virole, soit quand on la tourne à droite, en buttant contre l'oreille taraudée soit quand on la tourne à gauche, en buttant contre l'arretoir. Il faut, quand le pivot butte contre l'oreille de la virole, que le petit pontet, a, fig. 33 de cette virole, coïncide avec l'entaille, qui coupe le bourrelet, pour donner passage au tenon: c'est sa principale destination. C'est donc en mettant la virole dans cette situation, qu'on peut déterminer avec certitude la place du pivot.

248. This requires the ring in place on the socket with the screw in place. The workers call the pivot [stop-pin] 'the small vice', c, Fig. 2, which is fitted on the socket, and which limits the movement of the ring, either when it turns to the right, abutting the tapped 'ear' or when turned to the left, abutting against the stop [shoulder]. It is necessary, when the pivot abuts the 'ear' of the ring, that the small bridge, a, Fig. 33 of this ring coincides with the notch which cuts through the bead to give passage to the tenon on the barrel: it is its principal destination. It is thus by putting the ring in this position that we can determine with certainty the place of the pivot [stop-pin].

249. La virole montée sur la douille, et la douille sur le mandrin d'acier, le limeur fixe donc le mandrin horizontalement dans l'étau, et met la virole dans la situation qu'on vient de dire. Alors il frappe avec un poincon, un point qui sera le centre du trou qui logera le pivot.

249. The ring is mounted on the socket and the socket on the steel mandrel; the filer then fixes the mandrel horizontally in the vise and puts the ring in the situation just described. Then with a punch he marks the point that will be the centre of the hole that will house the pivot [stop-pin].

250. Il profite de cet état de choses pour blanchir et polir à face extérieure de la circonférence de la virole dans la partie qu'il n'avoit point encore travaillée.

250. He takes advantage of this state of things to clean and polish the outside parts of the circumference of the ring he has not yet worked on.

Page 54

251. Ensuite il retire le mandrin de l'étau et de la douille; et il ôte la virole. Il place la douille dans une mordache en bois de deux pièces à charnière, qui se serre dans l'étau. La douille y est droite, la lame en haut. Enfin il perce au foret et a l'archet le trou du pivot, en appuyant sur la pièce que les serruriers nomment conscience; et il taraude ce trou avec un petit taraud a manche de vrille.

251. Then he removes the mandrel from the vise and the socket and he takes off the ring. He places the socket in hinged two-piece wooden jaws and which he tightens in the vise. The socket is vertical, the blade uppermost. At last he pierces the hole of the pivot with the drill and the bow, pressing on the piece which the locksmiths call a breastplate; and he taps this hole with a small tap with a gimlet handle.

11. POLIR LE CORPS DE LA DOUILLE
11. POLISHING THE SOCKET

252. Le limeur remet le mandrin dans l'étau, et le fixe de nouveau dans la situation horizontale. Il passe la douille dessus, sans la serrer. Il la fait tourner au contraire sur le mandrin, en tenant de la main gauche la lame près de sa base, tandis qu'il emploie de la droite une lime plate ordinaire. Il continue avec une lime demi-douce, et sur le corps de la douille et sur le bourrelet; et il termine enfin avec une lime douce.

252. The filer puts the mandrel back in the vise and fixes it again in the horizontal situation. He passes the socket on it, without tightening it. On the other hand, he turns it on the mandrel, holding the blade near its base with his left hand, while he uses an ordinary flat file in his right. He continues with a half-soft [second-cut] file, and on the body of the socket and on the bead; and he finally finishes with a fine file.

253. Il polit ensuite particuliérement avec une lime douce a deux faces demi-rondes, la partie de la douille qui s'élève à la naissance du coude.

253. He then polishes particularly with a fine file with two half-round faces, the part of the socket which rises at the base of the elbow.

12. PLACER LE PIVOT **12. FITTING THE PIVOT [STOP-PIN]**

254. Le limeur prend un petit bout de fil de fer d'une ligne et demi de gros; il le met dans l'étau, en en laissant sortir au-dessus des machoires environs deux lignes. Il prend une petite filière a manche, et il feuillette ce fil, sur une ligne environ. Il le retire alors de l'étau, et il le visse dans le trou taraude qu'il a précédemment fait à la douille.

254. The filer takes a little piece of wire of a line and a half wide; he puts it in the vice with two lines above the jaws. He takes a small die with a handle, and he cuts a thread for about one line. He then removes it from the vise, and he screws it into the tapped hole he previously made in the socket.

255. Il le remet enfin dans l'étau, en le pinçant a deux lignes de la douille, qui y demeure attachée; et il le coupe en arrasant, dans l'intérieure, avec une lime demi-ronde. Il le scie ensuite a l'extérieur avec une scie a main sans monture, a une ligne et demi de la surface de la douille.

255. He finally puts it back in the vise, pinching it two lines from the socket, which remains attached to it; and with a half-round file, files it flush with the inside of the socket. He then saws it outside with a rimless handsaw, at a line and a half from the surface of the socket.

Page 55

256. Il en ôte ensuite les bavures avec un petit outil à fraiser; ce n'est qu'un petit bout d'acier emmanché, qui a petit creux en entonnoir évasé, taillé en lime et trempe.

256. He then removes the burrs with a small milling tool; it is only a small piece of which has a conical recess at the end, cut with file teeth and hardened, and fitted over the end of the pin and rotated.

13. BLANCHIR L'INTÉRIEURE DE LA VIROLE
13. CLEANING INSIDE THE RING

257. Vela se fait avec un mandrin de grosseur convenable, et taillé en lime a sa circonférence sur la longeur d'un pouce: on monte ce mandrin dans un vilebrequin, et on le fait passer dans la virole, en tournant le vilebrequin. La virole est pincée pour cela dans l'étau, par le tête.

257. It is made with a mandrel of suitable size, and cut with file teeth at its circumference over the length of an inch: this mandrel is mounted on a hand brace, and is passed through the ring while turning the crankshaft. To do this, the ring is pinched by the head in a vise.

14. FINIE LA VIS — 14. FINISHING THE SCREW

258. La limeur commence par acier en deux portions égales la petite pièce, qui en fournit quatre, et qui est encore telle qu'elle est sortie de la forge.

258. The filer begins with steel in two equal portions, the small piece, which furnishes four, and which is still as it came out of the forge.

259. Il prend dans un étau a main par son extrémité l'une de ces moites qui produira deux vis. Il arrondit à la lime la tige opposée, en vérifiant le diamètre avec son calibre: et il lime aussi l'embase de cette tige arrondie, ou la face intérieure de la tête de vis.

259. He takes in a hand vise by its end one of these portions which will produce two screws. He rounds the opposite stem with the file, checking the diameter with its gauge: and he also files the base of this rounded stem which is the inner face of the screw head.

260. Il prend la tige qu'il vient de limer dans l'étau a main, et il opère semblablement sur l'autre tige.

260. He takes the stem he has just filed in the hand vise, and he operates similarly on the other stem.

261. Il prend une petite filière a manche, et il feuillète celle-ci sur une longeur d'environ trois lignes; il la met ensuite dans l'étau a main pour feuilleter pareillement l'autre.

261. He takes a small die with a handle, and he threads it for a length of about three lines; he then reverses it in the hand vice to thread the other end.

262. Cela fait, il scie la pièce par la moitie; l'une de ces moities sera la vis dont il a besoin; l'autre servira pour une autre virole.

262. That done, he saws the piece in half; one of these will be the screw he needs; the other will serve for another ring.

263. Il prend la première dans l'étau de son étable, pour y limer le plat de la tête, et pour en faire l'entaille avec une lime fendante; il desserre l'étau et y replace sa vis par la tête, pour le mettre de longeur et pour arrondir son extrêmité a la lime, en goutte de suif.

263. He takes the first step using the vise on his workbench, to file the flat of the head, and to cut [the slot] with a key file; he loosens the vise and grips the screw by its head, to adjust its length and to round its extremity with the file, using a drop of tallow.

Page 56

264. Il la visée ensuite dans le petit outil a manche, fig. 40, pour la terminer avec plus de facilite.

264. He then uses the small tool with handle, Fig. 40, to finish it with more ease.

265. Il met dans l'étau un petit morceau de bois plat, sur lequel il pose la circonférence de la tête de la vis; et, en faisant tourner son outil, il lime cette circonférence.

265. He puts in the vise a small piece of flat wood, on which he places the circumference of the head of the screw; and, by turning this tool, he files this circumference.

266. Il place ensuite l'outil droit dans l'étau, et il lime le dessus de la tête en l'arrondissant légèrement en goutte de suif, ce qui se fait en balançant la lime en tout sens.

266. He then places the right tool in the vise, and, adding a drop of tallow, he files the top of the head by rounding it slightly, which is done by swinging the file in all directions.

267. Ces opérations répètent avec une lime demi-douce, et enfin avec une lime douce.

267. These operations are repeated with a second-cut file, and finally with a smooth file.

15. ACHEVER DE BRUNIR L'OUVRAGE
15. BURNISHING THE WORK

268. Le limeur monte la douille sur le mandrin d'acier, la virole sur la douille, et la vis dans la virole.

268. The filer mounts the socket on the steel mandrel, the ring on the socket, and the screw in the ring.

269. Ce n'est qu'alors qu'il blanchit et termine le sommet de la tête de la virole. Il la lime pour cela dans le sens de la longeur de la vis, en donnant a la lime les degrés d'obliquité nécessaires pour former la courbure, et en la balançant,

de plus, légèrement d'avant et d'arrière, et sur-tout au sommet. Il répète cette opération avec las differentes especes de limes, jusqu'à la lime douce.

269. It is only then that he cleans and finishes the top of the head of the ring. He files it for that in the direction of the length of the screw, giving to the file the degrees of obliquity necessary to form the curvature by swaying it slightly from before and behind, and especially at the top. He repeats this operation with the different species of files, finishing with the smooth file.

270. Cela fait, il enduit légèrement d'huile d'olive, avec une barbe de plume, toutes les parties apparentes de la douille, de la virole et de la vis; il les saupoudre d'écaille de fer tamisée, en tournant le douille sur le mandrin, pour en mettre partout; il prend un morceau de bois de peuplier d'Italie, on d'un autre bois blanc déjà imprégné de cette matiere, et en tenant la bayonnette de l'autre main, par la base de la lame, il en frotte toutes les parties avec vivacité.

270. This done, he slightly smears with olive oil using a feather, all the visible parts of the socket, the ferrule and the screw; he sprinkles them with sifted iron scale, turning the socket on the mandrel, to put it everywhere; he takes a piece of Italian poplar wood, or another white wood already impregnated with this material, and holding the bayonet with the other hand, by the base of the blade, he rubs all the parts with it vigorously.

Page 57

271. Il polit ensuite les deux orifices de la douille, d'abord à la lime demi-douce, puis a la lime douce, après avoir introduit la douille dans la mordache de bois a charnière, qu'il serre dans l'étau.

271. He then polishes the two orifices of the socket, first with the second-cut file, then with the smooth file, after having inserted the socket into the hinged wooden jaws, which he holds in the vise.

272. Cela fait, il ébarbe, avec une petite lime douce, toutes les bavures qui pourroient encore se trouver sur les angles de la pièce, aprés avoir replace pour cela la douille sur le mandrin d'acier, et le mandrin horizontalement dans l'étau.

272. That done, he trims, with a small fine file, all the burrs that could still be on the corners of the piece, after having replaced the socket on the steel mandrel, and fixed it horizontally in the vise.

273. Il passe ensuite dans la douille le mandrin a tenon, pour vérifier si tous les mouvemens sont bien doux et bien réguliers.

273. He then passes the mandrel with a tenon into the socket to check if all its movements are very smooth and very regular.

274. Il saupoudre enfin tout son ouvrage de cendre, et l'essuie avec un linge bien sec.

274. He finally sprinkles his work with ashes and then wipes them with a dry cloth.

La bayonnette finie doit peser à-peu-près neuf onces.

The finished bayonet must weigh about nine ounces.

ARTICLE DOUZIEME et dernier ARTICLE TWELFTH and last

274. On reporte les bayonnettes au magasin, pour être encore soumises à l'examen du contrôleur d'armes blanche.

Il vérifie, s'il le faut, au calibre, les dimensions de toutes les parties qui viennent d'être limées.

Il éprouve la douille sur son mandrin, pour voir si les entailles sont justes au tenon.

Il prend la lame a la main, et il frappe la douille sur un billot de chêne, une fois sur le pontet pour en éprouveè la solidité, et une autre vers l'orifice supérieur, a l'endroit de la soudure. S'il y avoit un défaut de soudure masque, ces coups le décèleraient.

Page 58

Il tourne la virole pour voir si le pivot est bien place, si elle tourne sans ressaut et sans trop difficulté.

S'il a du soupçon, il détourne la vis pour s'assurer du taraudage.

Il fait casser les douilles de rebut; mais si les défauts sont remédiables, il se contente de les indiquer avec de petites empreintes convenues de marteau. Toutes les pièces recues sont marquées de nouveau de son poincon, au coude de la douille, sur la coussinet de laiton.

Enfin, toutes les pieces sont soumises a l'examen de l'inspecteur, qui les fait frapper aussi de son poincon.

274. The bayonets are carried back to the store for further examination by the bladed weapons Inspector.

He checks, if necessary with the gauge, the dimensions of all parts that have just been filed.

He tests the socket on his mandrel, to see if the slots are correct for the tenon.

He takes the blade by hand, and he hits the socket on an oak block, once on the bridge to feel its solidity, and another towards the upper orifice, at the site of the welded joint. If there was a masked defect in the welding, these blows would detect it.

Page 58

He turns the ring to see if the pivot [stop] is well placed and if it turns smoothly without too much difficulty.

If he has any suspicion, he turns the screw to ensure correct tapping.

Rejected sockets he has broken; but if the defects are remediable, he is content to indicate them with small agreed marks of a hammer. All the pieces accepted are marked again with a punch on the elbow of the socket, on the brass cushion.

Finally, all the pieces are subjected to the examination of the [chief] inspector, who also strikes his mark.

Appendix 3

The Guardian, 1855, 10th Jan, p.6

THE MANUFACTURE OF BAYONETS, &c MANCHESTER AND BIRMINGHAM. In the *Guardian* of the 27th ult. we briefly referred to the fact that a spindle and flyer manufacturer of this city, had received from the government an order, for the manufacture of 80,000 bayonets, and 130,000 ramrods, to be finished and delivered with the utmost possible despatch. We added that in Birmingham and elsewhere, as we were informed, bayonets had always been made by hand: and on referring to an article entitled "The Supply of Arms", in the *Midland Counties Herald*, of December 28, we find it distinctly admitted that "hitherto, the process of forging the bayonet blade by hand, a necessarily slow and laborious one in itself, has been liable to all the other difficulties, which have impeded the operations of the gun makers".

Under these circumstances, the Birmingham bayonet manufacturers have been wholly unable to meet the requirements of the government; and in this juncture, a Manchester manufacturer of spindles and flyers, has come forward to supply the desideratum. We need no longer observe the delicacy of suppressing his name, for it is extensively known. Mr. Francis Preston, of Ardwick Spindle Works, an extensive establishment, which enjoys a desirably high reputation for the excellence of its productions, is able, when fully employed, to produce as many as 750,000 spindles and flyers (for throstle mules), per annum. But, finding that the present regular demand requires only about one-third of that number, Mr. Preston, learning the difficulty experienced by the government, in obtaining an adequate supply of bayonets and ramrods for muskets, within a reasonable time, availed himself of the circumstance of the Birmingham houses still adhering, chiefly at least, to hand labour in the fabrication of bayonets, to devote a part of his extensive premises to the novel process of manufacturing both bayonets and ramrods by judiciously planned and well-regulated machinery. This machinery includes Ryder's patent forging machines, of which a number are now at work in the Ardwick establishment and are advantageously employed in the forging and fluting of the bayonet; whilst the bosses, or sockets, are made and punched by new and powerful machinery secured by letters patent. The best proof of the expedition and perfection, and also of the low cost, at which Mr. Francis Preston's bayonets can be furnished, is, that after a careful examination by competent officers, the government have entrusted him with the extensive contract for bayonets and ramrods already noticed, in preference to other houses which had tendered for the contract. He has engaged to produce a larger quantity than any three of the old firms can supply within a given time, viz. 8,500 bayonets and 18,000 ramrods per month; at the same time submitting to the Board of Ordnance the offer, after the completion of his first order, to produce 12,000 bayonets and 20,000 ramrods per month, should they, unfortunately, be required.

This new rivalry, which at once throws competition into the shade, has already aroused the jealousy of the Birmingham manufacturers. Accordingly the *Midland Counties Herald*, in the article already cited, after describing a new machine, patented by a Birmingham house, for making bayonet blades at two "heats", leaving the socket, &c. to be completed by hand as heretofore, and by means of which machine 300 bayonet blades can be made per day, in the place of the 25 blades hitherto produced by hand labour, and at one-third of the previous cost, thus continues:

> *"These facts, we think, must be regarded, by every candid individual, as going a very considerable way towards proving the disposition which exists on the part of the trade in this town to meet those requirements of the public service with which a regard to their own pecuniary interests as well as a sense of public duty would induce a compliance; and in the present state of the case between them and the board, it may not be amiss to inquire into the return which the effort in question has met with. Looking at the matter from a common-sense and business point of view, we should have supposed that the authorities would have signalled their approval of the step which had been taken by a large outlay of money to meet their repeatedly expressed wishes, in some manner which should have been likely to act as a stimulus to still further exertions. So far, however, from this being the case, the board as an answer to the announcement of the enlarged means of Birmingham for increasing the supply of bayonets, have contracted with some firms at Manchester for a large number of these weapons, which might have been easily produced by the new mode, of which several of their officers had, we believe, witnessed the actual test.*
>
> *This proceeding would appear to indicate the absence of practical knowledge, and a total ignorance of the obvious and insuperable obstacles which will always present themselves to the sudden creation of any branch of industry, requiring skilled workmen, in a new district, where it has had no previous existence; and it may be reasonably doubted whether the conduct of the board towards the makers of small arms in this town has been marked by perfect candour and impartiality. It would rather appear that there is a desire in official quarters to create a prejudice against the Birmingham manufacturers for the purpose of promoting some ulterior objects; and for this and other reasons, the whole question will, no doubt, again be brought before parliament. In the meantime,*

> *we may mention, that the gun and gun material makers of the town are considering the most efficient means of co-operating together for the full development of the productive power in the several branches of manufacture, with a view to place at the disposal of the government every possible facility which they have at command for aiding the rigorous prosecution of the war. A committee, which has been formed, has already held one or two meetings; and it is possible that this body may find it necessary, in self-justification, to explain the real position of the trade with regard to the various matters which have formed the subjects of recent discussions."*

It will be seen that the Board of Ordnance are subjected to imputations of absence of practical knowledge, of ignorance, and of a want of candour and impartiality to the Birmingham houses. All this bespattering, however, will not conceal the real truth of the matter, that, notwithstanding the strong and confident opinion expressed before the Select Committee of the House of Commons last session that machinery might be more extensively employed than heretofore, not only to the fabrication of muskets, but also to the manufacture of bayonets, the Birmingham manufacturers would not, or at least did not, depart from their old modes of making these weapons, until they found there were others, not quite so supine, who were ready to take up a manufacture to which Birmingham had shown itself unequal. And now, when Manchester is making bayonets and ramrods at a rate with which Birmingham finds it impossible to compete, and when government has decided on erecting an extensive rifle manufacture of its own at Enfield, we find the Birmingham people getting angry that their trade is being taken from them, and meeting to consider what measures they shall adopt to keep it. How similar all this is to the history of machinery in its earlier application to many of our different manipulations and manufactures. It is like reading the same chapter over again, only substituting other names of materials and of seats of manufacture. Let the Birmingham manufacturers be assured that if they continue to oppose the introduction of machinery into their respective branches of the manufacture of fire and other arms, they will not thereby retain their present monopoly, but will see their trade depart from them to other seats, where there is less obstinacy of attachment to old modes or less prejudice against the introduction of improved means. Nothing can stay the march of mechanical improvement. Luddites may break looms; they only ruin the place of their abode; the looms migrate to securer localities, outlive poor Luddism, and clothe the World.

Appendix 4

Bayonet steel supplied by Thomas Firth and Sons, Sheffield

(From the Order Books held at Kelham Island Industrial Museum, Sheffield)

[Note: cwt. is the abbreviation for 'hundredweight' which is 1/20 imperial ton.]

Heighington and Lawrence

(p 44)	*Heighington and Lawrence* *5-cwt steel ¾ sqr. same quality as supplied to Astons for bayonets which we have tried and much approve of*	*Dec 14 / 54*
(p 53)	*Heighington and Lawrence* *10-cwt bayonet steel same as last 56/- net Be sure the quality is kept up*	*Jany 18 / 55*
(p 57)	*Heighington and Lawrence* *1/2 Ton bayonet steel Quality good and as soon as possible*	*Jany 31 / 55*
(p 132)	*Heighington and Lawrence* *5-cwt bayonet steel ¾ in sq bare of very good quality – last was not very good at present we have decided on using ¾ in sqr and will advise you of any future alteration*	*Sept 18 / 55*
(p 136)	*Heighington and Lawrence* *5-cwt bayonet steel ¾ in sq, bare, of very good quality please keep up the quality as well as the size of the steel*	*Oct 3 / 55*

(p 142)	*Heighington and Lawrence*	*Oct 1855*
	12-cwt bayonet steel square *Must be very particular to have it sound* *25 pairs of sword moulds to pattern*	
(p 170)	*Heighington and Lawrence*	*Jany 29 / 56*
	Please to send 10-cwt of bayonet steel *of the Ton ordered making 15cwt with that you just sent*	
(p 175)	*Heighington and Lawrence*	*Feb 11 / 56*
	10-cwt bayonet steel same as last supplied	
(p 187)	*Heighington and Lawrence*	*March 18 / 56*
	5-cwt bayonet steel same size as last– *must be of good quality*	
(p 189)	*Heighington and Lawrence*	*March 27 / 56*
	5-cwt bayonet steel ¾ sqr	
(p 195)	*Heighington and Lawrence*	*March 27 / 56*
	5-cwt bayonet steel as last *Immediately*	
(p 198)	*Heighington and Lawrence*	*April 10 / 56*
	1 Ton bayonet steel ¾ sqr	
(p 209)	*Heighington and Lawrence*	*May 19 / 56*
	5 b'dles bayonet steel per return for certain *but quality must be good*	
(p 212)	*Heighington and Lawrence*	*May 27 / 56*
	5 b'dles bayonet steel same as last *And please to send it immediately to oblige*	
(p 214)	*Heighington and Lawrence*	*June 3 / 56*
	5 b'dles best cast steel for bayonets *same as last as soon as possible*	
(p 218)	*Heighington and Lawrence*	*June 17 / 56*
	5-cwt bayonet steel same as last *Please to send a receipt*	

(p 223) *Heighington and Lawrence* *July 2 / 56*
5-cwt bayonet steel – immediately

(p 236) *Heighington and Lawrence* *Aug 1 / 56*
6-cwt bayonet steel just the same quality (ie very best) as that you now supply us with but same size as piece of steel now enclosed much wanted – pray mind quality

(p 238) *Heighington and Lawrence* *Aug 11 / 56*
5-cwt bayonet steel as usual ¾ in sqr immediately send the 6-cwt ordered on the 1st inst – we are quite out

(p 246) *Heighington and Lawrence* *Sept 2 / 56*
5-cwt bayonet steel as usual
Bare ¾ sqr good quality

(p 253) *Heighington and Lawrence* *Sept 22 / 56*
5-cwt bayonet steel ¾ in sqr bare as soon as possible – mind the quality

(p 259) *Heighington and Lawrence* *Oct 11 / 56*
½ ton of bayonet steel of usual size and quality to be forwarded with the least possible delay

(p 283) *Heighington and Lawrence* *Jany 14 / 57*
10-cwt bayonet steel ¾ in sqr bare as usual. pay particular attention to quality

(p 273) *Thos Lawrence, Albion Works* *April 15 / 57*
Liverpool St Birmingham
7-cwt bayonet steel same as before – first rate quality – immediately

(p 273) *Thos Lawrence,* *May 20 / 57*
5-cwt bayonet steel, ¾ in sqr bare – good quality
Please to send on receipt and oblige

(p 283)	*Heighington and Lawrence* *5-cwt bayonet steel as usual – immediately* *Please to pay special attention to quality*	*June 19 1857*

Chas Reeves & Co

[It is not known what the 13⁄16-inch square steel was for but it is clearly very close to the ¾ -inch square used for Patt. 1853 bayonets.]

(p 85)	*Chas Reeves & Co* *1 Ton Best Cast Steel for swords* *in moulds to pattern 72/-* *5 cwt Cast Steel for Bayonets 7/8G exact, 56/- net* *Mark all with name*	*April 19 / 55*
(p 143)	*Chas Reeves* *5cwt Bayonet Steel 13⁄16 square* *1 bundle Sword Steel to pattern.*	*Oct 1855*
(p 143)	*Reeves Birmingham* *½ Ton Bayonet Cast Steel 13⁄16 sqr*	*April 10th / 56*
(p 216)	*C Reeves* *10 cwt Bayonet Steel ¾ exact be very* *particular as regards its regularity and* *thickness, each bar not less than 15 or 16 feet long* *we have no fault to find with the quality* *of the last lot but the size is most irregular –* *bars vary in thickness and some too short*	*June 11 / 56*
(p 280)	*Charles Reeves Birmingham* *½ Ton Bayonet Steel 13⁄16 as soon as possible* *Be particular in regard to quality, temper, etc.*	*Sept 10 / 56*

Geo. Salter & Co

(p160)	*Geo Salter & Co West Bromwich* *Order 863* *1 Ton Best Bayonet moulds tilted exact to pattern* *Keep free from veins and full size and regular to pattern*	*Jany 1st 1856*

½ Ton Best Bayonet Steel ¾ in full square
We are entirely out of moulds – send some at Once Also the
¾ square if you have it by you or a part as sample

(p 242) *Geo Salter & Co West Bromwich* *Aug 26 / 56*

20cwt Best Bar Steel for bayonets as before
20cwt Best Bayonet Moulds – send some of
each on receipt
we are unexpectedly quite worked out

(p 282) *Geo Salter & Co* *Jany 10 / 1857*

1 Ton of Best Bayonet sqr steel in bars as before
1 Ton " " moulds
Send off 4 or 5 cwt of bars on receipt if possible

(p 300) *Geo Salter & Co* *Mar 2 / 57*

1 Ton Steel moulds same weight as
Mr Salter wrote about
1 Ton of sqr steel as before

Royal Small Arms Factory, Enfield

(p 140) *Royal Small Arms Factory, Enfield* *Oct 10 /55*

3-cwt. Cast steel ¾ inch sq. for bayonets
3 " " wire for Ramrods, hammered and rolled
3/8 inch diameter full
By railway, addressed as before and sent to Captain Dixon
when goods are sent off

(p 158) *Royal Small Arms Factory, Enfield Lock* *Dec 20 / 55*

20-cwt. Bar cast steel 11/16 sq. of a quality suitable for bayonets
as a trial of the quality of your steel for this purpose. You will
receive authority for the above in a few days from War Dept.
Direct to Captain W. M. Dixon, Superintendent.
Wanted as soon as possible.

(p 205) *Lt Col Dixon* *May 6 / 56*

Royal Small Arms Factory, Enfield
60-cwt Cast Steel for Bayonets ¾ in square
A formal order for the above in a few days
Send off 1 ton as early as possible.

(p 212) *Royal Small Arms Factory, Enfield* *May 28 / 56*
Jas. H. Burton, Chief Engineer

5 tons cast steel for bayonets ¾ inch sqr

(p 229) *Royal Small Arms Factory* *July 22 / 56*
Jas H Burton, Chief Engineer

10 Tons Best Cast Steel for Bayonets ¾ inch full square
(a form of tender will be forwarded as usual which you will fill up)

(p 271) *Royal Small Arms Factory* *Nov 17 / 1856*
Enfield Lock

[Various steels for tools plus]

15 Tons Best Cast Steel for Bayonets ¾ inch full square
To be delivered at the rate of 3 Tons per month
The first delivery to be made as quickly as possible.

(p 316) *Bill of Best Cast Steel for Bayonets and tools* *April 25 / 57*
to be supplied by Messrs. Thomas Firth
and Sons, Sheffield, for the service of the
Royal Small Arms Factory, Enfield Lock

13 Tons ¾ in. full square Cast Steel for Bayonets
5 Tons 305/1000 in. round, G[auge] to be supplied,
CS [cast steel] for Ramrods in lengths of multiples
of 37 ½ inches.
The Bayonet steel to be delivered at the rate of 4 Tons per
month
The Ramrod steel at the rate of 2 Tons per month from
date of order
the whole to be delivered at the Royal Small
Arms Factory, Enfield Lock, free of charge.

Appendix 5

Pattern 1853 rifle muzzle diameters in inches (measured with digital vernier caliper) (Royal Armouries Collections)

Acc. No.	Date and place	Dia. at muzzle	Dia rear of f'sight	Difference
		Enfield		
XII.1998	1857	.780	.782	.002 / 0.26%
XII.384	1859	.778	.785	.007 / 0.89%
XII.376	1859	.773	.782	.009 / 1.15%
XII.387	1860	.778	.785	.007 / 0.89%
XII.999	1861	.775	.782	.007 / 0.9%
XII.1985	1861	.777	.785	.008 / 1.02%
XII.377	1869	.775	.782	.007 / 0.9%
		Tower		
XII.3064	1854	.773	.785	.012 / 1.53%
XII.6707	1855	.776	.781	.005 / 0.64%
XII.9085	1855	.779	.785	.006 / 0.76%
XII.6778	1855	.777	.783	.006 / 0.77%
XII.9074	1855	.780	.785	.005 / 0.64%
XII.9087	1856	.776	.781	.005 / 0.64%
XII.9094	1856	.778	.783	.005 / 0.64%
XII.3912	1856	.777	.789	.012 / 1.50%
XII.6757	1856	.770	.782	.012 / 1.53%
XII.1999	1858	.770	.785	.015 / 1.91%
XII.6756	1858	.773	.784	.011 / 1.40%
		Liege		
XII.11812	1856	.788	.789	.001 / 0.13%
XII.9120	1856	.780	.780	0
XII.9102	1856	.783	.784	.001 / 0.13%
XII.2980	1856	.780	.786	.006 / 0.76%
		Windsor		
XII.1628	1856	.772	.779	.007 / 0.9%

Appendix 6

Three patents relating to manufacture of a socket bayonet in one piece

Introduction

Three patents are worth mentioning if only for their ingenuity since there is no evidence to suggest they were ever put into practice; Higgins and Whitworth's, 1854,[1] the Browns', 1855,[2] and Deakin's, 1855.[3] Considering their dates, and from the illustrations, they all seem to have been inspired by the 1853 Pattern bayonet and have the common feature of proposing to make it in one piece without any welding between blade and socket.

Higgins and Whitworth

The process described in the Higgins and Whitworth (not Joseph Whitworth) patent commenced with creating a bar of steel of roughly 'dumb-bell' section, Fig. 1.

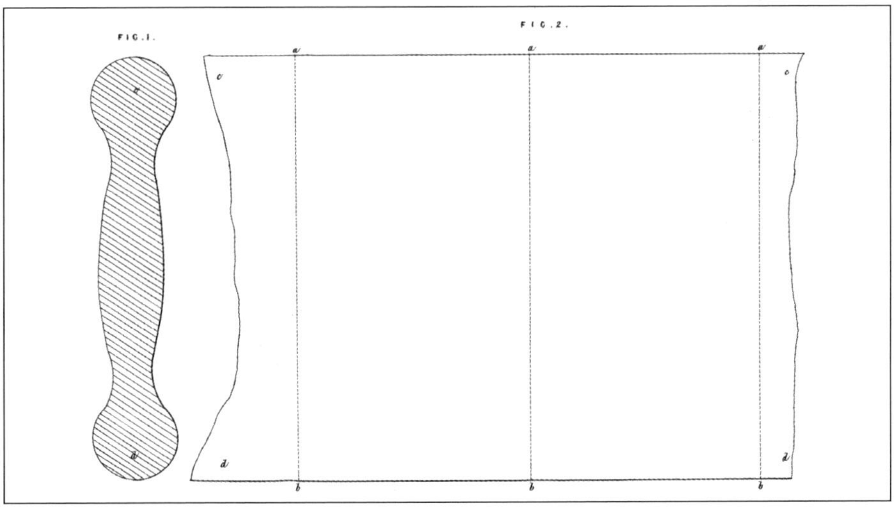

Fig. 1. Steel bar used as the starting point in the Higgins & Whitworth proposal.

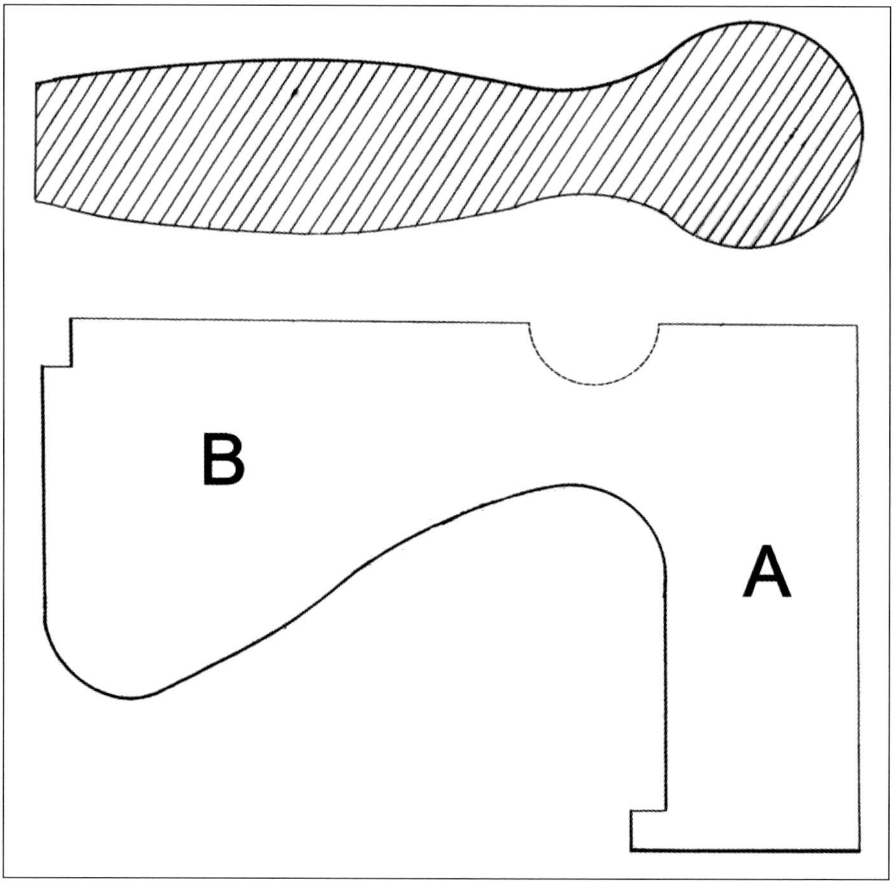

Fig. 2. The bar cropped to produce two identical pieces.

This was then cropped into two identical pieces having the forms shown in Fig. 2.

In Fig. 2. it can be seen the rudimentary 'socket', A, has been formed along with the adjacent waisting, which was to form the elbow or neck, while the remainder, B, would be formed into the blade.

The Browns' patent

This consisted of a two-stage rolling process to create a rudimentary bayonet. The first stage utilised the rolls shown in Fig. 3. In the front elevation, the space between the rolls A and B, takes the fanciful profile of a rondel dagger. A heated bar of steel of appropriate length was inserted between the rolls after raising the upper roll by means of the foot-operated lever, H, shown in the side elevation in Fig. 3. Once in place, the roll was lowered onto the bar of steel and rotated once. The rolls were mounted slightly eccentrically on their shafts and rotated in the same direction and therefore their mating surfaces revolved in opposite directions. This caused the bar of steel to be rotated on its axis, prevented from being ejected by the retaining buttresses, K and L.

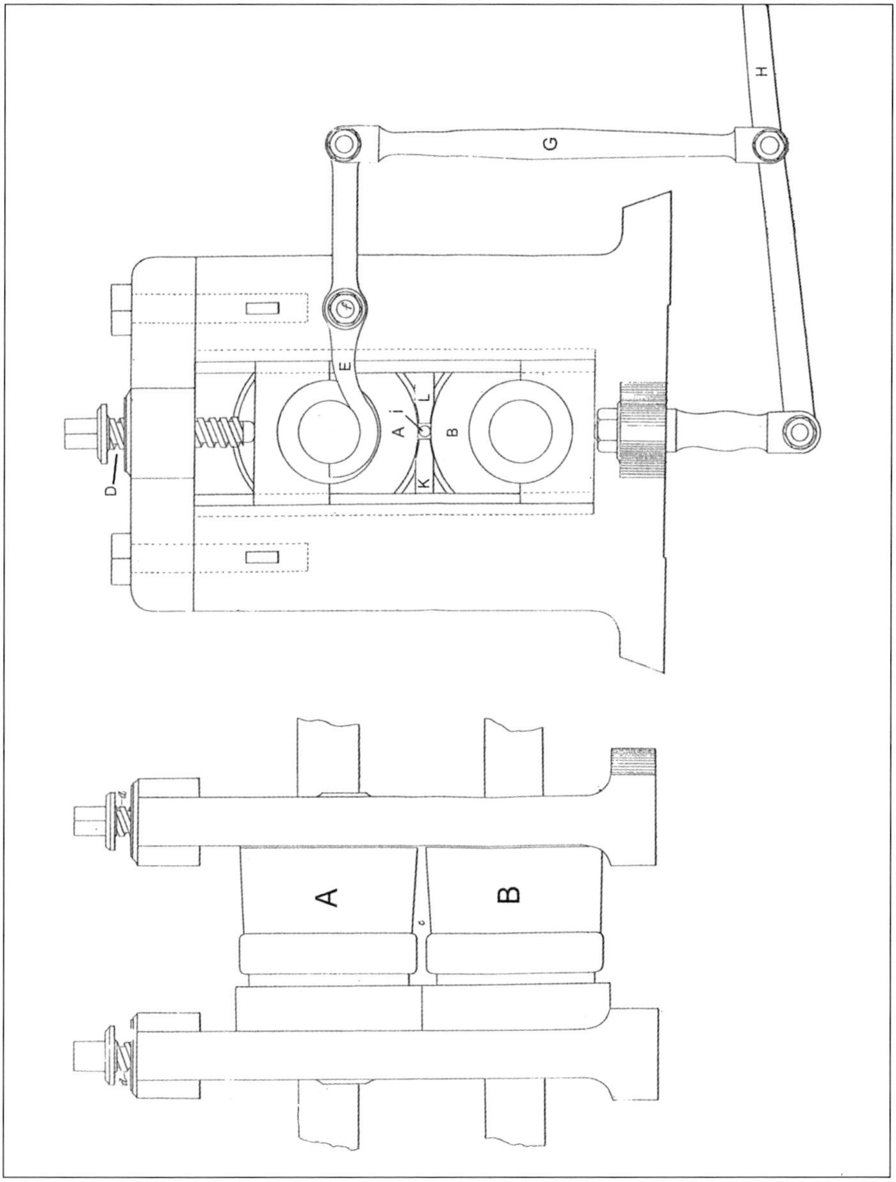

Fig. 3. Front and side elevations of the first of the Browns' rolling mills. (Re-annotated patent drawing)

A second rotation of the rolls resulted in the steel being formed into the shape shown in Fig. 4.

It can be seen that a long conical portion has been produced. This was to become the blade and was formed into the triangular section with hollow faces in a second rolling operation using a set of rolls the details of which are shown in Fig. 5.

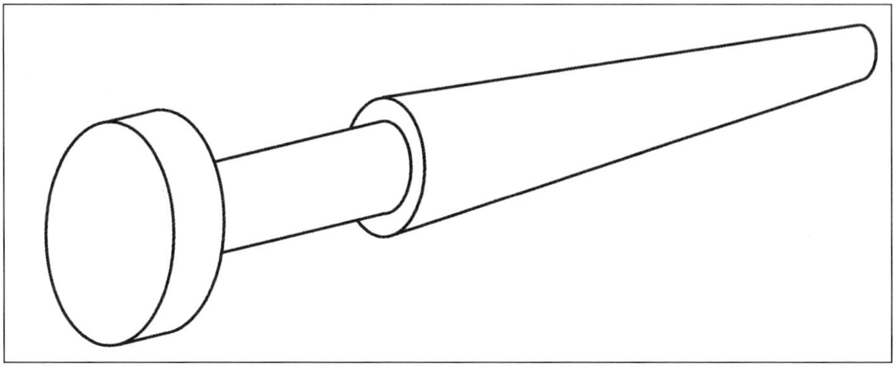

Fig. 4. The result of the first rolling operation. (© P. Smithurst)

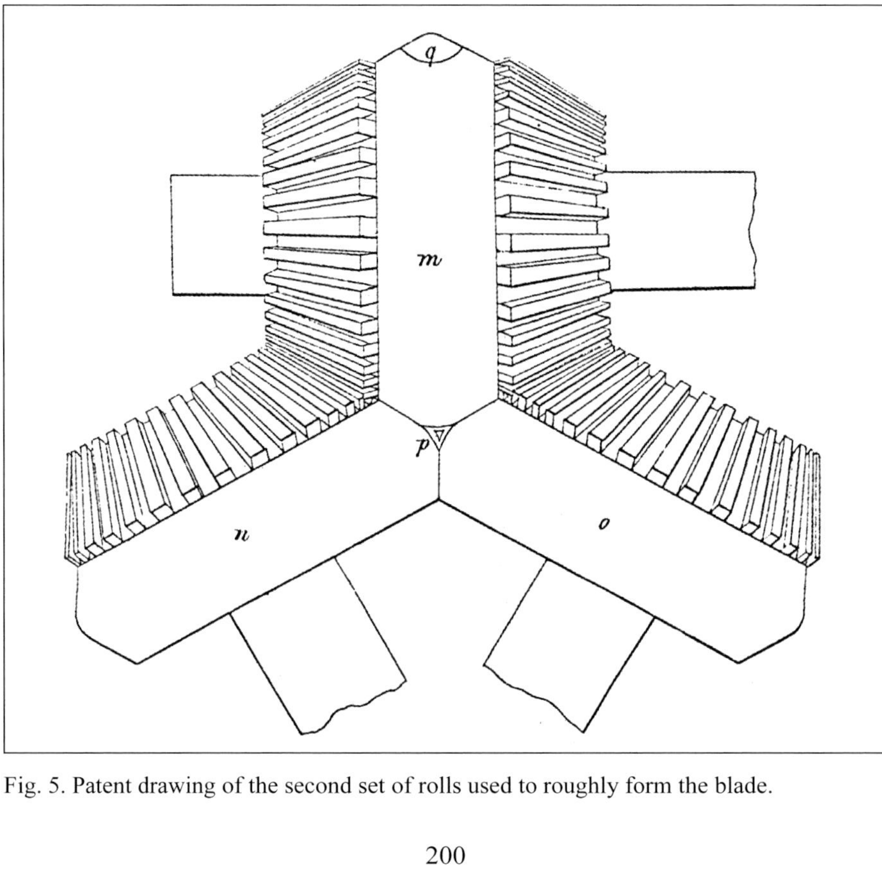

Fig. 5. Patent drawing of the second set of rolls used to roughly form the blade.

It will be seen that there is a triangular space, P, with concave sides formed by the rolls, Fig. 6.

The rolls also have a gradually increasing raised convex rib on part of their periphery, Fig. 7.

These rolls were so constructed that the mating faces rotated towards the operator – in Fig, 7 the roll would rotate clockwise. The way in which they were used was that, after heating the pre-formed steel piece, Fig. 4, it would be inserted between the rolls when the space was at its widest so that the widest part of the conical portion was in contact with the rolls. As they rotated, the tapered rib would act on the metal causing it to become triangular with hollow faces, resulting in a form approximating to that shown in Fig. 8, and would travel towards the operator allowing it to be withdrawn.

Clearly, more work was needed to convert the item into a finished bayonet but that forms no part of the patent.

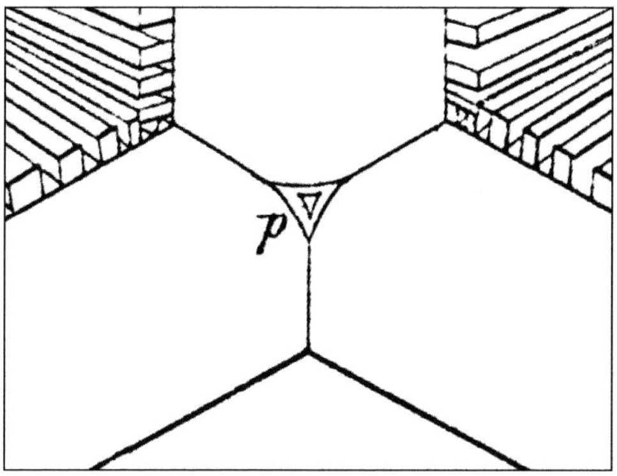

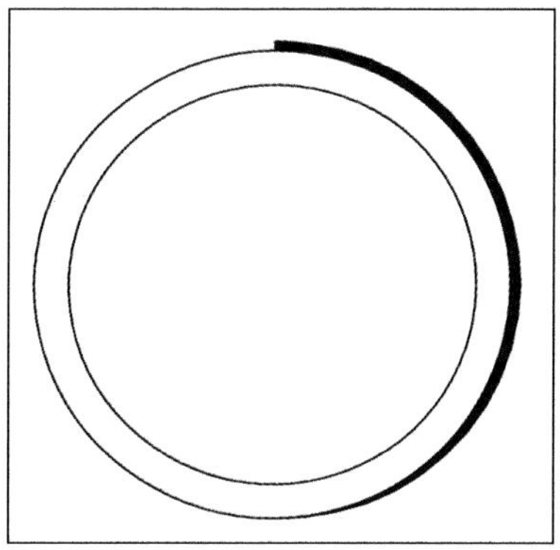

Above left: Fig. 6. Detail showing the space, P, between the mating faces of the rolls.

Above right: Fig. 7. Detail showing the inferred nature of the peripheral rib.

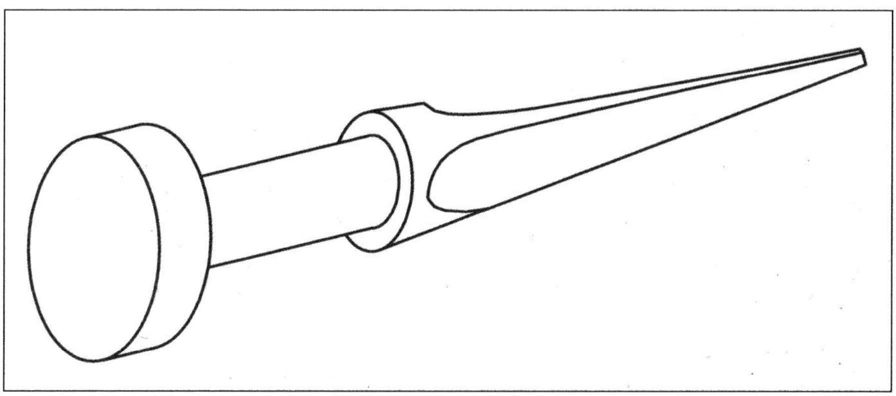

Fig. 8, The result of the second rolling operation. (© P. Smithurst)

Deakin's patent

In this Deakin also proposes to make the bayonet in one piece, but in what appears to be a more conventional form. He utilises what he refers to as 'cams' which are given a 'to and fro' rocking motion by a system of levers and crankshafts. There are two sets of these cams, which might be viewed as segmental rolls. The first are shown in Fig. 9.

It can be seen that both cams have matching cavities cut in their faces and which correspond to the socket, neck and shoulder on the bayonet. He does not elaborate on the mode of operation except to state that the piece of metal (steel?) is first formed into a 'T' shape with the vestigial socket at right angles to the neck and the blade. It is presumed the operator first heats the metal to red heat and when the cams are in the correct position, inserts the hot metal between them and when they revolve, form the socket, neck and shoulder as shown in Fig. 10.

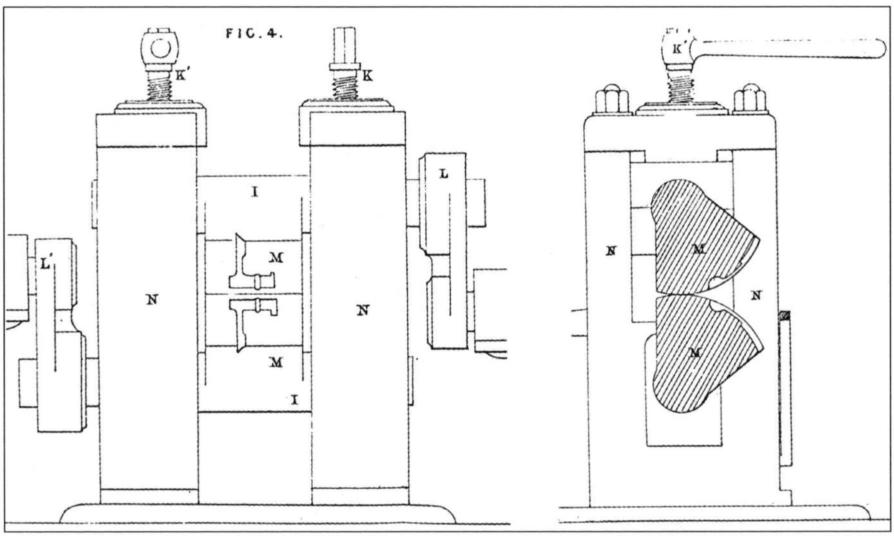

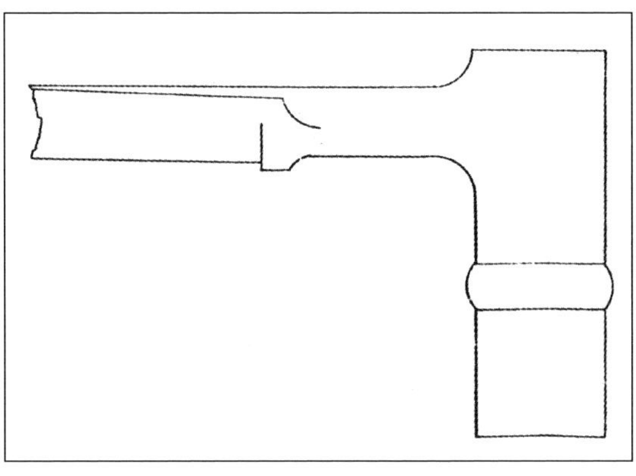

Above: Fig. 9. Deakin's first set of 'rocking cams' as shown in his patent.

Left: Fig. 10. Product of the first stage.

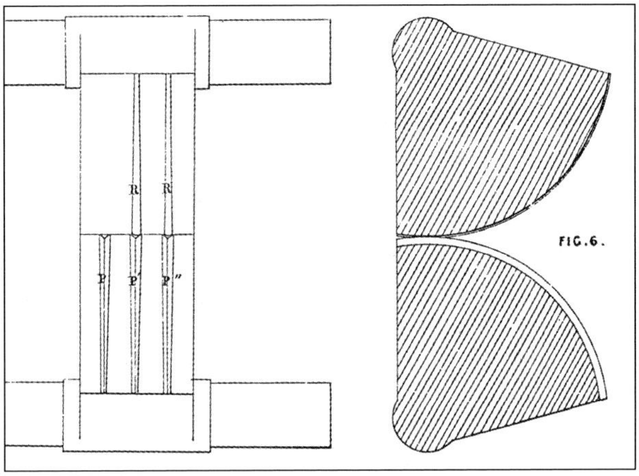

Fig. 11. Deakin's second set of cams for forming the blade; *left*, elevation of the cams; *right*, section through the cams corresponding with the two grooves on the right in the elevation.

The next stage was to form the blade, and this was accomplished using cams, Fig. 11.

It will be seen that the lower cam is cut with tapering grooves and the upper cam has two convex ribs formed and which correspond to the grooves on the right in the lower cam. The groove on the extreme left in conjunction with the plain face of the upper cam would simply form a plain triangle tapered along its length. The remaining two grooves are formed with convex inner faces and, in conjunction with the upper cam having two convex ribs on its surface, would then form hollows in the blade.

However, Fig. 11 is a misleading drawing in some respects insofar as the blade needs to be inserted from what may be taken as the rear of the elevation, left, or from the left of the sectional drawing, right – in other words, when the grooves are at their widest. The cams shown on the right in Fig. 11 would the rotate to the left, compressing and tapering the blade and releasing it into the hands of the operator. The first groove on the left, in conjunction with the plain face of the top cam, would allow the creation of a tapered blade of plain triangular section. After being worked upon by the second and third grooves the blade would be fully formed with concave faces ready for further finishing.

Comments

While these patents show a great deal of ingenuity in contriving to attain their goal of making the bayonet in one piece, they employed a varyingly extensive array of machines to overcome one basic operation – the welding of a steel blade to an iron socket. To a skilled forger – and there were countless numbers of them at the time in question – this process was simple. It also added another dimension – to make the socket of steel would add to the overall cost since wrought iron was cheaper than steel. This in itself would have been anathema to any government, and who but governments would require bayonets in such large quantities to defray the capital outlay for extra machines?

Endnotes

Chapter 1

1. Rauch, 1793, p.9
2. Rauch, 1793, p.15
3. Rauch, 1793, p.14
4. Rauch, 1793, pp.18-23
5. Rauch, 1793, p.18
6. Rauch, 1793, p.19
7. Rauch, 1793, p.19
8. Rauch, 1793, p.20
9. Rauch, 1793, p.17
10. Rauch, 1793, p.20
11. Rauch, 1793, p.21
12. Rauch, 1793, p.22
13. Rauch, 1793, p.28
14. Rauch, 1793, p.29
15. Rauch, 1793, p.35
16. Rauch, 1793, pp.30, 34
17. Rauch, 1793, p.30
18. Rauch, 1793, pp.31, 34
19. Rauch, 1793, pp.34, 35
20. Rauch, 1793, p.36
21. Rauch, 1793, p.37
22. Rauch, 1793, p.32
23. Rauch, 1793, p.32
24. Rauch, 1793, p.39
25. Rauch, 1793, p.35
26. Rauch, 1793, p.35
27. Rauch, 1793, pps.47, 48, 49
28. Rauch, 1793, p.50
29. Rauch, 1793, p.50
30. Rauch, 1793, p.42
31. Rauch, 1793, p.44
32. Rauch, 1793, p.45

33. Rauch, 1793, p.45
34. Rauch, 1793, p.50
35. Rauch, 1793, p.52

Chapter 2

1. Gamel, 1826, (translated version) p.76, footnote 2
2. Gamel, 1826, (translated version) p.133, footnote 3
3. Return, House of Commons, 1863
4. Gamel, 1826, (translated version) p.125
5. Zagorski, 1982, (translated version) p.344
6. Gamel, 1826, (translated version) p.119
7. Gamel, 1826, (translated version) p.120
8. Gamel, 1826, (translated version) p.121
9. Gamel, 1826, (translated version) p.121
10. Gamel, 1826, (translated version) p.122
11. Gamel, 1826, (translated version) p.122
12. Gamel, 1826, (translated version) p.123
13. Gamel, 1826, (translated version) p.123
14. Gamel, 1826, (translated version) p.124
15. Gamel, 1826, (translated version) p.126
16. Gamel, 1826, (translated version) p.127
17. Gamel, 1826, (translated version) pps.15 & 126
18. Gamel, 1826, (translated version) p.126
19. Gamel, 1826, (translated version) p.127

Chapter 3

1. Ordnance, 1862, p.319
2. *Illustrated London News*, Supplement, Jan. 26th, 1855, p.97
3. Report, 1854, p.237
4. Report, 1854, p.27
5. Report, 1854, p.489
6. Report, 1854, p.27
7. It has not been possible to ascertain when the term 'fullers' began to be applied to the hollows on blades; antiquarian encyclopaedias and dictionaries simply define 'fuller' in relation to the 'fulling' of cloth. The term may be a corruption of 'furrows' which they clearly resemble; equally it may derive from – or be the source of – the blacksmith's 'fullering' tool used to create curved channels in metal. However, it is equally clear that the term 'hollows' in relation to sword blades was in use at least as early as 1690 with the formation of the 'Hollow Sword Blade Company' at Shotley Bridge (Jenkins 1934) and was still in use in the mid-19th century.

8. Ryder, T., 1841
9. Report, 1854, pps.31-34, 76, 77
10. *Illustrated London News*, Supplement, 1855
11. *The Engineer*, 1859
12. Smithurst, P., 2016
13. Preston, F., 1854, *Bayonets, and machinery for their manufacture*, British Patent No 2758
14. *Illustrated London News*, 1855, Supplement, Jan. 26th, p.97
15. Lawrence, T., *Manufacture of bayonet blades*, British Patent No. 1756, 1854
16. Preston, F., 1856, *Machinery for shaping and rolling metal,* British Patent No. 274
17. *Illustrated London News*, 1855, Supplement, Jan. 26th, p.97
18. Morse, S., 1863, U.S. Patent No. 38, 119
19. Petrie, Captain M., 1866, p.42
20. *The Engineer*, 1859, p.384
21. These order books are held by West Yorkshire Archives in Leeds, UK
22. *The Engineer*, 1859, p.384
23. Fitch, C., 1882
24. Pratt & Whitney Co., 1917, *Precision Machine Tools,* Catalogue, pps.66, 67
25. *The Mechanics' Magazine*, 1861, p.144
26. *The Mechanics' Magazine*, 1861, p.144
27. *Illustrated London News*, Supplement, Jan. 26th, 1855, Fig. 4, p.97
28. *The Mechanics' Magazine*, Sept 8, 1855, p.217
29. *The Mechanics' Magazine*, August 28th, 1861, p.144
30. *The Engineer*, 1859, p.384
31. *Illustrated London News*, Supplement, Jan. 26th, 1855, p.98
32. *The Mechanics' Magazine*, August 28th, 1861, p.144
33. Report, 1854, p.489
34. Priest, G., 1996

Appendix 6

1. Higgins, J. and Whitworth, T. S., *Manufacture of bayonets etc.*, British Patent No. 2588, 1854
2. Brown, D. and J., *Manufacture of bayonets,* British Patent No. 1870, 1855
3. Deakin, T., *Machinery for the manufacture of bayonets, matchets, and swords,* British Patent No. 2150, 1855

References

Brown, D. and J., *Manufacture of bayonets,* British Patent No. 1870, 1855.

Deakin, T., *Machinery for the manufacture of bayonets, matchets, and swords,* British Patent No. 2150, 1855.

Fitch, C., (1882), *Report on the manufacture of firearms and ammunition, Extra Census Bulletin*, Washington.

Gamel, J. (1826), *Описание Тульского оружейного завода с учетом исторических и технических аспектов*, [Description of the Tula Weapon Factory in regard to historical and technical aspects]. Moscow: August Semen Press.

Gamel, J. (1988), *Description of the Tula Weapon Factory in regard to historical and technical aspects*. Moscow, August Semen Press, 1826. Translated reprint, E. A. Battison (Ed.), published for the Smithsonian Institution Libraries and The National Science Foundation, Washington D.C. by Amerind Publishing Co. Pvt. Ltd., New Delhi, 1988.

Higgins, J. and Whitworth, T. S., *Manufacture of bayonets etc.*, British Patent No. 2588, 1854.

Illustrated London News, Supplement, Jan. 26th, 1855, p.97.

Lawrence, T., *Manufacture of bayonet blades*, British Patent No. 1756, 1854.

Morse, S., (1863), U.S. Patent No. 38, 119.

Ordnance, (1862). *Minutes of the Ordnance Select Committee.*

Petrie, Captain M., (1866), *Equipment of Infantry,* H.M.S.O., London.

Pratt & Whitney Co., (1917), *Precision Machine Tools,* Catalogue, New York.

Preston, F., (1854), *Bayonets, and machinery for their manufacture*, British Patent No. 2758.

Preston, F., (1856), *Machinery for shaping and rolling metal,* British Patent No. 274.

Priest, G., (1996), *Crowned A is for America,* Society of American Bayonet Collectors, Vol. 16, pps.16 – 19.

Rauch, F.-A. (1793), *Procédés de la fabrication des armes blanches,* Comité de salut public, Paris, De l'Imprimerie de Département de la Guerre. (Available as Reprint by Hachette Livre (BnF) available online from Bibliothèque Nationale, Paris. http://gallica.bnf.fr/ark:/12148/bpt6k6125146w)

Report, (1854), *Report of the Select Committee on Small Arms.* House of Commons, London.

Return, House of Commons, 1863.

Ryder, T., (1841), *Apparatus for forging, drawing, moulding, or forming spindles etc. in metals*, British Patent No. 8835.

Smithurst, P., (2016), *Thomas Firth & Sons – steelmakers to the arms industry. Part 1 – smallarms – Enfield, government contractors and others*, Arms & Armour, Leeds, Royal Armouries, pps.143 – 156.

The Engineer, (1859), The Royal Small-Arm Manufactory, Enfield, *The Engineer*, London, pps.204, 258, 294, 295, 348, 384, 422, 423.

The Mechanics' Magazine, Sept. 8th, 1855.

The Mechanics' Magazine, August 28th, 1861.

Zagorski, 1982, (translated version) p.344.